TRESPASS

ECOTONE ESSAYISTS BEYOND THE BOUNDARIES
OF PLACE, IDENTITY, AND FEMINISM

FOREWORD BY **MAY-LEE CHAI**

LOOKOUT BOOKS
University of North Carolina Wilmington

First printing, November 2018
ISBN: 9781940596297 | E-BOOK: 9781940596303

Cover design by Meg Reid
Cover artwork by Danielle Clough
Interior design and typesetting by Kathryn M. Barber, Katy-Whitten Davidson, Sofie Harsha, Kinzy Janssen, Kate McMullen, Jeff Oloizia, Caroline Orth, Daisuke Shen, Caitlin Rae Taylor, and Matthew Thies for The Publishing Laboratory

Library of Congress Control Number: 2018958676

ART WORKS.
arts.gov

Lookout Books gratefully acknowledges support from the University of North Carolina Wilmington and the National Endowment for the Arts.

LOOKOUT BOOKS
Department of Creative Writing
University of North Carolina Wilmington
601 S. College Road
Wilmington, NC 28403
lookout.org

CONTENTS

TRESPASSING IN GOOD COMPANY

I visited Nanjing last summer at the age of fifty-one after an absence of thirty years. I knew the city had changed greatly—hadn't we both?—and I was curious as to what I'd find.

As a twenty-one-year-old college student, I'd left the United States to live in the city of my paternal grandparents. Both Ye-ye and Nai-nai had died by then, and I was still mourning their loss. I'd been bullied as a teenager in my predominantly white high school, and only my grandparents' love had sustained me. I ended up spending two years in the city, studying at Nanjing University, then teaching English in a local high school.

Back then, in the 1980s, goods from cooking oil to bicycles were rationed and required special coupons to purchase. Dogs as pets were outlawed as "bourgeois affectations" (rabies vaccines were rare and expensive), and students took to demonstrating in the streets to protest the slow pace of reform. But now, everywhere I looked people were clearly more prosperous, wearing designer clothes and walking small dogs or even carrying them on their arms. Cars outnumbered bicycles, and skyscrapers crowded the horizon. Only the tropical heat and leafy plane trees lining the streets remained the same.

This time around, I'd come to Nanjing as a guest lecturer, not a student. I'd been invited to talk about my books, including *The Girl from Purple Mountain*, the family memoir I'd co-written with my father about my grandmother. Speaking on the campus of Nanjing University, I asked graduate students to name the biggest changes they'd seen in their lives. Some commented on the quality of material life, while others complained about academic pressure and increased competition for jobs.

But one young woman shook her head, disagreeing with her classmates. "No, it's the changes in how women are treated. Now my grandfather is as proud of my achievements as he would be of any grandson. It wasn't always this way."

I understood immediately what she meant.

When my grandmother was a young woman, two generations earlier, she'd been one of the first eight women admitted into what is now Nanjing University when the college went coeducational in 1920. She'd always credited her mother's love for her success: when she was a little girl, her mother had insisted she be educated alongside her brothers, still a rarity in the first decades of the twentieth century in China.

Nai-nai remembered that her mother walked with a limp her whole life because her feet had been bound at age three. Her toes had been wrapped and bent toward her heels, the bandages tightened every week in order to break the arch and prevent the foot from growing past the ideal "three-inch golden lotus" shape.

Yet Nai-nai also recalled her mother's resistance. As a child she'd cried so ferociously that her family eventually agreed to let missionaries from the United States unbind her feet just to stop her screams from disturbing their peace. In return, the missionaries promised to educate my grandmother's mother, so that when the time came, she'd be a modern bride, appealing to a similarly Western-educated young man. This was the woman who'd insisted that her own daughter be educated like a son. My grandmother was eternally grateful.

Surveying the graduate literature students who'd come to hear me speak, I could see that more than half of them were young women. They were fashionably dressed, equally adept at Mandarin and English, bold enough to match the young men question for question.

Yes, I realized, this was the greatest change, the story I needed to understand about twenty-first-century China. It was not just skyscrapers and shopping centers. It was a generation of young women eager to claim their place in the world.

Throughout much of human history, women have been told to stay in their place—a place defined by societal norms, often as dictated by elite men, and whose boundaries were enforced brutally. The safe space for women to be "good" and thus alive was often so narrow that any normal human behavior could be enough to inadvertently send a woman across its boundaries and into an unsafe, unsustainable space.

Think of the ways that women have been held in their place throughout human history: by stoning, by beating, by burning, by foot binding, by suttee, by rape, by law, by lack of education, by lack of access to healthcare, by too much work, by too little food, by social convention, by Constitution, by precedent, by ignorance, by misogyny, by poverty, by design.

Things women have been accused of causing: the fall of humankind from God's grace, the fall of dynasties, birth defects, infertility, witchcraft, moral lassitude, their own rapes, their own harassment, crop failure, gossip, anything that goes wrong.

In China, during my grandmother's youth, Confucian values required women to submit to the "three obediences and four virtues" (三從四德): as daughters they had to obey their fathers, as wives their husbands, and as widows their sons, while maintaining "wifely virtue, speech, appearance, and work." Most women lived a life of endless work with no access to education.

Meanwhile, in the Western world, since antiquity men have

written that the female body is inherently dangerous. One among many examples is Michel de Montaigne (1533–1592), who, in the very *Essays* hailed for legitimizing this literary form, warned of the dangers of the female imagination (here translated by Donald Frame):

> We know by experience that women transmit marks of their fancies to the bodies of the children they carry in their womb.... There was presented to Charles, king of Bohemia and Emperor, a girl from near Pisa, all hairy and bristly, who her mother said had been thus conceived because of a picture of Saint John the Baptist hanging by her bed.

Yet women from the beginning have resisted their second-class status. Women like my grandmother's mother, who screamed until her family unbound her feet.

Even without access to literacy, women have sung their stories, woven them into cloth, stitched them into quilts, embroidered them into paj ndau, danced them in ceremonies, chanted them alone and in groups. Women in various cultures have invented their own forms of writing. Some archaeologists now believe that the oldest known cave paintings were made by women, based on analysis of handprints on the walls.

We have trespassed throughout history so that our minds could be free and so that our stories could be told.

In this spirit of resistance, *Ecotone*, the acclaimed magazine that centers writing about place, has teamed up with Lookout Books, its sister imprint at the University of North Carolina Wilmington, to offer this remarkable collection of essays selected from the first fourteen years of award-winning writing published in the magazine. Here twenty contemporary women writers trespass across various confines—imposed upon body, gender, race, sexual orientation, class, national origin, and more—to explore the theme of place in their lives: the places they travel, the places they call home, the places they have carved for themselves in the world despite every obstacle. From campus open-carry laws to the health of the planet to the way women's bodies are treated and patrolled, the essays touch upon the most urgent issues of our times, in prose that is incandescent. Together these essayists create a sense of place that transcends all previously imposed boundaries.

For example, Belle Boggs challenges the stigma of infertility for women and the limited role for women that such a stigma implies in "Imaginary Children":

> We count on literature to prepare us, to console us, but I am shocked by how little consolation there is for the infertile, or even for those who are childless by choice and trying to live in a world that is largely fertile and family driven. Old ideas and prejudices persist—a woman without a child is less feminine, less nurturing.

Meanwhile, essayists Camille Dungy and Aimee Nezhukumata-thil address issues of belonging—who gets to decide who belongs, and where and when. In "Differentiation," Dungy describes a visit to Alaska, giving a visceral sense of what it's like to be one of exactly two black people in a small town there:

> "Are we being segregated?" Sean asks as we seat ourselves in the brightest corner we can find. This is the fancier eating space, like a room reserved for company. "I think we are being seg-regated," I say, though we both know we are being set apart because we are outsiders, not (just) because we are black.

And Nezhukumatathil recalls, in "Monsoon and Peacock," how her love for peacocks as an eight-year-old visiting Kerala did not translate well back in her life in Arizona. After drawing a peacock, the national bird of India, for a classroom assignment, she finds that her teacher disapproves: "My teacher walks up and down the aisles, checking out notebooks. When she stops at my desk, I hear a smoky sigh, and her long maroon nail taps on my notebook: two short taps. I have no idea what this means."

In a different classroom, in a different era, Arisa White recalls in "Fake IDs" the steps that she and other queer teens had to take to find a place of their own. In her first year of high school, she's uninterested at first in a guest speaker from the Gay and Lesbian Community Center, bearing brochures and condoms: "Gym class was the occasional self-conscious snicker, whispered remarks that

Nobody's gay in here, and the snapping of latex." Years later, though, it's one of those brochures that helps her connect with a new and supportive community.

But perhaps Terry Tempest Williams most directly addresses the themes at heart in so many of these essays: the limits of safety even within one's own body. In "A Disturbance of Birds," she writes of being diagnosed with a brain tumor: "How strange the way change comes, without warning, and never the way we think. Like a flash flood in the desert, it doesn't have to be raining before the water hits."

Change indeed can come in what seems like a flash, within a body or a family, a society or a civilization, as my visit to Nanjing this past summer underscored for me. In this thrilling global moment, women across the world are speaking up and rejecting the old restrictions on the spaces they're expected to occupy.

Likewise, in essay after essay, women here trespass boldly, asserting their right to tell their stories, to critique, to explore, to assert their place in the world. I am honored to join them on this journey.

MAY-LEE CHAI
September 2018

IMAGINARY CHILDREN

Belle Boggs

I t's ten o'clock on a Tuesday morning in December, and I'm waiting to see a matinee performance of that holiday classic, *Who's Afraid of Virginia Woolf?*, with twelve of my AP English students. The drama teacher is next to me; she has brought her class also. The kids sit one row in front of us, but we don't have to monitor them too closely. From where we sit, on steep risers, we can see the tops of their heads as they lean together to talk.

I've taught at a small charter school in a rural North Carolina county for three years; though the school has since grown, when I started there were barely ten students in most of my classes. Our principal has warned us against getting too involved in their lives, but the very structure of the school makes it tempting to feel like the students are our own children—we drive them on field trips in our cars, eat lunch with them, counsel them about boyfriends, girlfriends, problems at home. The same principal, in years past, prepared Thanksgiving dinner for the whole school and their families. The students have our cell phone numbers; they know where we live and call some of us by our first names. They can get emotional, fighting with us over grades, attendance, wardrobe choices. Once a student called me a bitch for criticizing a project he was proud of; I sent him out of the room and he cried for an hour, truly remorseful, in the guidance counselor's office. We know the things that motivate or upset them, and if they imagine that their teachers talk about them when we gather for casual chats, they're right. Like parents, we constantly strategize about how to strike the correct balance between what they want and what they need. Today I'm worried about an earnest, religious girl who last year recused herself from several reading assignments because of instances of sex or strong language (when we read *Huck Finn*, another student helpfully blacked out the offending words in her copy of the book). I wonder if she'll walk out on this performance, what I'll say when I follow her.

I have loved this play since I first read it as a sophomore in college, though it means something different to me now. Back then, it was about the shock of George and Martha's dysfunction—*you make me puke*—and how they made their way back, after all the fighting, the rounds of "get the guest," to something approaching love. I suspect that is what interests my students—the verbal histrionics, the cruelty—but I realize that they must also recognize, from the literature we've read together, a familiar idea within this story of a childless, miserable couple: failing to have children has a socially distorting, morally corrosive effect on people's lives, especially on the lives of women. Four years into my own experience with infertility, I can admit that I once saw this play through the same lens. Now I'm attuned to another part of the narrative: the missing child, and what they do to survive his absence.

A couple of months ago, I left these same students to drive twenty miles to the hospital in Chapel Hill where I'd been receiving fertility treatments for almost a year. No one knew where I was going—who would I tell?—only that I'd be back by lunchtime. I remember feeling hopeful and excited in the clear, crisp light of early fall, a time of year that reminds me always of childhood and fresh starts. This was to be my fourth intrauterine insemination, or IUI, as I'd learned they are called; after days of testing my urine in the school bathroom using an ovulation-predictor kit, I'd finally achieved the digital smiley-face that indicated I was about to ovulate, and made my appointment. My husband had already been to the hospital, early that morning, to provide his sample of sperm, which would be washed in a special machine that left only the most capable swimmers. Our chances for conception were slim, perhaps 5 percent, but the procedure was relatively affordable and easy to manage. Both financially and in terms of time, scheduling an IUI was like getting a new set of tires—even if sometimes every month. In vitro fertilization, our next step, would be like buying a new car, or several new cars. No one I know has attempted IUIs expecting them to work the first, or even the second, time; because our clinics were not required to keep data on IUI success rates, we had only the stories of cumulative success or failure shared on message boards or around the hospital conference room where we meet with our support group each month. Three failed attempts were nothing—I knew women who had been successful after five, six, or seven IUIs. Eventually, I hoped, we'd be successful too.

When the doctor led me not into the dim room with the familiar examination table and stirrups, but into a separate, brightly lit conference room, with only chairs and a table, I knew that my hope had been foolish. I barely looked at the numbers he circled on my chart as he explained the futility of trying the procedure again.

"I think it's time," he said, "to move on to something else."

I knew we weren't ready—financially, emotionally—for IVF. For now, we were done. I took a handful of tissues and drove back to school. It was lunchtime, warm enough for the students to eat outside. I walked to my room without speaking to anyone, closed and locked the door. I don't remember if anyone tried to come in, but I do know that none of my high school students has ever asked me why I don't have any children. Perhaps they think they are enough.

IT DID NOT OCCUR TO ME, when I first read Albee's play, to wonder why George and Martha could not have children. I was nineteen years old, and the mechanics of reproduction had little meaning in my life aside from the birth-control pills I took daily. I suppose I realized that Martha, in her early fifties, was beyond her fertile years, but that fact is never discussed directly. In act 3, when their childlessness is laid bare to their guests, George and Martha express themselves with uncharacteristic reserve. Nick asks George, quietly, "You couldn't have...any?" "*We* couldn't," says George. "*We* couldn't," Martha echoes, with "a hint of communion," according to the stage directions.

George and Martha are past the crisis point of infertility—childbirth is a ship that long ago sailed—and we are not invited to wonder why they did not have children, or what they might have done to treat their condition. Instead, the couple represent an idea about what the rest of a childless marriage looks like—the subversion of the traditional heterosexual relationship, the one that progresses, as the schoolyard chant goes, from kissing to love to marriage to baby carriage. They are a dangerous couple because they lack the anchoring affect of family. They are inappropriate, vitriolic, unfaithful, lewd, alcoholic. They are thwarted—George in his career, Martha in the expectations she had for George's career—and in their unhappiness, they bring out the worst in their guests, Nick and Honey. They get the guest because they are so unanchored.

"Who's afraid of Virginia Woolf," sings George, near the end of the second act. Honey joins him.

"STOP IT!" screams Martha.

Honey leaves the room to vomit.

The house lights come up at intermission, and our students turn to us, blinking and smiling, a little exhausted. Though the actors in this university production lack a certain sex appeal—Martha is too thin and angular, and George is short, bald, and narrow-shouldered—I can tell our kids are enjoying the production. They laughed when George mocked Nick; they gasped when Martha came on to him. I am too busy monitoring their responses to pay much attention to my own. You okay? I mouth to my wary student. She nods, then leaves with a friend for the concession booth.

LITERATURE OFTEN ASKS US TO IMAGINE the way childlessness affects its protagonists. By the time my AP English class gets to George and Martha, they have already read several accounts of childless women and couples, each of them reinforcing this un-anchored, subversive quality. Though we have no textbooks, I choose their reading based on suggestions from our state curriculum, availability of opportunities (like the chance to see this production), and my sense of what these students—these stand-in children—will like. It's a selfish move, at its core; I want to see the students claim the characters I love so much as their own, but I also want to be the teacher who introduced them. I was thrilled when a girl who does not always do her reading sauntered into class one morning, gleefully impersonating Dickens's shriveled, rejected-at-the-altar Miss Havisham—cruelly exhorting her stand-in daughter, Estella, to break Pip's heart.

And we talked for days about Lady Macbeth, another appealing villain. The Macbeths are presumably not past their childbearing years, and they imagine the children they might have with a kind of perverse and violent pillow talk. Lady Macbeth tells her husband that, if they did have a child and he'd asked her to kill it, she'd "have pluck'd [her] nipple from his boneless gums" and dashed its brains out. Macbeth responds by fondly telling her she should "bring forth men-children only." They are childless all the same, and plagued by it, surrounded as they are by happier, more virtuous families. Macbeth, heirless, sees Banquo's line of kingly succession as an affront to his own happiness and success. And what does he get up to, spurred by his own ambition and the goading of his childless wife? Murder of Duncan, murder of Banquo, murder of Macduff's whole family—all his "pretty ones." As with

George and Martha, as with the brooding Miss Havisham, what the Macbeths lack makes them dangerous.

Sitting in the darkened theater, considering my own state of childlessness, it occurs to me how many of the female characters we have talked about most—Hester Prynne, Miss Havisham, Sethe—have been defined by their relationship to children, a subtle reinforcement, for my students, that who they are is at the center of someone else's life, their very identity. In reality, this is both true and not-true; some have doting parents, while others have parents who have disappeared into work, addiction, or other relationships. Still, even the most neglected cannot seem to imagine a life that does not involve parenthood as a milestone. At seventeen or eighteen years old, they already know the number of children they would like to have and the age they'd like to be when they have them, and most of their plans replicate the family structures they were born into. Those with one sibling think they'd like to have two children, while those from large families imagine the same for themselves. Even the most romantically inexperienced among them are certain that they will one day have a family.

Until a few years ago, I saw my life the same way. Like my parents, my husband and I would live in a little house in the country. We'd have two children (a boy and a girl). I imagined taking them on long walks to the river, or to visit the horses and goats on nearby farms. I knew the books I would read to them—*Frog and Toad* along with *Eloise*, *Owl at Home*, and *Mouse Soup*—because they were the same books my mother read to me.

My husband Richard and I have the little house in the country, but instead of two children, we have two cats (a boy and a girl). We take the long walks to the river or to feed apples to our neighbors' horses by ourselves. I used to read those books to my first-graders, and I have been known to read Toni Morrison and Charles Dickens to my high-school students. But the afternoons and evenings, the weekends, can be long. I wonder sometimes, how do we fill our time? Richard writes songs about our cats and works too much; I read too much, go out too little, and am alternately anxious, accepting, and despairing.

We are both thirty-six; we have been married for ten years. We met in high school, at a summer camp for the verbally talented (one could imagine George and Martha, despite their age difference, meeting under similar circumstances). We were among the first in our social group to marry, and for years we didn't feel in any rush to have children. There was always some element of imaginary parenting in our life together, though—when we first lived together, in Los Angeles, we had a collection of small stuffed animals that began with a scarf-wearing bear who came, inexplicably, with my engagement ring. To keep the bear company we added a toy panda, two stuffed hamsters, and a rabbit dressed in pirate costume, and we invented personalities for each of them, bringing them out on holidays for family-style celebrations. We made them tacos on Cinco de Mayo and bought them lottery tickets for Christmas, and we never felt strange about it—it was just something we did—though we never told anyone either.

Now that we are older and disappointed by our childlessness, we are painfully aware of the way our rituals and traditions might appear to other people, continuously reminded that our life together does not resemble the lives of our parents at this age, or any of our aunts, uncles, or cousins. Increasingly, our life is less and less like the lives of our married friends, who have entered a new and somewhat exclusive world of play dates and birthday parties and bedtimes. Because we still want children, and are trying expensive and time-consuming medical interventions to have them, our life does not resemble our single or childless friends' lives either. We live in a constant state of waiting: for the next cycle, the next appointment, the next support-group meeting. We don't travel far; we save and save. We calculate—if this treatment is successful, we will be this far along in June, this far in August.

Sometimes I catch us talking about our imaginary children. It's not something we did before we started trying, or even before we started failing. We didn't have a list of baby names; we never mentioned children or trying to other people. But now I find myself saying "What if she…" or "What if he…" How old would she have to be to kayak with us? How much would it cost to build a skate ramp in the woods? Then I'll get my period—it always arrives, if not exactly like clockwork—and we're back to where we started.

WE COUNT ON LITERATURE to prepare us, to console us, but I am shocked by how little consolation there is for the infertile, or even for those who are childless by choice and trying to live in a world that is largely fertile and family-driven. Old ideas and prejudices persist—a woman without a child is less feminine, less nurturing. She is defined by what she does not have, and she confronts, again and again, a culture that reinforces the wrongness of her circumstances, which may be biological or social, temporary or permanent, something she treats or something she accepts.

For the infertile-but-trying woman, even the way she chooses to treat her condition is subject to literary commentary, literary example. Think of the Biblical Sarah, barren to the age of ninety, who endured and even blessed Abraham's procreation with the maid before God finally gave her a child. The allegorical message of her story is that by accepting God's will with patience and faith, Sarah was rewarded with the birth of Isaac, long after it should have been biologically possible. Though Abraham's wife had little other choice than to wait, the act of waiting transformed her—from Sarai to Sarah, from childless and grieving to the mother of nations.

The myth of Sarah infects our literature and our thinking, and it offers insight into what makes the spectacle of Albee's Martha, who responds to her childlessness by inventing a son, so pitiable and grotesque. Conception is transformative but also mysterious, endowed by God rather than planned by the woman. To interfere is to be unnatural, greedy, grasping.

Looking back on my first book of short stories, I see how thoroughly the myth was part of my own thinking. I did not anticipate trouble becoming pregnant when I wrote the stories, but motherhood, that long-expected stage of life, must have been on my mind. I include three characters who happen to be infertile, and one character who is accidentally pregnant.

It's interesting to me now how thoroughly those characters replicate received wisdom about fertility. Loretta is a nurse who is saving for a boat, the *Mattaponi Queen*, to enjoy in her retirement. Though she and her late husband had no children, she accepts her infertility stoically. Accompanying her elderly patient, Cutie, to the Dairy Queen, she remembers going out for soft serve with her husband on Friday nights: "We would sit on the cement benches and eat our cones like a dating couple, never mentioning that it would have been more fun if we had children with us." Though a few readers have told me that they find Loretta prickly or dishonest, she is as close to a hero as the collection has, and the stories in which she appears honor the way she accepts her condition, mourns it privately, and focuses her energy on other kinds of care-taking. Of course there is nothing wrong with Loretta's acceptance and privacy, or with finding her emotional strength and resourcefulness admirable. Her story becomes problematic for me in the context of a minor character who appears in another of my stories.

Jessica is the infertile daughter of Melinda, whose husband, Jonas, is in the process of gender reassignment. Writing the story, I worried a lot about portraying Jonas's and Melinda's experience accurately; I did extensive research about middle-aged couples like them, and about the hormone therapy and surgeries in Jonas's future. In contrast, I hardly remember researching Jessica's condition and treatment at all; I suppose I thought I knew enough.

Jessica is only twenty-two; while not impossible, it's rare for someone her age to be infertile. She takes fertility pills for six months, then has a "half-dozen fertilized eggs...implanted in her womb" and—in Melinda's words—"lies on her side all day and gives herself injections in the butt." I'm not sure how I came up with this course of treatment, but I now know it to be inaccurate. More damning is my portrayal of Jessica; she is narrow-minded, desperate, and emotionally unavailable to her family, and her pursuit of infertility treatment is directly linked to these characteristics. "Stress is the enemy of conception," she warns her mother before hanging up on her, right after Melinda delivers the news about Jonas's sex change. The treatment has not only isolated her, but has also made her less attractive and feminine in the eyes of Melinda, who laments to her sister that Jessica "wears sweatpants to the grocery story and goes out without her hair done."

If Loretta is like the Biblical Sarah, patient and accepting and stoic, then Jessica represents a newer stereotype that has accompanied medically sophisticated infertility treatment: the desperate, uptight woman who blindly pursues conception at all costs, destroying her relationships and her dignity in the process. If I could go back and rewrite her, I would. Though I'd still want her character to provide a contrast to her open-minded mother, I would not choose to make IVF the means of expressing Jessica's selfishness. At the very least, I would get the details of her treatment right.

WHY DIDN'T I CONCERN MYSELF with portraying Jessica's treatment accurately? I suppose the answer may be because popular culture has provided us with so many consistent portrayals of the IVF patient—needy, self-focused, materialistic, unnatural—that I assumed they must be accurate. But I think that there is an even more compelling, and more troubling reason, that connects back to George and Martha, back to the Macbeths, and back to Sarah.

As a culture, we in the Western world have imagined human conception as mysterious, even magical. We can hope or pray for a child, but it is nature or God who will ultimately decide whether that child is conceived and born. This way of thinking has a positive social effect; it makes mothers and fathers feel chosen and special, and may help soothe the burden of unplanned or unwanted pregnancies. But think about the infertile couple: despite their prayers, hopes, or wishes, they have not been selected by God or nature to have a child. There is something wrong with them—biologically, maybe morally. They are broken, unsuitable for parenting. Perhaps their love is not strong enough, or perhaps they want different things. Perhaps they are too concerned with witchcraft and regicide, like the Macbeths. Maybe they are too old, like George and Martha. Maybe they fight too much.

And if they choose to intervene, are they defying God? Defying nature? In 1962, the year that *Who's Afraid of Virginia Woolf?* premiered, scientists were still more than a decade away from the first successful in vitro fertilization treatment, yet the specter of the test-tube baby is present in George's debates with Nick. "You people are going to make them in test tubes, aren't you? You biologists," George accuses. More recently, Catholic teaching, which regularly addresses questions of bioethics and medicine, has opposed many forms of assisted reproduction, including IVF, staunchly and consistently. The wide-ranging objections raised by Catholic bishops and bioethicists to IVF include the creation and destruction of unviable or unwanted embryos; the genetic screening and selection of embryos; the profiteering of doctors; the use of donor eggs or sperm; the temptation of human cloning; and the idea that it is all too technical and artificial. Even Jesus, according to the Nicene Creed, was "begotten, not made." The root objection, however, appears to be the way that assisted reproduction interferes with natural conception, which is seen as a gift from God. In 1987, Pope John Paul II issued the Donum Vitae (full title: Instruction on Respect for Human Life in Its Origin and on the Dignity of Procreation), which asserted that IVF deprived procreation "of its proper perfection." In 2012 Pope Benedict XVI, who cowrote the Donum Vitae, expanded on this idea in an address to two hundred scientists and members of the Pontifical Academy for Life at a conference on "the diagnosis and treatment of infertility." He likened IVF treatment to "taking the Creator's place" and encouraged infertile couples to "find a response that fully respects their dignity as persons and spouses."

I am not Catholic, or even religious, but I notice that my state-provided health-insurance coverage for infertility matches recommendations in the Donum Vitae: hormonal and surgical treatment of my body is okay, but "any means of attempting pregnancy that does not involve normal coitus" is not. Further, before experiencing infertility myself, I can see that I had somehow taken on this bias against assisted reproduction, which is in itself a bias against the many infertile couples who have sought treatment. It is more comforting to imagine a baby who arrives (for free!) via chance or grace or biology than one who is created, at great (and for many, prohibitive) expense, in a sterile laboratory. And it is true that many of the rituals and practices of assisted reproduction lack dignity; they are not what I imagined, anyway, when I thought about having children. It is undignified to inject yourself with hormones designed to slow or enhance ovarian production.

It is undignified, also, to have your ovaries monitored by trans-vaginal ultrasound; to be sedated so that your eggs can be aspirated into a needle; to have your husband emerge sheepishly from a locked room with the "sample" that will be combined with your eggs under supervision of an embryologist. The grainy photo they hand you on transfer day, of your eight-celled embryo (which does not look remotely like a baby), is undignified, and so is all the waiting and despairing that follows.

But many things in life, and especially in marriage and medicine, are undignified. One could argue that certain diets lack dignity, as do going to the gym, having a colonoscopy, and performing many kinds of home repair. And when was sex ever dignified? I don't think that when the former pope advises couples to find a more respectful response to infertility, he is concerned about a woman's feet in stirrups or her eggs in a dish. I think the real trouble is with the unfulfilled desire—the grasping, the wanting, the circumventing. It's the idea that she is so dissatisfied with how things are that she would turn to elective medicine (as I have) or to the imagination (as Martha did). Better to wait, like Sarah (mother of Isaac), like Hannah (mother of the prophet Samuel), like Elizabeth (mother of John the Baptist).

Resistance to the things that are, particularly resistance that fails, is undignified. One of the things I love about Albee's play is the gradual way it allows us to discern, within Martha's rawness and apparent lack of control, an essential gravity and fortitude. When she admiringly characterizes Nick's study of biology as "less...abstruse" than mathematics, George corrects her—"Abstract"—and she fires back "ABSTRUSE! In the sense of recondite," then sticks out her tongue. She is dignified on her own terms, and it is up to the audience to catch up to her.

Initially, some playgoers and critics struggled with the details of George and Martha's marriage, and with Martha's character particularly. The first review heard by Albee and some members of the cast, received and transcribed via telephone, was from Robert Coleman of the *Daily Mirror*, who wrote "This is a sick play about sick people. They are neurotic, cruel and nasty. They really belong in a sanitarium for the mentally ill rather than on the stage." The play was recommended, in a *New York Daily News* headline, FOR DIRTY-MINDED FEMALES ONLY (which only served to increase ticket sales); later, calling the play "filthy" and rejecting its nomination, the 1963 Pulitzer board refused to award a prize for theater. Aside from the profanity and the vociferous, unabated arguing of George and Martha, many were troubled in particular by the presence of the imaginary son. Some argued that George and Martha represented a homosexual relationship in disguise (Albee, who is gay, rejected this idea); Richard Schechner, writing for the *Tulane Drama Review*, asserted that the "illusory child" was "neither philosophically, psychologically, nor poetically valid."

This debate over the validity of the imaginary child threatened the film version of *Who's Afraid of Virginia Woolf?* too. Ernest Lehman, the producer and screenwriter, proposed dealing with critical discomfort by making George and Martha's imaginary son real. In Lehman's unrealized version, Jim would have hung himself in a closet at the age of sixteen. The wallpapered-over closet would have served as a crass physical representation of the question of "truth or illusion" that George and Martha spar over throughout the play.

Edward Albee, adopted as an infant by wealthy parents he later described as emotionally distant, had some reason to think about infertility and its consequences. "The whole family was barren: the end of the line," he has said of the Albee clan. "Skidding to an awful halt. The whole lot of them." (His father's sister was also infertile.) Albee knew of his adoption from an early age, and he experienced his role in the family as somewhat imaginary—that is, he was meant to fill a particular role. "They bought me," he said of his parents. "They paid $133.30." It's not difficult to imagine that Albee might sympathize with George and Martha as well as "sonny-Jim," the child who does not exist, and it must have felt strange to him, the same way it does to me now, to hear a central element of his play dismissed as unrealistic or, worse, invalid.

Before the play was produced, Albee wrote to Leonard Woolf to let him know that his late wife's name would appear in the title. Woolf wrote back with his approval, and after seeing it performed in London wrote back again, asking if Albee had read one of

Virginia Woolf's stories, "Lappin and Lapinova." "The details are quite different but the theme is the same as that of the imaginary child in your play," Woolf told him. The story is about a newly married couple, Ernest and Rosalind, who cope with the pressures of married life by inventing, as the story puts it, "a private world, inhabited, save for the one white hare, entirely by rabbits." As Lappin and Lapinova, the king and queen of their imagined world, they are able to feel connected in the face of an alternately dull and threatening reality. Like George and Martha, they agree to tell no one: "that was the point of it; nobody save themselves knew that such a world existed." But the strongest connection between Albee's play and Woolf's story (which Albee said he had not read) is the destruction of the imaginary world, which is also accomplished by the husband. Lapinova has been "caught in a trap," he tells her, "killed." Rosalind is no longer allowed to live in a fantasy world, and their marriage (unlike, we presume, George and Martha's) is destroyed.

In their book, *Infertility and the Creative Spirit*, Roxane Head Dinkin and Robert J. Dinkin write that "envisioning a fantasy child is not as unusual as one might think, and fantasy children appear not only in fictional works but in the lives of actual people." Among the writers they identify who actively imagined children are Ella Wheeler Wilcox, who invented, with her husband, the life of a daughter named Winifred; Katherine Mansfield, who fantasized with her husband about a boy named Dicky; and Dr. Seuss, who with his wife Helen had an imaginary child named Chrysanthemum-Pearl.

In Los Angeles, the stuffed-animal family Richard and I collected lived in our bedroom on a shelf made to hold CDs, like a dollhouse. Eleven years later, in North Carolina, I put the bear, the panda, the rabbit, and the hamster in a basket, along with their losing lottery tickets and old Christmas candy, and shoved the whole thing under the bed. Sometimes Richard mentions them—"We haven't seen them for a while"—and I'll make excuses about the lack of space, my aversion to clutter. In truth, I don't want to think about the way our peculiar habit would look to outsiders, or contemplate the possibility that we'd still be making tacos for stuffed animals while our friends went to school plays and graduations. At our infertility support group, no one talks about imaginary children; we spend our precious two hours discussing more pressing matters, like the benefits of acupuncture and how to inject Follistim with the least amount of discomfort. We have time only for the body, never the imagination.

IN THE CLASSROOM, it took a while for my more literal-minded students to understand that George and Martha's bouncing baby boy isn't real. "What?" they said, turning back pages. "He's dead? He's *not* dead? He never existed?" But in the darkened theater, as the devastation of act 3 unfolds before them, they understand; I watch them bracing themselves as George announces, with menacing triumph, "I've got a surprise for you, baby."

George and Martha's son is a product of sorrow and disappointment, but also of imagination. They do not have enough to do; they must fill their days and nights somehow, and it's easy for me to imagine how idle talk and speculation about the child they might have had transformed itself into a boy with a name and a twenty-first birthday. He is so real to them that, like some people's actual children, he becomes a weapon. In front of their guests, George insinuates maternal smothering that borders on sexual abuse, while Martha suggests that in fact, he might not even be George's son.

There is sweetness in their imagining, too—when Martha says the boy, away at college, only writes to her, George claims to have a stack of letters from his son, and Martha describes his "easy birth," his "full head of black, fine, fine hair which, oh, later, later, became as blond as the sun." But her most vivid imaginings are the memories she conjures of the woman she might have been—the couple they might have been—had they had the child they wanted. "He walked evenly between us," she remembers, "a hand out to each of us for what we could offer by way of support, affection, teaching, even love." How painful it is for me when she recounts the banana boats she made for him on Sundays, "a whole peeled banana, scooped out on top, with green grapes for the crew" and "along the sides, stuck to the boat with toothpicks, orange slices...SHIELDS."

Here's one question the play provokes: are George and Martha the way they are because they could not have children, or are they denied children because of the way they are? It is a chicken-and-egg dilemma that goes back to the Macbeths, back to Sarah, back to the insensitive comments every infertile couple dreads.

And here is another: how are we to read George's killing of their son, with the made-up telegram, before their stricken guests? If we read their son as a symbol of what is wrong in George and Martha's relationship, of lies and deception and the refusal to see things for how they are, the killing is an act of mercy. That's how I read the play, years and years ago, and it's how most of my students read it now.

"Who's afraid of Virginia Woolf..." George sings softly.

"I...am...George," says Martha. "I...am."

The house lights come up. The drama teacher and I quickly wipe away tears.

"He had to do it," our students say, on the way back to school. "He had to do it so they could face reality, so there could be some hope left, in their marriage."

"Is there hope?" I ask. "Do you think tomorrow will be good for them?"

"Maybe not good," they demur. "Better?"

Instinctively, my students understand Martha's creation of an imaginary son as transgressive, intuiting the same cultural logic that former Pope Benedict relied on when he dismissed IVF as beneath human dignity. Her creation of the boy is a refusal to accept things as they are. What my students don't understand, because they are so young, is that there are many ways to live in a marriage, and many things you must do to survive a long one. What if Jim is necessary? What if his green eyes and those banana boats are all that Martha and George have that is good? What if, by killing Jim, George is killing something vital?

That's the way my husband reads George's killing of Jim—as violence, as cruelty. He tells me that it's for this reason that he finds the play painful and difficult to read. The life of the imagination is more important to him than the destruction of illusions.

I agree with him, though I don't believe Albee would. Act 3 is, after all, called "The Exorcism," and Albee has carefully woven in admissions from Martha that there is more to sustain their marriage than cruelty and games: "There is only one man in my life who has ever…made me happy," she tells the disbelieving Nick.

But then, what do you do with the play's title, with the ghost of Virginia Woolf? I make a note to tell my students more about her: that she was brilliant, that she influenced generations of writers. I could tell them I first read her when I was their age; maybe we have time to read *To the Lighthouse* or *Mrs. Dalloway*. Maybe they already know some things about her: that she was married and had no children, that she suffered from mental illness, that she walked into the River Ouse with a heavy stone in her pocket and drowned.

(Who's afraid of Virginia Woolf?)

(I am.)

FOR HALLOWEEN THIS YEAR, I dressed for school as Miss Havisham, wearing a yellowed, lacy debutante dress and carrying a plate of spiderwebbed cake and a deck of playing cards. "Break their hearts!" I hissed at my students from beneath my veil. Most of the teachers at my school dress up for Halloween, and our choices usually reveal something about what we teach or how we perceive ourselves—the outdoor education teacher comes to school as a "canoe accident," covered in fake blood and bruises; the vain and handsome Latin teacher comes as Superman. The year before, I was Lady Macbeth, binding my hair, coating my hands with red, and sleepwalking through the halls.

Our participation in what is essentially a childhood ritual— dressing up, pretending—delights the students, who see us as extensions of their families. They want to carpool with us and camp with us and watch episodes of *Doctor Who* with us at evening lock-ins. They want us taking pictures at their dances and proms. They ask to be our Facebook friends. I have had students, frustrated by the reasonable or unreasonable actions of their real parents, beg me to adopt them.

I don't remember looking for the same kind of access to my teachers when I was their age, but I have always been close to my students, baking for them, inviting them to museums and plays. My classroom's family atmosphere is my creation and an expression of my need, too. I know that the stories I put in front of them—and, to a lesser degree, that the stories I write—matter. They are patterns not only for how to live, but also for how to see the world. For all the variety, beauty, and brilliance of the works read in a typical high school English class, though, there is a sameness to their treatment of reproduction and reproductive choices. Maybe that sameness reflects a need to understand ourselves within the contexts of our families—we are each of us (even Macduff) born to someone—but what happens when one of them, like me, cannot have a child? What if she needs medical intervention to conceive? What if she chooses not to? What will she read then?

On Halloween, we offer the students extra credit for dressing in historic or literary costumes, and some of them annoy me (on purpose, I believe) by dressing as characters from *Harry Potter* or *Twilight*. But this year, one girl wore a long gown in a printed African cotton and painted a birthmark in the shape of a stemmed rose around her eye. I knew right away that she was Toni Morrison's Sula, who embraces a more openly unconventional life—sexually liberated, without a husband or children or a permanent home—than any of my students has ever admitted considering for herself.

"I'm Sula, fool," she said, when one of her classmates asked about her costume. Then, more kindly: "I love her."

My students nodded; eventually, they had all loved Sula. But we'd struggled with that book at first. Morrison's deeply imbedded authorial perspective, her lack of exposition, her very casualness—about sex, about drugs and death and mental illness and racism—challenged them. I'd finally broken through by sitting on the edge of a desk, as I used to when I taught younger students, and reading whole chapters aloud while they sat with their heads resting on their arms, like schoolchildren. Like my children.

DIFFERENTIATION

Camille T. Dungy

Sean wants to eat chicken and waffles above the Arctic Circle, so we set out walking toward Osaka in the dark. This is Barrow. February 10. The sun won't rise until around eleven, and we have a wealth of hours in which to wander before anyone is scheduled to look for us.

The previous day, we'd taken the morning Alaska Air flight that shuttles from Anchorage to Fairbanks to Prudhoe Bay (northern terminus of the eight-hundred-mile Trans Alaska Pipeline System) and then into Barrow. The plane would return to Fairbanks and fly on to Anchorage, then turn around to make the run again, dropping and collecting oil- and coal-field workers, university professors, scientists, tourists, and members of the community.

Passengers on our flight knew each other—if not by name, then by type. "Those guys from Prudhoe Bay are coming off three-week shifts," said the Iñupiaq woman sitting next to me. "They'll be drunk and rowdy by the time they get to Anchorage." There were families on the plane, but this didn't matter to those oil guys, she said. "How's your mother?" she asked the young man in the row to our left, starting a conversation that didn't include me. I turned to the window and tried to make sense of the tundra well enough to identify the pipeline.

With Sean, a friend and fellow poet who teaches at the University of Alaska in Fairbanks, I was scheduled to conduct a writing workshop and deliver a reading at Barrow's Tuzzy Consortium Library later that afternoon. When we got off the plane, temperatures outside were well below zero. The two of us were greeted warmly by Rita, the library's administrative assistant. She left the SUV running while we checked into the Airport Inn. When she took us to lunch at Osaka, she plugged in the car's block heater.

Sean and I ordered two plates of yaki soba, plus a spider roll and some ikura to share. I love the way salmon roe explode in my mouth, tasting like the ocean would taste if the ocean were jelly. I try to be mindful about my consumption of seafood, aware that the global appetite for sushi is threatening aquatic life—all of our lives, really. But I won't deny that I love the crunch of soft-shell crab wrapped in sushi rice and chewy seaweed. Rita had told us this was one of the best restaurants in Barrow. Who was I to refuse the town's offerings? After we'd already ordered, Sean noticed Osaka's American menu. "I've got to try the chicken and waffles," he said. "They'll probably just be some Eggos and a couple of frozen chicken nuggets, but I've got to try them."

I didn't want Rita to think we were gluttons. She'd told us the library was picking up the tab for lunch, but only after we'd ordered. Food prices in Barrow are exorbitant. Each of our plates of yaki soba was $24, and we had the sushi, too. "We'll come back for breakfast tomorrow," I'd said, which is why we are out walking two hours before sunrise.

Despite a banner on the front of the building that declares, OPEN 8:00 A.M. TO MIDNIGHT, Osaka is closed when we arrive, so we triangulate back to Sam & Lee's, the red, two-story restaurant we'd passed on our way.

Sean and I take off our hats and gloves in the entryway and peer through our steamed-up glasses into a bright, crowded dining room. People talk across tables like they've known each other a long time. The hostess stands in the rear of the room with her back to us, talking on the phone. We wonder if we ought to seat ourselves in one of the open booths, but an old man sitting next to the hostess looks at us and points to the ceiling.

There is a stairway to our left, but it is dimly lit, unpromising. We look toward the dining room's open tables. The old man points to the ceiling more emphatically.

We have our pick of tables upstairs. The lights aren't on, and dawn is just beginning to brighten the windows.

"Are we being segregated?" Sean asks as we seat ourselves in the brightest corner we can find. This is the fancier eating space, like a room reserved for company. "I think we are being segregated," I say, though we both know we are being set apart because we are outsiders, not (just) because we are black.

For a long time, we are alone. I send Sean downstairs, asking him to tell the hostess we'd be happy to move so she doesn't have to turn on the lights up here. I've always been troubled by the resource consumption segregation demands. In the last decade of the twentieth century, I lived for three years in Greensboro, North Carolina, a town of about 275,000 with more than five colleges. One of the colleges had been founded as the state college for white women, a counterpart to the state university for white men fifty miles up the road. Another was founded as a private college for white women. A third remains a private college for black women, and a fourth was founded as the public college for black students. A fifth college, founded by the Religious Society of Friends, was the first to admit everyone. All that brick and all those radiators. The pipes for plumbing and the water drawn for all those playing fields. The multiple libraries, the redundant classrooms. Imagine the resources that might have been conserved if people weren't so set on separating students based on race and class and gender.

Sean returns quickly, without having delivered his message.

The hostess is still on the phone. "She turned around long enough to point to the ceiling."

When she finally comes to our table I say, "We didn't want to waste your electricity by making you turn on the lights just for us."

She sets down our water and menus with a grunt, then flicks the lights on as she heads down the stairs. When she comes back, we order eggs, and toast, and reindeer sausage.

In North America, we use the terms reindeer and caribou interchangeably, or if we do differentiate it is because we call the domesticated creatures reindeer and the wild ones caribou. It is the reins that convert a caribou to a reindeer here in North America, but in Old Norse, from which the term *reindeer* is derived, *hreinn* means horned animal. Unlike other deer species, both female and male caribou sport antlers. Males lose theirs in late fall and slowly regrow them. Rudolph and Dasher and the others pulling Santa's sleigh were probably female reindeer—male reindeer would be without antlers at Christmas.

I've read about people refusing to eat reindeer sausage while visiting Alaska because of their associations with Rudolph and the rest of Santa's crew. But harnessing caribou is not part of indigenous North American culture—rather, harvesting them is. Here in Alaska, great herds of wild caribou move over the tundra, rein-free. They are not considered "labor power" by the Iñupiat, according to reindeer scholar Shiro Sasaki, but are "food material." Caribou are hunted for their meat (which is lean and nutritious), hides (which are used in protective clothing), and sinew (which is used in bows and spears and skin boats). Somewhere in Alaska, reindeer must be farmed for sausage, because reindeer sausage is on every menu. But commercial reindeer sausage is mixed with pork or beef or both, to cut down the toughness and gamey tang of caribou flesh. Sean and I like the idea of eating a local staple, but the animal on our plate, alongside the eggs that had to have been flown into Barrow from Anchorage or the Lower 48, has been converted from a wild creature into something tame as a feedlot cow.

As Sean and I zip up our parkas and prepare to walk into more cold, I overhear a local girl, who appears to be half black, beg her mother to sit at the big tables upstairs. "No," says her mother, pushing past us into the crowded lower dining room. "Everyone's down here."

THE SUN IS NEARLY OVER THE HORIZON, and the ice in the distance glows. We explore the shoreline. Where we would find sand in the Lower 48, there is snow and ice. Where we would find water, snow and ice.

Though it looks substantial to us, we know the ice is shrinking and thinning exponentially each year. Polar bears come into town more frequently, looking for places to rest because they've had to swim so far without the ice pack they rely on. Police chase the bears beyond the city limits, trying to prevent the stressed animals from threatening human residents. Sometimes, persistent animals are shot.

The ice has taken on the pinkish-yellow cast of the rising sun. I am squinting. "Do you think you would be able to spot a polar bear if one was nearby?"

"No," says Sean. "I don't think I could."

Sean is soft-spoken, and I almost lose his words to the roar of a snow machine pulling up behind us. The driver pauses between two ornamental palm trees, fronds fabricated out of bowhead whale baleen. The wooden house they are planted in front of is gray-blue with well-insulated windows. A dream catcher is hung near the doorway, and next to that is a ceramic cutout of a white whale. I am not sure whether or not I am supposed to experience all of this as authentically Alaskan, but I take a picture to share with my family back home.

"There's a polar bear out there," says the driver. He is standing on the footrests of his snow machine as if about to bring his hand to his forehead and scan the horizon for evidence of life. He says the bear hauled up near the college, which we understand is fairly far from where we are now. I ask how he identifies bears against all that snow and white ice. He says their fur is sort of yellow, then he smiles as he revs the throttle and takes off. Looking for bears.

Sean and I want to go with him. We'd love to see a wild polar bear. But neither of us is bold enough to ask for a ride. Instead, we head into the Fur Shop so I can buy a postcard for my daughter.

I choose a postcard with an artic fox leaping in the air over its prey. "I'll leap this high when I see you again, and I might just eat you up," I write on the back of the card.

Sean and I buy hats that say BARROW, AK to give to our parents. I buy a compact mirror with the Alaskan flag because the dipper part of the Great Bear is the one constellation I can always recognize, and I think the blue field and yellow stars on the state's flag are pretty.

The flag was designed in 1927 by a thirteen-year-old orphan named Benny Benson, but it makes me think of Karen Nyberg's family. Nyberg is an astronaut who spent six months on the Space Station last year, when her son and my daughter were both around three years old. Nyberg's husband is an astronaut too, and on clear nights he'd take their kid outside to wave at the light coming from the Space Station. Imagine being able to look at the stars and locate your mother.

Benson, whose mother died of pneumonia when he was three and whose family home burnt down soon after, said the blue field on the flag "is for the Alaska sky and the forget-me-not." Sometimes, my daughter says she wants to see where I've gone when I travel. We have a world map at our house. Before my trips, my husband, Ray, and I mark the places I'm going with pins. It's not the same as walking outside and pointing to a beacon in the sky, but it's the best we can do.

When I get home, I'll let my daughter play with the mirror.

The day the director of the 49 Writers reading series contacted me about extending a scheduled trip to the University of Alaska, Fairbanks, so that I could read in Anchorage and Barrow, I asked my husband if it would be okay. The hardest thing about accepting the offer was the idea of leaving my daughter for nine days. Ray said it wasn't his decision to make, but he thought I would be crazy not to go. I asked him the next day, and he said the same thing. When I asked him the third time—sometimes it's hard for me to recognize his support—he grew exasperated and reminded me that for three of our first six months together I was on the road promoting or researching the books I'd worked so hard to write. He had no illusions that my travels were going to stop just because I'd married him and had a child. He said I should go, and he assured me he would take good care of our daughter. She was his daughter, too.

In an interview with *Parenting Magazine*, in which she talked about leaving her son with his father for the six months she would be on the Space Station, Karen Nyberg said that "after going through it in my head for a long time," she realized "this is a dream I had since I was a young child, myself. I don't think I would be setting a very good example for my son if I were to give up on my dream." Even a NASA-trained astronaut had reservations about prioritizing her career. For some reason, this is heartening for me to know.

"Those Good & Plenty were three dollars," Sean says as we leave the Fur Shop. "They better be good. There better be plenty."

"Did you buy them?" When he was at the counter, I'd been occupied fitting my souvenirs into my purse, putting on my hat.

"No," he says. "I took a picture."

We've heard that transit costs to Barrow and frequent spoilage due to freezing drive up prices on staple items—a carton of milk can cost thirteen dollars. We want to see this for ourselves. Our next stop is the AC, the grocery and supply store. I suggest that if we walk toward the church we'll eventually arrive at the store.

I remember the church from our tours the day before. The Presbyterians were the first missionaries in Barrow, arriving in 1890, and their church stands in what I understand to be the center of town. The town's distance signposts are yards from the chapel. (Los Angeles: 2,845; Fairbanks: 555; Paris: 4,086; North Pole: 1,250; South Pole: 11,388).

"If my parents were here, they would have gone to services," I tell Sean. But I'd been afraid the people wouldn't be friendly. "Sometimes these small communities don't want outsiders," I say.

Several parishioners walk out of the church as if summoned to greet us. One woman stands, arms outstretched and head tilted toward the sky. The white wooden Utqiagvik Presbyterian Church behind her, she cries, "The sun! The sun!"

In the northernmost town in North America, the sun set on November 19 at 1:36 pm, and it didn't rise again until January 22, when it stayed up for twenty minutes and four seconds. Each day since the twenty-second, the sun has stayed up longer. Barring overcast weather, which is common up here, we will get six hours and six minutes of daylight today, nineteen days after the year's first sunrise. "Look at that glorious sun!" the woman exclaims. Then she puts a foot on the running board of a black, extended-cab truck and pulls her short body inside.

Sean says, "I don't think we're going the right way."

"The store is just over yonder," I insist, though we both realize I don't know what I'm talking about. We don't even know how to find the Airport Inn.

The sun singer is driving toward us. We flag her down and ask the way.

"WHO INVITED YOU?" the woman asks. We are in the cab of her truck now.

Her name is Ida, and though she can remember Sean's name, she calls me Amelia. I correct her twice, and then answer to what she calls me.

"Is there a word in Iñupiaq for when you are speaking to an elder?" I ask. "Where we come from, Sean and I might use *aunt* or *uncle*." Sean and I aren't from the same place, but we are from the same type of people. It would be strange—rude, even—for us to call a church-going woman of roughly our mothers' age by her first name, using no mediating honorific.

Our driver tells us the word we should use, but she says it so fast I can't get the hang of it.

"Are you nurses from the hospital?"

"No, Ms. Ida. We're writers," I say from my seat in the back of the cab. "We spoke at the library yesterday."

"Hmph," she says. "Who invited you to Barrow and left you standing on a corner?"

"We wanted to go for a walk this morning," I explain.

"We're doing a bit of exploring," says Sean.

"Whoever invited you didn't give you a tour?"

"We were driven around yesterday," I assure her. "That's how we knew about your church."

She is not satisfied. "You're not going to tell me who it was who invited you, are you? I can't believe they just left you on your own."

"We really didn't mind wandering by ourselves, ma'am. We know there was a death in the community recently and many of the people who would have hosted us this weekend are home with family."

Ms. Ida nods solemnly. She tells us the boy was related. Perhaps he was her husband's cousin's nephew's stepson—I don't remember the whole chain. "I've been at the family's house all week, but this morning I had to get away, to go to church," she says. "When I went into church it was dark outside. Now, look at all this beautiful sun."

For a while after she speaks, we are all quiet, admiring the open sky.

"That's our hotel," says Sean, pointing to the Airport Inn.

"Hmph. They have you staying there?" says Ms. Ida. She keeps driving, pointing out buildings. "This is our new hospital. It's a really nice hospital. When I first saw you I thought you were new nurses from the hospital."

"No, ma'am," says Sean. "We're writers."

Ms. Ida keeps driving in what I understand to be the opposite direction of the grocery store. "My people learn from seeing things," she tells us. "That's why I used to have so much trouble in school. They had us reading all these books, but I never got good at reading. If I couldn't see it, I didn't understand. It wasn't until I started reading the Bible that I learned to really see what I was reading about. Isn't that interesting?"

"Do you think it's because the parables and stories help paint a picture for you?" I ask.

"When I started reading the Bible, the things I read just made perfect sense," she says, continuing to drive. She hasn't answered my question, but she has answered my question.

"Out there is our satellite farm." Ms. Ida indicates the row of satellite dishes at the southeast edge of town.

I recognize the place. Erin, our host librarian, brought us out to the sat farm late last night, after our reading, so I could see the aurora borealis without the interference of streetlights. Erin had been underwhelmed by the night's show. She'd seen much grander displays. She kept the car running and stayed in the driver's seat. But I was awed by the green light waving through the night sky. I'd heard about the dancing lights, but I understood the aurora borealis to be a cloud, and clouds in my experience move as if they are solid masses. They do not jump and spin and dive as if each particle is in visibly independent motion, like dancers doing isolations. What I saw, when I saw the northern lights, was an observable enactment of the volatility of matter. In my solid world of cars and books and glasses of wine, I know each atomic particle, each cell and each nucleus, is an independent body engaged in independent, often erratic, motion. Still, the riggings appear so inflexible that I can't apprehend motion. The aurora is the result of particles colliding with other particles and, though each explosion happens in something akin to a unified field, I could observe discrete activity.

I tried to take a video of the lights to send to my daughter, but the flowing tangibility of sparks of differentiated matter didn't convey in the replay.

"That's how we communicate with the rest of the world," says Ms. Ida, driving her Toyota Tundra past the sat farm at the same steady speed she's been driving since we climbed into the truck.

WHEN WE FIRST ARRIVED at the library, Erin said, "Welcome to Barrow. Have you already been on four tours?" We told her Rita had shown us around. Barrow only has about 4,500 people. It didn't seem like there was much we needed to see. "You haven't really been to Barrow until you've been taken on four tours," Erin argued. "After your workshop, if you want, I'll drive you around so you can take photos."

How to describe Erin? She was of indistinguishable age, somewhere between twenty-eight and forty-six. In the manner of a woman who has grown used to not being seen, she wore practical flannel-lined Carhartts and a thick sweater that disguised her physical form, but her energy was a bubble machine of exuberance that seemed less middle-aged, more twenty-something. She had a sort of plains-state can-do attitude, the kind I'd come to recognize in people from the Lower 48 who move to Alaska and stay.

Her tour of the library started in the children's room: a cozy space with small chairs. Though she made sure to have plenty of Samoan romance novels in the adult collection, to satisfy the library's substantial client pool of women from the South Pacific, and she'd organized our event to target Barrow's surprisingly robust poetry-loving population, Erin was devoted to the children's program. This room boasted lots of children's books and also plenty of YA classics to keep the kids engaged well into high school. She nearly leapt for joy—I am not exaggerating—when I pointed to a prominently displayed copy of *Mama, Do You Love Me?* Set in Alaska, the book follows the adventures of a girl who tests the extent of her mother's love. "I'll love you until the umiak flies into the darkness, till the stars turn to fish in the sky," I said to Erin, quoting some of the mother's lines.

"I'm so glad you know that book!" said Erin.

I told her that reading the book to my daughter, the illustrations had seemed fanciful, but here in Barrow, I've seen women and children dressed in parkas like the girl's and her mother's, I've seen dolls like the child's, and I've seen real umiaks, the skin boats used to ply these Arctic waters.

"It's the best book. I just love it!" she said. Then her attention jumped. "We should show you where you'll be giving your workshop," and she bustled us into a quiet conference room with five waist-to-ceiling windows overlooking the frozen Isatkoak Lagoon.

A group of six children on four snow machines gathered just before the lagoon, waiting for something. Sean took their picture. A kid of about five, seated behind his brother, noticed us first. A few of the children turned and waved, looking at us like we were exotic lizards in a terrarium. Sean took pictures until the children bored of us, turned their attention back to the snowfield, popped down over the berm, and drove their machines into vastness.

"This week a boy in our community was shot," Erin told us.

"Yes, I read about it in the paper down in Fairbanks," I said. The papers said the accident had involved a hunting rifle.

"The kids have been skipping school and riding around together," she said, though this was a Saturday. "It's like therapy for them." Erin sat still for a long moment, one of the longest I'd see in two days. "He was a really good kid. Everybody loved him. He used to come to the library a lot. Only thirteen. It's really devastated the community, but so many of the teachers here are from outside. They come to teach, and then they leave when the term is over. They just don't seem to care."

What could we say to that?

"Do you need water? The bathroom? Something to write with?" Erin was up and moving again. "I am so excited you're here. Oh, golly, this is going to be great."

On our second tour of Barrow, Erin took us to stand between two jawbones that arched far over our heads, framing the Arctic Ocean from one vantage, the town of Barrow from the other. "This is the iconic Barrow photo spot. You have to have a picture of yourself by the whale bones." She took us to the Presbyterian church and the nearby signpost with arrows pointing toward the rest of the world. And she took us to Ilisaġvik, the northernmost accredited community college in the United States—the only tribally controlled college in Alaska.

Erin was proud of the college and how it served the community. Signs around the halls were written in English and Iñupiaq, supporting the college's mission to "perpetuate and strengthen Iñupiat (Eskimo) culture, language, values and traditions." We learned that the word for February is Siqiññaasugruk, which means "the month of longer sunshine," and that this is a time "to celebrate a successful hunting season." Erin gave us a poster that praised community self-sufficiency. She made sure Sean took a picture of a sign that described what to do if confronted by a polar bear.

Erin drove us out to the satellite farm, past the new hospital, past the ruins of the burnt-out Top of the World Hotel. There used to be a restaurant in that hotel, called Pepe's North of the

Border, where you could get a certificate that said you'd been to Barrow, the northernmost city in North America. (My grandparents visited Barrow once. Somewhere in their unsorted boxes I could probably find their North of the Border certificate.) Since the 2013 Top of the World fire, nothing quite so intentionally constructed for tourists has taken its place. Most of the outsiders in Barrow are there to work in the hospital or the schools, or they're passing through to work on one resource-extraction project or another, mostly jobs having to do with carbon-based fuels.

Erin drove us from photo op to photo op, trying to make sure we saw the best parts of her adopted town. Barrow has its share of interesting human-made structures, including the oldest frame building in the Arctic, built in 1893 as a whaling station and trading post. Not far from Osaka, we saw the remains of 1,000- to 1,500-year old Iñupiat dwelling mounds. But, for the most part, human construction is not what makes Barrow remarkable. Most of what we saw was human-built and imposed—buildings made from shipping containers or frame structures stilted above the permafrost, which, in this part of Alaska, can be as much as a half-mile deep. Or, like the baleen palms or the jawbone arches, dead things imposed on the landscape. Most of what we saw was desolate, lifeless, and frozen. In spite of this, standing by the bone arch with our feet near the icy Arctic Ocean, we marveled aloud at how beautiful everything was.

"I just love you guys," said Erin. "You are so cool."

We were grateful that she liked us but weren't sure what made us stand out from other guests.

"You'd be surprised," she said. "People come here and hate it. They say it all looks bleak. They say everything looks the same."

"Why wouldn't we like it here?" I asked. Sean and I looked out toward the Northwest Passage which, somewhere beyond where we stood, was growing more navigable each year.

"The last person I brought up here wrote a blog post about the trip. She said Barrow looked like a bombed-out town after Armageddon," said Erin.

Sean and I enumerated the different colors of white we had

perceived that afternoon, the varying shades of blue and gray, the saturation of brightness where the ice sheet met the darkening sky at the farthest point of the horizon.

Later, I'd ask Ms. Ida how she could tell when the frozen field changes from sea ice to land ice. "You can just tell," she said, looking out over the crystalized water.

I wanted to see the difference as easily as she could.

Sean walked toward, or maybe onto, the frozen ocean. At the height of the freeze, the sea ice should be thick enough to support a three-ton whale, but all I know is unpredictable pond ice. I stood at the edge, where I believed the land met the water, too skittish to wander out far.

"THERE'S THE GROCERY STORE," says Ms. Ida, pointing to the AC. "Did you still want to stop?" It's a rhetorical question. She hardly slows the truck.

I understand, now that we're in the middle of this fourth tour of the town, that we could have walked to the AC the way we'd been headed, but there were no roads leading in that direction. We would have had to walk straight across the frozen lagoon.

Ms. Ida stops the car at the Iñupiat Heritage Center, next door to the library. I finally know where we are. Erin had taken us to the Heritage Center the night before to see Barrow's collection of taxidermied tundra beasts. Inside, we saw a polar bear and a scale model of a bowhead whale. But Ms. Ida takes us to the back where women sew parkas and fur hats. Outside, near the trash pile, is the beheaded carcass of a seal.

"Are they throwing that away?" I ask.

"It's storage," she tells me. Today's high temperature will be −6. Why bother with a deep freezer? I keep being surprised by what comes to seem obvious once I realign my perspective.

In Anchorage, the director of 49 Writers lent me a hat she'd gotten in Nome. It would keep me warm as I traveled farther north. Sealskin on the outside plus a beaver-pelt lining meant hardly any cold got in. Ropes of stiff yarn ending in fur pompoms brought the earflaps nearly to my chin. When we finally do get to the AC, an Iñupiaq woman selling colorful handmade parkas (at six hundred dollars, I won't buy one, though I will be sorely tempted) will ask to look at the hat. Upon inspecting its craftsmanship, she will compliment the maker. I won't admit it is just mine on loan. I like the idea of someone thinking such a fine, warm hat belongs to me. Wearing the right hat for Barrow helps me feel less out of place.

Ms. Ida, too, makes me feel like less of an outsider. Our quickly constructed friendship builds for us a bridge. She tells me she met her husband at a bar in San Francisco's Mission District. I gasp and ask which one. Turns out, the restaurant where I first met Ray is just four blocks from the bar where Ms. Ida met her husband. She was attending secretarial school across the bridge in Oakland at the time, she tells us. Sean and I have both lived in Oakland too. We each know the area where Ms. Ida shared an apartment with two other women, though Sean and, later, Ray and I walked those streets years after Ms. Ida and her husband moved back to Barrow.

"I don't live in California anymore," I tell her. "My family moved to Colorado this summer."

"Colorado? Near Denver?" she asks. "My husband was sent to the BIA school in Denver when he was a boy." I have to work that out in my head and am ashamed when I realize I was too dense to immediately recognize the abbreviation for the Bureau of Indian Affairs. "He says they treated him well there." She is quiet for a moment, and I imagine she is considering the alternative treatment her husband might have suffered. I've heard reports. "He has good memories of the place," she says.

In one version of a story told in Sean's partner's family, they say her grandfather's mother ran an Indian school in Denver. Perhaps it was the very school where Ms. Ida's husband was sent as a boy. The Earth is small.

We get back in the truck and Ms. Ida drives slowly past particular houses, looking in the yards. The polar bear hunter doesn't have anything. The body at the Heritage Center is the only seal we see. "I'm going to take you to my house," she says.

Sean says nothing, just slightly nods and looks toward Ms. Ida and also out the window. Later, he will tell me he had been afraid to climb into the truck when we'd met Ms. Ida at the church.

Where he's from in Georgia, black men would be wise not to jump into strange women's cars.

Outside the truck window, I can see the lagoon stretch on either side of the causeway we are crossing. I am beginning to understand where we are in relationship to where we have been. Soon we'll pass the jawbone arches again.

WHEN WE PULL INTO Ms. Ida's driveway, there are three caribou-gut piles in the yard from where her sons dressed the animals. At the top of the stairs that lead to the house, her husband smiles quietly, holding open the door to welcome us. Inside, Ms. Ida walks directly to her kitchen. Sean and I linger in the living room looking at family pictures. Ms. Ida with her children. Ms. Ida as a child. I carry my phone to the kitchen and show off the photo Ray sent of my girl at the breakfast table that morning, her cereal bowl just inside the frame.

"I'm so happy I married a Native man," Ms. Ida says of her husband. As she speaks, she chops hunks of caribou with an ulu, a wood handled knife with a curved metal blade. "We never have to argue about what's for dinner. This is what's for dinner." She walks out to the back porch, returning the caribou, which she's wrapped in butcher paper, to a bench and retrieving some similarly wrapped salmon filets. She also brings in a big hunk of meat that turns out to be bowhead whale. The salmon goes into a skillet, and the whale lands on a piece of cardboard at the head of the table. Her husband puts more cardboard at each of our places. This, I learn later, is a typical way to serve muktuk, one of the local foods Ms. Ida will offer us this afternoon. "Give them plates!" Ms. Ida chides and, without a word, he takes the cardboard away and replaces it with Corelle dishes.

Her husband leaves the kitchen and comes back with two lapel pins that announce we've been to Barrow. "I was mayor for about thirty years," he tells us. "Now, I'm emeritus."

Sean and I can't quite believe our luck. We've stumbled into a first-class adventure when all we'd planned was to kill some morning hours. We hadn't asked for any of it, but we're enjoying everything.

Soon Ms. Ida has finished cooking the caribou and salmon, and we gather at the table. She uses her ulu to slice small pieces off the frozen hunk of whale. This is muktuk. It looks like the miniature slices of watermelon I find in my daughter's toy kitchen, a wedge of greenish-black skin on a triangle of pinkish blubber. The pink is flecked with bits of black that broke off the skin as the ulu sliced through.

Because Ms. Ida's husband was the whaling captain until he grew too old and one of his sons inherited the position, he and Ms. Ida get the best cuts, including flipper, which is thin and not as difficult to chew as other muktuk. We eat it all raw, like whale sashimi. The skin is the texure of tough calamari, and the blubber melts on my tongue as I chew. Ms. Ida gives us more slices of meat—this time with no skin or blubber. She cuts these from a frozen block of whale steak. Small bites, thin and red like carpaccio, rich with the taste of protein and iron.

I understand this is an experience I shouldn't be having. Or, to borrow an overused word, I understand how unsustainable it would be if a bunch of outsiders, like me, had ready access to the meal I am enjoying.

You can't just walk into a restaurant in America and find whale on the menu. People are trying to make sure you can't walk into a restaurant anywhere in the world and find whale on the menu. For good reason. Whales need our protection, not our appetites. They are threatened. The ways of life of people whose traditions rely on the animals are threatened as well. I accept the food Ms. Ida offers because I am curious, and because I don't want to be rude, but also because it tastes good, and because I appreciate that my window of permission is small.

FOR CENTURIES, the people who live here have used hand-thrown harpoons and block and tackle to harvest a whale that will feed the community for a season. Nothing is wasted. Whalebone is used to rig the harpoonists' boats, caribou tendons are used to sew water-tight sealskin around that rigging. But, sitting at the head of his table, Ms. Ida's husband tells us the whale hunt might not go well this year. The ice is too thin. Even if the hunters catch a whale, the weakened shelf might not support its weight. If they can't pull the whale onto the ice, it will rot before it can be butchered. "A waste," he says.

Ms. Ida brings out a bucket of seal oil. Suspended in the oil, which is the consistency of what you might find in a stoveside jar of bacon grease, are three-inch-long pieces of dried seal meat. I think it is bearded seal. Left to render in the salty oil, these slabs of flesh are tender, with just enough meaty taste to balance the salt. Seal confit. We dump a spoonful of the seal oil on our plates and rub it on the caribou before we eat it.

While Sean uses one of Ms. Ida's homemade rolls to wipe every trace of seal oil from his plate, she asks me how I prepare meat for my family at home.

I don't cook red meat very often, I admit. I think meat is too messy, practically as well as ethically, though I don't tell her this. My squeamishness would ring hollow as I gobble rare, community-sustaining meat off her table.

Ms. Ida is eating a fish she calls cisco. "This is my favorite fish."

"Some people call it butterfish, or whitefish," her husband tells us.

I want to cut myself another slice of muktuk, but when I try rocking the ulu over the bowhead, I find I can't use the knife Ms. Ida wields so effortlessly. "You have to be strong," she says, cutting a few slices of muktuk and handing them to me. She slices her cisco and gives one piece to me, another to Sean. "You don't have to like it," she says.

Raw and still frozen from its time on her back porch, the buttery white fish melts on our tongues. "That is delicious!" I exclaim.

I'll look up the Arctic cisco while waiting for the flight out of Barrow the next morning. Like other salmonid fish, it is anadromous, returning to freshwater to spawn. But unlike salmon, Arctic cisco can make the journey from saltwater to freshwater multiple times. The fish are abundant in the Beaufort Sea near Point Barrow, where they are a key component in the diets of the Iñupiat of Alaska's North Slope, but climate change and oil and gas development are beginning to threaten their numbers.

Seated across from me at her kitchen table, Ms. Ida cuts us each another piece from the fish on her plate, then offers us no more. She eats the rest herself, popping the eyes out with her ulu and savoring them like I savored my ikura the day before, like Sean will savor the fluffy waffles and perfectly fried chicken quarter he will order at Osaka around nine that evening.

Sean and I can't stay with Ms. Ida forever, though sitting in her warm kitchen, we wish we could. We are due to go cross-country skiing with one of the librarians and his friend, a woman who moved to Barrow from Colorado. Thinking we were only walking to Osaka for breakfast and then going to the grocery store we believed to be just down the road, we'd left the Airport Inn without their numbers, but Barrow is small and, without much trouble, our ski partners will find us. Sean and I will stand in Ms. Ida's foyer and hug her good-bye. I will promise to stay in touch, inviting them to stay with my family in Colorado should her husband ever revisit his old boarding school. I will thank her, again, for inviting us into her home. She will tell us, one more time, that it was a relief to have a break from the community's grieving. She will tell me to travel home safely. I will tell her how excited I am to see my daughter. We will hug again, and I will thank her husband for my pin, which is embossed with a walrus, a whale, and a compass rose like the pole star in the Alaskan flag, indicating each of the cardinal directions.

At 3 p.m., Sean and I, full and warm from our meal at Ms. Ida's, will venture onto the tundra on borrowed Nordic skis. The high fat and protein content of the whale and seal and seal-oil–soaked caribou will regulate our blood flow and body temperature. Surviving, even thriving, in cold climates is the reason people eat such food. Our insulin will release at a steady pace, keeping us from growing sluggish in the frosty wind. As the sun dips close to an orange-tinted horizon, before the first stars appear in the long night sky, we will ski past the mile-long snow fence. When I look to my right and beyond me, I will see ice and compacted icy snow and tussocks of Arctic grasses mounded in snow. My unaccustomed eyes will see nothing distinguishable enough to identify as a landmark. If I let it, the vastness would terrify me.

Out there alone, I would be lost.

Events do indeed take place; they bear meaning in relation
to the things around them. And I, too, happen to take place,
each day of my life, in my environment. I exist in a landscape,
and my existence is indivisible with the land.
—N. SCOTT MOMADAY

Say, who are you that mumbles in the dark?
And who are you that draws your veil across the stars?
—LANGSTON HUGHES, "Let America Be America Again"

TO SEE THE WHOLE: A FUTURE OF ENVIRONMENTAL WRITING

Lauret E. Savoy

I was fourteen years old when I first read *A Sand County Almanac* by Aldo Leopold. That his 1949 book was hailed as landmark or, in Wallace Stegner's words, "a famous, almost holy book in conservation circles," I knew nothing about. What appealed to my adolescent sensibilities were the intimate images of land and seasons in place, as well as the seeming openness of this man's struggle to frame a personal truth. In the book's last essay, "The Land Ethic," Leopold enlarged the community's boundaries "to include soil, water, plants, animals, or collectively: the land." His call for an extension of ethics to land relations expressed a sense of responsibility and reciprocity not yet embraced by this nation but embedded in many Indigenous traditions of experience.

These ideas forced new questions and suggested troubling possibility. In a book so concerned with America's past, why was it that

39

the only reference to slavery, to human beings as property, was of ancient Greece? Only uncertainty and estrangement felt within my teenage reach, as if the book's "we" and "us" excluded people with ancestral roots in Africa, Asia, and Native America. If, as Leopold wrote, "obligations have no meaning without conscience, and the problem we face is the extension of the social conscience from people to land," then what part of this nation still lacked conscience broad enough to realize the internal change of mind and heart, to embrace what Leopold had called an "evolutionary possibility" and "ecological necessity"? Why was it that, in the United States I knew at age fourteen, human relations could be so cruel?

We all carry history within us, the past(s) becoming present in what we think and do, in who we are. Ecological interdependence between human beings and the land is framed by this history, which informs our senses of place and our connections with each other. Deeply rooted values and economic norms institutionalized exploiting and manipulating the natural world—by fragmenting ecosystems, threatening biological diversity, and changing the atmosphere's nature through fossil-fuel burning. And too few honest self-reflections have yet considered how the roots of our "democratic" values and institutions link to sanctioned violence for power and profit, to class conflict, to the exclusion of peoples of color in a still deeply racialized United States.

The compromising of nature, and the compromising of human beings by racial separatism and inequities in political and economic power, in large measure define our American past-to-present. Witness poor communities of color that continue to suffer disproportionate levels of environmental pollution and toxicity. Witness the ongoing curtailing of civil rights and cutting back of even basic assistance to the poor and disenfranchised.

Yet we, in every aspect of our lives, have ecological ancestors, because we all have been in relation in time and place, whether acknowledged or not. And environmental thought, activism, and writing in the United States have old, diverse roots that leave a legacy far richer than the contributions generally noted. It is essential to recognize the biodiversity of self and of others over time, and to resist any monoidentity or monoculture of mind, self, and knowledge. Euro-American ecological ancestry is not the whole.

Consider these examples:

The writings of those who escaped slavery in the early to mid-nineteenth century, Frederick Douglass among them, also considered how the oppressive agricultural system of plantations distorted relations to land, degrading both the enslaved and the soil.

More than a century ago, Zitkala-Sa (of Lakota-Dakota heritage) and Sarah Winnemucca (of the Paiute) wrote of the close ties between the racism shown by some Anglo-Americans and their attitudes toward the land.

W. E. B. Du Bois's essay on the African roots of the First World War, which appeared in the May 1915 issue of the *Atlantic Monthly*, is as much an environmental essay as is any piece written then on the need for a national park system. But it's never been thought of as such. Du Bois even wrote about his own sense of nature and his visits to Grand Canyon and Acadia national parks in the book *Darkwater*. But how many people know this?

This past is not past because the same types of segregation of ideas, and of people, continue. The perceived lack of other voices in environmental writing and action, beyond a traditional Anglo-American context, continues to reflect a societal structure of inclusion and exclusion based on color, culture, gender, and class. In recent years, though, some of the hardest-hitting works have come from the environmental-justice movement's grassroots activism.

I think self-protective silence and denial have kept too many from even knowing who "we the people" really are, and have kept a language of possibility impoverished. By this denial, this not-remembering, we are dis-membered, broken into pieces.

✳

ONE OF THE HARDEST THINGS to cultivate is a capacity to ask significant questions about our lives in a larger world, and about lives not our own. Yet it *is* possible to refrain from dis-integrated thinking and living, from a fragmented understanding of human experience on this continent. It *is* possible to refuse what alienates and separates.

Perhaps a future of environmental writing begins in trying to meet all people where they are, wherever they are. Not where you think they are, or where you think they should be. It's acknowledging and honoring difference as enriching, and at the same time finding, across divisions, common interest and common humanity. Diversity is a condition necessary for life, so why not bring difference to bear? Such writing would attempt to call into dialogue what has been ignored and silenced, what has been disconnected or dis-membered—whether by a failure of imagination, by narrowed -isms and -ologies, by loss of memory-history, or by an unwillingness to be honest.

In reimagining and enlarging our language and frames it might be possible to have creative interaction with many audiences, a calling back and forth, an exchange. So we can be in contact with and confirm each other. So through the multiplicity of true voices, we can limn larger stories that all of these are part of. So that—from land distribution, poverty, suburban sprawl, to even how and by whom so-called nature or environmental writing is defined—we can dismantle the patterns of living in this country that fragment and exclude and allow people to believe they don't have to think about or care about...some *other*.

Perhaps a future of environmental writing resides in two words taken to heart and made real: respect and responsibility. Respect, the willingness to look again (and again); responsibility, the ability to respond, the capacity to attend, to stand behind one's acts.

Perhaps a future of environmental writing is in those who haven't yet spoken, and in those who haven't yet been heard. So many, like stars in the sky.

CARRY

Toni Jensen

I.

In the memorial garden, my colleague Michael Heffernan bends to tend some short, once-green plants that, to my untrained eyes, remain mysterious. He is quiet and pours the water with care. He is so quiet. In this, the first week of classes, my first on this campus, I don't yet know Michael well, but already I know *quiet* to be, for him, the most unnatural of states.

The moment before, I was sitting in my office near his in our building, Kimpel Hall, and he was trying to exit the door next to my office, his hands filled with water glasses. I said, "Thirsty?" And he said, "Do you know about the garden?"

When I shook my head, he nodded toward the window, to a grassy patch, and I had work to do, new names to memorize, grading to finish already. Another colleague had just been in my office too, talking about a female graduate student, describing her as "a bag of snakes." At first, I'd misunderstood. "She *has* a bag of snakes?" I said. "In the building?"

On the topic of snakes, I'm surprisingly neutral. But if this student kept her snakes, say, in her office down the hall, I felt I perhaps should be prepared.

"No, no," said the colleague, "she *is* a bag of snakes," and when I presented to him my blank-faced silence, he waved his hands around in my doorway as if clearing a swarm of bees and took himself back down the hall. I understood him fine, of course. He was trying to tell me the student is difficult, is trouble, is to be avoided. But the phrase "bag of snakes" and his casual delivery made me want to defend her. I thought, if this is how her faculty are, how brave she must be to have only brought with her one bag of snakes. I thought, she needs to go home on the weekend and collect the other three bags.

So when Michael holds out his water glasses, says *garden*, I'm still thinking snakes and more snakes, and now I'm thinking Arkansas, Bible Belt, strangeness, and I don't want to follow. I don't. But Michael is more than seventy years old, and how will he open the door with glasses of water in both hands? So I take one of the glasses; I follow.

In the garden, after the careful tending of the plants, Michael tells me about his friend, John Locke, who was killed in our building, on this campus, the University of Arkansas, on the first day of classes in fall 2000. The memorial garden, like me, is new to campus in fall 2010.

After the tending, Michael and I sit on a concrete bench, the August sun heating the concrete, the concrete heating the backs of my legs. He tells me about his friend's life, as a father, as a professor of comparative literature for thirty-three years, as a teller of elaborate jokes, as a mentor.

"He could listen," Michael says. "He heard you."

Michael's eyes are wet behind his glasses, and we sit across from the memorial grass, the memorial koi pond, the small plaque. We sit like that, the sun on our heads, the concrete warming my legs, until Michael nods and pats me on the arm, and we head back inside, each of us carrying a water glass emptied.

After, I learn more details: a graduate student, about to be expelled from the program, shot John Locke in his office, and then, a few minutes later, shot and killed himself. In the faculty vote on the student's expulsion, John Locke had been the only person to abstain, the student's only supporter. John Locke's office was Kimpel 231, and my new office is Kimpel 221.

This year, in spring 2018, in the first week of classes, according to new law, anyone who's licensed can come to Kimpel Hall carrying a handgun, to my office, to Kimpel 221, carrying a handgun, to my classroom carrying a handgun. Similar laws exist in nine other states as well, affecting thousands of campuses, hundreds of thousands of students, faculty, and staff. But on this, the campus that is supposed to be mine, I'm supposed to be concerned with the mine, with the now. As Americans, we're all supposed to be concerned with the now over the past, with the mine over the ours. So to consider the mine, the now, anyone with a license now can carry his gun and sit to warm himself on this concrete bench. Anyone with a license can look out, with his hand on his handgun, and enjoy the memorial garden.

II.

MOST OF THE GREAT STATE OF ARKANSAS was once Quapaw land, but the northwestern corner where I reside—including the town, Fayetteville, and the university campus—was Osage territory, not formally ceded until 1818. This particular patch of territory had been long contested, first between the Osage and Quapaw and then between the Osage and Cherokee. So the earning of it had been hard fought, hard won. The eventual ceding of this territory to the United States government, of course, happened at the sharp point of the bayonet or down the wide barrel of the earliest muskets and longarms, known as Northwest Guns, Mackinaws, fusils or fusees or Hudson's Bay fukes.

The southern border of this space we call campus, the University of Arkansas campus, is now called Martin Luther King Jr. Boulevard, but was once best known as the Trail of Tears.

From the Library of Congress to Wikipedia, through the history books in between, the language describing Removal is a study in power dynamics.

> In 1830, President Andrew Jackson signed the Indian Removal
> Act and began the Era of Removal of the five southeastern tribes
> from their homelands to reservation land in Oklahoma.
> The Choctaw were removed in 1831.
> The Seminole were removed in 1832.
> The Creek were removed in 1834.
> The Chickasaw were removed in 1837.
> The Cherokee were removed in 1838.

Note, in this, the language of the official record, how Jackson is the only one assigned an action, albeit a polite action: he signs; he begins. Note how passive is the language of Removal: "were removed," "were removed," "were removed." Note the absence of guns from this official record, official narrative. There is no mention, for example, of the seven thousand United States soldiers who arrived in Cherokee territory in 1838, who forced the removal of thousands of Cherokee people. There is no mention of how sharp the points of the soldiers' bayonets.

According to *Webster's*, the first known use of the word *campus* occurs in 1774. Definitions include:

> 1: the grounds and buildings of a university, college, or school
> 2: a university, college, or school viewed as an academic, social, or spiritual entity
> 3: grounds that resemble a campus <a hospital ~ > <a landscaped corporate ~ >

In 2017, there are ten states that allow guns on school campuses: Arkansas, Colorado, Georgia, Idaho, Kansas, Mississippi, Oregon, Texas, Utah, and Wisconsin. Though there are competing narratives about motive and means, all agree the campus carry movement begins after the shootings at Virginia Tech. In a decade, the movement grew from one state, Utah, to ten, at roughly the rate or speed of one state added per year.

Though the University of Wyoming wouldn't open its doors

until 1886, the first remains of the dinosaur known as *Campto-saurus* were found in Wyoming in fall 1879. The *Camptosaurus* is a plant-eating, beaked dinosaur of the Late Jurassic period, of western North America and possibly Europe. The name means "flexible lizard" or "flexible-backed lizard." Scientists believe a full-grown *Camptosaurus* could move at roughly the rate or speed of fifteen miles per hour.

To study a familiar moment in time: a woman tells someone how she met her husband through a mutual friend, at a restaurant, and that someone smiles politely. If the same woman tells that same someone how she met her husband while they were students together on a campus, same someone smiles and sighs and says, "Oh, how nice." Their children will be encouraged to attend this campus, to be that charmed presence universities call legacy. Their children and their children's children and on. Oh, how nice.

To study the tangled history of this space considered campus is to study the sigh, the smile, the "Oh, how nice." To study the tangled, contested history of this space considered campus is to enter into a deep conversation about why some spaces are considered hallowed when they are, in fact, stolen.

III.

I'M TEACHING IN PITTSBURGH at Chatham College in 2007, at my first tenure-track job, when a college senior at Virginia Tech, an English major, brings his guns to campus and begins shooting. My friend Mimi is an MFA student, a teaching assistant at Virginia Tech.

I have a newborn daughter. I am the godmother of Mimi's teenage son, Daniel. That morning, as the news blares from the living room television, I walk circles around my dining room table because this is a thing my daughter likes. The room holds stained-glass windows—red, green, and gold-patterned—and my daughter likes to follow the patterns they make on the hardwood floor, the wall, the table. So I walk and rock her, and she follows the patterns, and in between, I dial Mimi's number and I dial and I dial. I get busy signals, I get her cheerful voice, recorded, I get more busy, more signal.

It is late afternoon when I hear her voice, when I learn that Mimi has been in lockdown one building over from Norris Hall, the main site of the shooting. It is late afternoon when I learn she has spent her morning hearing shots, instructing her students not in the art of narrative forms, but in how to get down and stay down, in how to remain so very quiet.

In Pittsburgh, in the later afternoon, in my rental house, the light through the stained glass casts lovely, colorful shadows onto the hardwood. It is time to go to work, so I hand my daughter off to her father and leave the light to them.

Pittsburgh lies about three hundred miles north of Blacksburg, of Virginia Tech, by car. If the crow is flying, the distance is shorter and includes the hills known as the Allegheny Mountains and the Monongahela National Forest, which were long home to the Shawnee and to the Cherokee before Removal.

I don't drive to Blacksburg, though this is my impulse. Instead, I drive across Pittsburgh, its rivers and bridges, its hills and hollows, to the campus I'm supposed to consider mine.

To my graduate fiction class that night, I bring my wrecked face, my hair caked with baby spit, and my talk on the art of narrative forms. A student, Amy Fair, sits among the group. Teachers are not supposed to have favorites, but in this private school space, on this private school campus, I do. Amy is from West Virginia, is tattooed, and swears like it's as necessary as breathing. She's not from money, either, or even from the middle class, and therefore she is as rare a creature on this campus as would be a *Camptosaurus*. She has brought the right amount of snakes.

Back in the fall semester, at the end of my pregnancy, when I had to miss a few classes to stay home and lie on my left side, Amy organized and co-led one workshop in my absence. Already, after one prior bed-rest episode, some students were complaining about my absence. Why, they wondered to the program administrator, could I not work right up until my due date? Why was I not there for them?

When I asked Amy to sub for me on what would be my second absence, she said, "Some of these bitches are going to hate that. Do you care?" "No," I said. "I trust you." "Good," she said, "perfect. Fuck those complaining bitches, anyway." Both our faces stretched wide a second before we looked away, before we examined with care the tops of our shoes.

Eight years later, in fall 2015, during the first week of that quarter's classes, when a student brings his guns to Umpqua Community College in Oregon, Amy is teaching an English class in that building, in Snyder Hall. She has just returned from a sabbatical. She is working on a book about the history of tattooed women.

Roseburg, Oregon, and the surrounding area are and were the territory of the Cow Creek Band of the Umpqua tribe, whose tribal headquarters are in Roseburg. The one hundred acres of the college campus is land taken from the Umpqua.

That fall day, 2015, the shooting begins in the room next door to Amy's classroom. One of her students in the front row is an army veteran, Chris Mintz, who blocks the shared door between the classrooms with his body. Amy leads students, quiet, so quiet, out of Snyder Hall in one direction. Chris leads students out the other way, each of them knocking on doors along the way, quiet, so quiet, with their *get down*s, with their *follow me*s.

After, Chris is rightly valorized, and Amy happily ignored, because she tells all the reporters to go fuck themselves.

Which is to say, each of them lives, though Chris Mintz is shot five times helping evacuate fellow students from the campus library, and Amy takes a leave of absence to heal from posttraumatic stress. Each of them lives, but this is not a happy ending. There is no way to gerrymander this narrative into the frame of the simple, the jingoistic, the most American of our narratives.

IV.

MY FIRST CAMPUS is the University of South Dakota in Vermillion. Much of the Great Plains, including South Dakota, was and is Lakota, Dakota, and Nakota land. This corner of South Dakota, in particular, was Yankton Sioux or Dakota land. This word *vermillion* in Lakota means "the place where the red clay is gathered." All of which is to say, this campus sits on their land.

Before I left my no-stoplight hometown in rural Iowa for this campus, my sister had left for another, larger campus. When she went, she forgot her bag of snakes at home, or maybe she left them for me, knowing I would have a need. She didn't stay at school more than a semester. When it was my turn, the snakes went along, and I still was unprepared, but I stayed.

My first college roommate took one look at my father and then started working the phrase "Indians get" into every conversation, every corner of our room. "Indians get free computers." "Indians get free school." "Indians get all the scholarships." "You would know this," she said, "if you lived West River." In South Dakota parlance, West River means west of the Missouri River, which divides the state, east/west, with most of the reservation lands on the western side. She is playing both sides—if I'm Indian, I'm a taker. If I'm not Indian, I should know the Indians are the takers. She is here to give me an education. I give her my blank face. I give her more and more time in the room without me. I give her no answers.

On this, my first campus, on my first visit to my faculty advisor to choose my classes, the woman is behind schedule, so I wait in the hall while student after student files into her office. Sometimes this professor flits by, all scarves and long, flowing skirts, on her way to fetch more coffee. The students remain in her office.

When my turn comes and I go to schedule my classes, creative writing and Native literature, in which I'm planning to major, the professor comes back to her office with her full cup, and says in a voice not quiet—"Get out." She recovers herself and says, "I need a minute. Please wait in the hall."

I've been waiting in the hall, and I go back there. From inside the office, there are the sounds of shuffling and rifling.

When the door reopens and she waves me back in, her purse has been moved to the other side of her desk.

"I'm sorry," she says, by way of explanation, "but things have been taken lately from people's offices."

I sit through my advising session very carefully, my file in front of her, which includes my demographics. I think of my friend from Pine Ridge who's scheduled to come to this office the next day, and if this is how I'm treated with my light skin and blue eyes, how is it going to be for her? I'm thinking how I'll tell her the story—the scarves, the skirts, the crazy eyes. I'm thinking that we'll laugh, and so I sit in the chair but remain unadvised.

The next semester, I get a new roommate and a new advisor, and the roommate is fine, and the second advisor, instead of proffering advice, offers his hand on my knee, his traveling hand, and I leave the building again unadvised and go back to my room to tend my snakes.

I'm attending this campus on a scholarship, and to keep this scholarship, I work at the university paper. The advisor is a woman who swears and paces, and I love her and fear her in equal measure until the day she trusts me with the story of her son, a grown man, accused of sexual assault in Nebraska. He has to go to court, she says. It's such bullshit. He wouldn't do that.

At a party, a half block off campus, this man, the son of my advisor, drinks and drinks. One night, just before this conversation, I'm there, drinking and drinking. The house belongs to a good friend who falls asleep, and this man—we'll call him Doug—chases me around and around the futon couch like we're playing some terrible game of duck-duck-goose. There are no snakes present, no *Camptosaurus*, and my friend is asleep, is snoring from his recliner, and where have all the other people gone?

The way I get away from Doug is because I'm small. The futon has a large, wooden frame, and there are meant to be soft, comfortable pillows on the back, but they are absent, and I make use of their absence. Which is to say, I've lost the game of duck-duck-goose. I'm on the futon with Doug, and I only get to leave because the pillows are missing, and I wiggle out the gap and shake awake my friend, who walks me home, to my apartment just off this place considered campus. My snakes are waiting, and I think perhaps I will, this day forward, carry them with me in that space we call *always*.

The next week, I learn Doug will be acquitted on all charges in Nebraska. The next week, I learn he raped one of my friends at another party. I don't tell my newspaper advisor; she is in charge of my scholarship; she is happy her son is acquitted. Later that year when he is going through his twelve steps, Doug follows me around town, apologizing. At the bookstore: apology. At the bar: apology. At the diner: apology.

I tell him to move on to his next step without my forgiveness. I tell him I work the police beat now, and I mention statute of limitations, and he grows quiet, so quiet, and he moves on to the next step or does not, but he stops enacting the act we call *apology*.

This story is an ordinary, everyday-violence story from a space considered campus. It is hard to see this space as hallowed when it is filled with so much ordinary, everyday violence. It is hard to see this space, this campus, as mine when it so clearly is not, when it so clearly never was.

It is hard not to ask the question: Who benefits from having an armed presence on a place considered campus? It is hard not to answer it with the negative, with the absence: not the girls who become women while they tend their snakes.

They are waiting in the campus halls for someone to offer advice. They are waiting still.

WHAT LOOKS LIKE MAD DISORDER: THE SARAH WINCHESTER HOUSE

Joni Tevis

San Jose, California

Midnight, she knew, tasted of bitter water but smelled good as damp dirt. The dark hours had taught her that as she'd slid from room to room. A big house creates its own sink of nighttime silence, ponderous as weather; how quiet the place back east had been. But these rooms were noisy as she wanted, alive with the ring of dropped nails, chuffing saws. Hammers swung all night at her command.

She slept, if she slept, in a different bed every night, or else waited patiently at the little desk in the séance room. She went over accounts and sketched plans for the next day, chewing on dried apricots grown in her own orchards. Tough little suns, flat and orange; they caught in her teeth. One night she drew a spider web on a sheet of paper. It would be a design for a stained-glass window.

She must have seen something she recognized in the spider. How every night she spins herself a home, and every dawn destroys it. How she anchors herself in a sturdy spot, reels out a loop, and adds the weight of her body. From this triangle, everything begins.

ONCE UPON A TIME there lived a baby girl, the only child of parents rich beyond measure. But when she was just a few weeks old, that baby died. Some years later, her father died too, and her mother was left alone. The mother had been the hub of a small family and now was the center of nothing, drifting from room to room, eyes dimmed by grief, hands empty. Maybe she felt a curse had fallen upon her, and maybe one had.

So she went to the city, Boston, and found a soothsayer, who told her to move west, build a house, and never stop, lest the spirits that had taken her daughter and husband come for her. There were legions of those ghosts, the medium said, all the people killed by her husband's guns. For this grieving woman was heir to the vast fortune of the Winchester Rifle Company. Sarah was her name, Sarah Pardee Winchester, and this was her house.

WE'RE STANDING IN THE COURTYARD, my husband David and I, waiting for our tour to start. The fountain beside us sparkles and spurts. We hear occasional honks from the traffic outside on Winchester Boulevard, and kids squealing as they horse around in the Victorian Gardens—it's a busy place, and we squint in the sun, tickets in hand.

We're between jobs, all our things stacked in a storage unit across the country in a new state, in a town called Apex. *You have to go where the work is*, people say. Well, we've done that, following jobs from Texas to Minnesota to North Carolina. Will one of us get a steady job when the academic hiring season starts up again next month? If not, what then? "We'll get by," David says, but right now, I can't see how.

In the meantime, we're taking a few days off, finagling flyer miles and a spot on our friends' sofa into a California junket. When we started packing, we couldn't find our suitcases—they were buried too deep in that storage unit. So we stuffed our clothes in a box that a coffee pot had come in, taped it shut, and heaved it onto the baggage belt. An awkward fix, but it would have to do.

The intercom crackles: *Tour number seventy-one, prepare to depart from the side entrance.* Twenty of us line up, a mixed bunch— retired couples, a father with two children, a boy in a ZAPATA VIVE! T-shirt. Our guide, a stony-faced college student with her dark hair cut in sleek wings, lays down the law. "Keep up," she says. "Stay with the group. If you get lost, you'll have to find your own way out. Nobody will ever find you."

With that, we step inside, through what used to be a service entrance. Nothing grand, just this threshold over which Sarah used to walk, sometimes with her favorite niece but most often alone. And entering here, I feel off-kilter—will feel off-kilter for the whole mile-long tour, through this 24,000-square-foot mishmash of a house. No time to ponder that as we shuffle up the shallow Easy Riser steps, built late in Sarah's life to help with her arthritis; into the $25,000 Storeroom, as it's now called, still stocked with expensive wallpaper and stacks of stained-glass windows; along endless rubber-runnered halls, stopping here and there to hear paragraphs of the guide's spiel; and occasionally passing other groups, whose guides repeat the same anecdotes with the same scripted language. Does anybody believe this stuff?

Here's the first story they tell: workers left nails half-driven when they heard of Sarah's death. She'd paid them three dollars a day, in cash—double the going rate. Many of them lived on the property, either in regular servants' quarters or in apartments below the water tower. And she kept them working at all hours. The Boston medium's prediction included the warning that Sarah had to keep renovating her new house constantly. If the hammers fell silent, the spirits would come for her. So she made sure that never happened. When she moved into the house, it had eight rooms, and she was three years a widow. When she died in 1922, thirty-eight years later, it had one hundred sixty rooms, some of which she had remodeled six hundred times.

Right away someone asks, "Was she crazy?" The question sticks in my craw. It feels too knee-jerk, too dismissive. What can you call that level of revision but obsessive? And yet something in it resonates with me; maybe she just wanted to get it right. I tuck the question into my notebook and hurry to catch up with the rest.

We don't know which eight rooms comprised the original farmhouse; we don't know where she began. So start with a nail, one end blunt and the other end sharp, ready to bite its beam. I wonder if nails pleased her as they please me; I wonder if she found them waiting for her on the sidewalk or in the street, if, when she bent to pick one up, her dark veil belled around her face. If, all day, her fingers worried it in her pocket. Nails were newcomers here, in the Valley of the Heart's Delight, as she was; resourceful people had whittled pegs before. Now they prized crates apart and hammered nails free. A good nail could be used more than once.

How different things might have been had she married a maker of nails. But she had married a gun man, William Wirt Winchester, and after his death, she became the weapon his family had perfected, repeating, her hammers' plosive stutter reshaping the rooms. Walking these hot halls, past oscillating fans that don't do anything to move the air, I shift beneath the weight of the guilt Sarah chose to bear. What stories do we tell ourselves about who we are? If we repeat them often enough, we'll start to trust them.

"Recently," our tour guide says, "a psychic contacted Sarah, and do you know what she said?" She flicks her eyes over us, waiting. "'What are all these people doing in my house?'" As soon as she says the words, I know they're true.

IT STARTED WITH A MAN'S DRESS SHIRT: funny to remember that. Her father-in-law had found a way to make it fit better through the shoulders. From shirts he moved to guns, shot, bullets: Winchester Arms, the Gun That Won the West. Eventually, Winchester factories would turn out products as diverse as meat grinders, scissors, fishing tackle, and roller skates—"The Skate With a Backbone"—but then as now, the Winchester Products

Company was best known for its firearms. Back in 1866, the year baby Anne was born and died, the Gun That Won was underwriting Sarah's life in New Haven, Connecticut. That gun paid for roast duck, hothouse greens, down-stuffed bedticks; it kept her servants in board and uniforms; it paid for doctors, ministers, and, at the end, the sexton. That gun hired a stonecutter and paid for a small casket, lined with silk.

And a few years later, when her husband died, Sarah found herself alone. Maybe she knew she couldn't have built the $25,000 Storeroom without the warehouses of guns, ready to be loaded in crates, into railcars, into waiting hands ready to shoot Apache and Pueblo by the thousands. Lead soldered water pipes and joined panes of glass; lead made ammunition. In the Winchester Arms shot tower, seven stories of carefully engineered furnaces and molds and water tanks where the hot shot was dropped to cool, hissing and steaming. Soothsayers used to employ lead rings to divine your future, holding the circles aloft with threads, burning through the threads, and marking where they fell. But she had asked her questions of the Boston medium, who scratched out answers with a planchette one letter at a time.

By all accounts her days in California were busy ones. The weight of her body anchored her here, on thick rugs that showed no wear and polished floors that gleamed like gunstocks. Sarah became an entrepreneur, buying real estate, running her farm, selling walnuts by the barrel. She stored up spade and mattock and blade, oil and whetstone, homing pigeons and ivory leg cuffs, screws cast from solid gold. She invented a sink with a built-in scrub board, and a window clasp modeled after a rifle's lock, paying homage to both cleanliness and defense. And although she set up the house to be self-sufficient, with its workshop, water tank, and gas reserves, still she answered the call of the outside world—rosewood and teak for the floors, German silver inlay for doors, pipestone for a fireplace.

In the end, she knew none of it mattered. She signed her thirteen-page will thirteen times, leaving provision for the house to be sold at auction and the furnishings to be left to Francis, her favorite niece, who took what she wanted and sold the rest. A practical way to dispose of things. Leave the gaslight chandelier with thirteen jets; leave it all, with minimal instructions, so that mountain of stuff won't hold you back. Set aside a sum to hire a man to deal it all out once you're gone.

I love a good auction, the auctioneer's chant braiding buyers, goods, price. His chant is a ballad that lasts all day, and each lot is a verse. *What will you give me*, he cries, *what'll you give?* More, always more: rugs scrolled like scripture, bare-head lamps shorn of shades, books on orchardcraft, cobbler's tools. Sales used to be regulated by candles; bidding lasted, like a séance, until the flame guttered dry.

BUT FOR THE KITCHEN, the Grand Ballroom, and the séance room, it's hard to tell what most of the rooms were used for, and that's not the only thing that gives the Winchester House a rickety, kaleidoscopic feeling. There are shallow cabinets an inch deep, and others large as generous rooms; one door opens onto a one-story drop, another onto slats instead of flooring. One staircase ends blind in a ceiling, and another forks into a Y, eleven steps up and seven steps down. Despite the fortune Sarah spent, the house feels temporary as a badly pitched tent.

And here we stand in the Hall of Fires. It's lined with hearth after hearth, strange for central California, but the guide tells us that Sarah craved the heat to ease her arthritis. I think of her sitting on this bench, listening to her house: a medium taps out a message from the dead, coins snick like knitting needles, and a gun-shaped latch snaps home. Two swings tap a trim nail true. A burning log hisses, freeing drops of old rainwater. A signal card drops into a slot: Mrs. Winchester needs assistance in the Hall of Fires, and a nurse heads toward her. Radiators knock, carrying waves of warmth. The rim of a plate nicks into its stack, and the maid clicks the cupboard door closed.

BY APRIL 1906, Sarah had lived in her house twenty-two years. During that time, her workers had built, among many other rooms, the Grand Ballroom. Whereas the rest of the house follows no rules—chimneys stop shy of ceilings; an extravagant rock-crystal window receives only slantwise light—the parquet floor in the Ballroom is precise down to the hair.

"The floor builder used no nails," our guide tells us, "only glue." He would have worked a section at a time, fitting one piece of smooth wood against another in a neat herringbone. This must have been the one hushed corner in a house constantly worried by sound, and even now, I'd like to stand here awhile, quiet, in this sunny corner.

I wonder if he heard the remembered racket of other workers when he slept at night, as I have, the carnival jingles of the theater-lobby arcade, the burr and shriek of machine parts turning and dropping off the lathe. If he took the sound in without realizing it and heard it played back in his dreams.

Above the glowing floor hang two stained-glass windows with quotations from Shakespeare. From *Troilus and Cressida*: "Wide unclasp the tables of their thoughts"; from *Richard II*: "These same thoughts people this little world." According to legend, only three people ever entered the house through the richly carved front door: Sarah, the man who delivered it, and the door-hanger. When Teddy Roosevelt dropped by one afternoon to express his admiration for Winchester rifles, servants sent him around back.

But on April 18, 1906, just after sunrise, the earth shook. In San Francisco, the ground liquefied and houses crumbled, their fronts peeling off and their walls buckling and kneeling. There must have been screams and silence—people shaken from sleep and too surprised to speak. When the gas lines ruptured, walls of flame pushed up the city's hillsides; pictures taken just after the disaster show buildings planed open, whole city blocks blackened to rubble where houses had stood, rifts carved in the countryside, oaks rived open, fences fallen, barns sucked flat.

Later, some witnesses told of hearing "an approaching roar" at dawn, or feeling a cold touch upon the cheek. Others said dogs pawed at doors and birds flew strangely; earthworms wriggled to the surface and tied themselves in knots. And in the Daisy Bedroom, a fireplace shook loose and collapsed, and Sarah was trapped alone.

"Sarah believed she caused the Quake," our guide says. "She thought the spirits were rebuking her for spending too much time on the front part of the house." So, the guide goes on, she ordered those rooms to be boarded shut and never went there again. No one danced across the Grand Ballroom's smooth parquetry, no chamber orchestra warmed the walls with music, and no friend paused in front of the Shakespeare windows and asked Sarah what she meant in choosing them.

But the guide hustles us away too quickly from the earthquake-wrecked rooms, with their crumbling plaster and naked studding, lengths of ship-lathe and dusty little cobwebs. Light bends from a curved window. Torn wallpaper and scrawls of glue stain the walls, and I think of that old line from Pliny the Elder: "Hence also walls are covered with prayers to ward off fires." The floor creaks companionably, and there's no armchair to distract, just the bones of the tired old house. I'd stay here all day if I could.

A telling detail hides in the house's thirteenth bathroom: the spider-web window Sarah designed. The artisan rendered the web's arcs in curving sections of glass, but this is shorthand; in any real web, something more pleasing than symmetry develops. After all, symmetry leaves gaps, and if prey escapes, the spider starves.

Jean-Henri Fabre, a French naturalist writing during Sarah's lifetime, noted that the orb-weaver spider works in a method that might seem, to the untrained observer, "like mad disorder." After the initial triangle, spokes, and spiral, she rips out the preliminary threads, whose remnants appear as specks on the finished web. (In one added room of the Winchester House, you can make out the slope of a previous roof, a vestige of what the house used to be.) The spider fills out the web, testing its tension as she goes, finally building up the "sheeted hub," a pad near the web's middle where she rests and waits. Fabre calls this area "the post of interminable waiting." When night fades, the spider destroys the web, eating the silk as she goes. Says Fabre: "The work finishes with the swallowing."

The spider carries within her belly a store of this strong, pearly stuff, which nobody has yet been able to replicate. She dashes along an invisible line to bind a fly with bights of silk; she bluffs her foes by "whirling" or "shuttling" her web at them. Naturalists used to carry scraps of velvet to the field, so they could have a better backdrop for examining the webs they found. An entrepreneur once made wee cork-padded cuffs and fitted them to a spider's legs, then wound skein after skein of silk from her spinnerets until the creature ran dry. He repeated the process with thousands of spiders until he had enough material to weave a gray gown of spider silk, which he then presented to Queen Victoria. During World War II, British gun manufacturers used black widow silk to make crosshairs for rifle sights.

As for me, when spring comes, I keep a lookout for the "sea of gossamer," as it's been called, when spiderlings take flight. In summer I have spied many a tight purse or reticule in which a swaddled grasshopper still struggles, staining the silk with dark bubbles of tobacco juice. And in fall I watch big garden spiders move from holly bush to camellia, spooling out guy lines and waiting under the streetlight for miller moths. With articulate legs, they pluck strands of silk and load them with gum. When dawn comes they finish hunting and tear down their webs, swallowing the golems a line at a time.

THE WINCHESTER HOUSE was once a living thing, Sarah's shadow self, breathing in and swelling out, tough as twice-used nails. There are many threads to this story; many entrances, but only one safe exit. Not the door that opens onto a one-story drop, or the one that opens onto slats above the yellow kitchen. She knew the way out; she designed it. After she died, movers needed maps of the house to empty it.

The house's largest cabinet, the size of a generous apartment, is a useful place to examine how the house is and is not made. A cabinet is a container, a room with single-minded purpose. Pliny tells of a house built of salt blocks mortared with water; how the sun shining through those walls must have glowed red at sunset. A fitting shelter for ghosts: crimson, translucent, walled with tears.

Sarah knew her house to be founded on blood, invocations written on the walls, looping script of glue holding the heavy wallpaper tight. Such a house, built for the dead, turns itself inside out, night after night. Windows mutter curses, drains align with Saturn rising, nails turn from gold to lead. She moved veiled through her nights, knowing what others did not, and placing a coin on every tongue her guns had stopped. Some jaws opened easily, others she wrenched apart, still others (blown away) she could not find: for these she placed gold on the breastbone, flat as a plectrum. Lay a goose's tongue on a sleeping person, and he will confess every sin he has ever committed. If a robin dies in your hand, your fingers will always shake. You will forget what you meant to say. The hum of voices grew. Sarah heard them all.

Step through a little door. "Welcome to the séance room," the guide says, and something about it does feel mysterious. Not just because of the thirteen hooks in the closet, or the three entrances and one exit (two doors only open one way). Here was where Sarah moved the flat planchette across the divining board, spelling out messages from the dead. The room feels like a sheeted hub, a knot.

Samson spoke false when he said, *Weave my hair into the web of your loom, and I will become weak as any man,* but it would have been natural for Delilah to believe him; superstitions about weaving have been around as long as knots themselves. Part a bride's hair with the bloodied point of a spear. Forbid pregnant women from spinning, lest the roots of the growing child tangle. To treat infections of the groin, tie the afflicted person's hair to the warp of a loom, and speak a widow's name (*Sarah, Sarah, Sarah*) with every knot.

Move from legend to artifact and find hair jewelry, a practice that reached its obsessive height during the Victorian era, a way to keep a scrap of absent loved one close. Women wove locks of hair into watch chains, button covers, and forest scenes, or braided flat ribbons from forty sections of hair, weighting them with bobbins to pull them flat as they worked. In Boston, a man had two hundred rings inset with locks of his hair and had them distributed at his funeral; their inscriptions read "Prepare to Follow Me."

When Sarah searched for the center of her life she found her child, quick breath in her ear, warm weight on her heart. She remembered the slight rise and fall, remembered counting the breaths, standing in the dark nursery past midnight, holding her own breath to better mark her infant's.

She tucked a simple lock of baby's hair in a safe and knitted a house around it. Whose grief could be more lavish than hers? She wove a row of rooms—hummed calls toward the dead, boxes made of music, measure upon measure. Began, like a spider, with three: herself, her husband, their child. Or herself, the rifles, those slain. The séance room has three entrances, but only one exit. The Fates hold three lengths of line and a keen edge to cut them.

From three points, she moved outside of language, opening the priceless front door, stepping over the threshold and bolting the door behind her. Spoke notes and rhythm and commerce (per box of dried apricots, less the cost to grow them). In her youth, she had spoken four tongues, but now she spoke the language of nails, to which no one could reply. While her carpenters built, she spoke through them, though they remembered nothing beyond *worked on the kitchen today*. They cracked jokes about ghosts while they worked, but that wasn't what made them uneasy; it was the way she used them to get outside speech. A good enough reason for paying them double—once for building, twice for hiding her secrets. Her army of men, working day and night, could hide a nail for every bullet sown and not feel the debt of guilt she had to spend. No wonder she kept them working throughout the dark hours.

IN A GRAVEL-FLOORED AVIARY, Sarah kept tropical birds. To understand the speech of sparrows, touch a marigold to your bare foot on the appointed day. Tuck a bittern's claw into your lapel for luck. The blood of a pelican can restore murdered children to life.

I read Aesop's little-known fable, "The Lark Burying Her Father." The lark lived before the beginning of the world. Water stretched out before her; she hollowed a home in the mist. When her father died, she was forced to let him lie unburied six days, because there was no earth to cover him. Finally she split open her head and buried her father inside, and to this day, her head is crested like a burial mound.

Spared the problems of the birds who would come after her—the myrtle tree to ensnare, the gems to distract from food—the lark's difficulty was elemental. Just the primary problem of grief, and not a bit of dust at hand to help. Later, Aesop relates, she would tell her children, "Self-help is the best help."

The problem of what to do with the dead was one Sarah also confronted. She buried the bodies in the usual way, then moved across the country and built a living house in which she buried herself, again and again. Pliny records that magpies, if fed on acorns, can be taught to speak. Going further, he claims that they develop favorite words, "which they not only learn but are fond of and ponder carefully," he says. "They do not conceal their obsession." Did any of Sarah's tropical birds possess the power of speech? If so, what did she long to hear them say? Maybe *help* or *home* or *Mama*, a name no one had ever called her. We don't know if they were toucans or macaws or quetzals, whether they screamed or croaked, only that they were tropical and that they came, like Sarah, from far away.

AFTER A QUICK PASS through the basement with its ancient furnace and rust-stained cement floor, the house tour ends and we're escorted out a low door. Our guide takes her leave, and we're free to wander the grounds, crunching along gravel paths between the carefully clipped boxwoods, the thirteen palm trees, and the bronze sculpture of Chief Little Fawn. Press a button by the fountain and listen to the talking box tell its story. A boy of twenty, maybe a guide-in-training, studies a stapled script under an ancient grapefruit tree. It's a lot to remember.

You can see anything you want in Sarah Winchester. Craft a story from what bits and scraps you know. Her house is the only document left to show us who she was, and it's so easy to read it wrong. What was she trying to say? Was the house a letter to herself, or a cryptic message to the outside world?

Whatever the place is, it makes people uneasy. I heard it in the nervous banter of the other visitors. ("I think we should visit the firearms museum," a man said to his son. "I think *that* would be interesting.") ("She might have been *too* educated," a woman said to our guide, who ignored her.) I can't say whether the house is haunted or not, but it got under my skin.

Her naked display of long-term grief makes me flinch. Could I do any better; could any of us? When her husband and child died, she mourned them the rest of her life, and all her buying and selling couldn't distract her. She did not hope for heaven—*what will it profit a man if he gains the whole world and loses his soul?*—but let the world pass through her fingers: imported stone, brass smelted in faraway furnaces. Cared for none of it except as material bulk, something to make the house more than what it had been. Ordered the gardener to put in a new bed of daisies and hawthorn; paged through a catalogue offering English yew and monkey puzzle, catalpa and persimmon, whose bitter fruit she craved.

For me, the stories about Sarah are the worst of it. All the easy myths, free of real life's half-measures; the tour guide's flip answers, and the dismissive chorus: *She must have been crazy.* In fact, in her constant rebuilding of the house—an occupation with roots in the daily and domestic, but which she was able to take to new lengths because of her tremendous wealth—she looks a lot like an artist at work. If she'd been like her father-in-law, perfecting one object and mass-producing it, we'd remember her for her innovation and engineering. If she'd been like most upper-class women of her time, creating House Beautiful around her and then living out her life there, we wouldn't remember her at all.

But Sarah Winchester did something of both when she created her house. Because she didn't leave explanatory documents behind, all we have is the coded message of the house itself. Glance at it, and you might think it reads *crazy old woman.* But linger over its crabbed lines, fish-scale shingles, old-growth redwood painted over to look like birch, and you'll see she was doing what an artist does—leaving her mark and seeing what happened; working through an idea via metal, wood, and space; expanding the notion of what life is all about.

AFTER WE LEFT the Winchester House, we stopped at an Army-Navy store and bought a duffel bag to replace the battered old coffee-pot box for the trip home—a step in the right direction. But long after I dragged the duffel through the door of our new place and started unpacking, I couldn't let Sarah go. Dangerous, maybe, to take a big trip like that when you're between stages of your life, looking for work, unsure who you are. I kept coming back to a postcard we bought in the Winchester House gift shop, a reproduction of the one extant photo of Sarah. She's seated in a carriage behind a driver, and even though she's at some distance, there's a smile on her small, expressive face. She looks content, someone with work that needs doing. In that moment, she's far away from the morning she buried her child, farther still from her husband's rattling sickbed, and just like that she passes through the one safe exit into the realm where time shunts away, and hours, days, thirty-eight years pass, and she follows the unspooling line of her thought to its ragged end and looks up to see the marks she's made. Floor, ceiling, wall; this covers me; this crowns me; this pushes me forward. *Self-help is the best help*: maybe she believed it. But Sarah's story ends not with a tidy moral but a dashed-off map. The movers, at least, would find that useful.

She could have filled scores of rooms with visitors. But in the end, the memory of her lost ones was enough for her. We are the crowd she never invited. (*What are all these people doing in my house?*) Now every day is filled with the tread of feet, the whisper of hands sliding along her banisters, the hum of conversations she can't quite make out.

WE SIGNED A YEAR'S LEASE on a brick cottage outside Apex. I spent my days running between libraries: an elegant domed one with a smooth marble floor, barrister's tables, and an echo; the main one, eight stories and two sub-basements crammed with no-nonsense metal shelves; the zoology one, where I read Fabre in a cozy little carrel; the geology one with maps of historic earthquake activity and potted succulents growing in deep-silled windows. I read an article about scientists feeding LSD to spiders to see how it affects their webs. I read that earthquakes leave coded messages in the earth around them, and that San Francisco politicians tried to deny the Quake after it happened. That an old Roman myth tells of a gown made of moonbeams, and the pages, eyes sore and bloodshot, who carried it to Hera. That barbed wire used to be called "the devil's rope," and that you can tell the construction date of a house by the nails that bind it together.

At the time, it didn't occur to me that I was obsessing over the details of someone else's house even as I craved a place of my own. When our year's lease was up, we moved to yet another state, where we've been ever since. Now we live in a tidy little bungalow with green shutters and a tight roof we paid for ourselves, with gleanings from that steady job we scoured the country to find. And from this place of greater stability I see the Winchester House in another light. Maybe an art installation, as I initially believed, or maybe just something to fill her time.

Still, nights when I can't sleep, I walk the halls of a darkened library, a place Sarah bequeathed me. Her ramshackle house provided me plenty of work, paragraphs to draft and revise again and again, dry little suns to gnaw on, morsels sweet and tough by turns. Even now, telling these secrets, slick pages whisper beneath my fingertips and I smell marvelous old dust and glue. I breathe in air that speaks of words tucked between heavy covers, tales spelled out one letter at a time.

FAKE IDS

Arisa White

Jason Benjamin Josaphat, nineteen years old. Akyra Monet Murray, eighteen years old. Luis Omar Ocasio-Capo, twenty years old. I'm reading the forty-nine names and ages of the victims killed in the June 12, 2016, mass shooting at Pulse nightclub in Orlando. I am sad all over. I'm remembering when I was in high school, how my crew of friends snuck into lesbian clubs in New York City. I'm remembering that moment of stepping into the darkness: when the bass-beat hit my chest and some of my defenses let down their arms, and we danced our asses off.

Nineteen years old. Eighteen years old. Twenty years old. And Pulse is listed as twenty-one and over. *What were they doing in the club?* I know my own answer.

UNDERAGE, AND I GOT INTO HerShe Bar in Chelsea, Clit Club in the Meat Packing District, and Meow Mix on Houston. It was the mid-nineties, and I was seventeen in the fall, eighteen in the spring, a high-school senior. I got my fake ID in the West Village, near where Gray's Papaya used to be. I decided to make myself four years older, the year my oldest brother was born. Kept my birthday, which made it easy for me to remember. I was tall for my age, my demeanor calm, and I had no problem making eye contact with authority. I have eyes.

But four years earlier, my freshman year, while I watched my gym teacher pile the mats against the back wall, I wasn't looking forward to what the guest speaker from the Gay and Lesbian Community Center had to say about youth services, HIV testing, and free condoms. I wanted to practice my Taekwondo punches. Gym class was the occasional self-conscious snicker, whispered remarks that *Nobody's gay in here*, and the snapping of latex. My overly tanned black-belt gym teacher had invited the speaker so that, she said, "Regardless of being gay or straight, here are resources available to you." Despite my irritation, something must have registered from the talk because, unlike most of my classmates, who left their brochures behind or waited to toss them after we left, I kept mine.

IT WAS THE WINTER of junior year when things shifted for me. I'd just arrived home from Israel, where I'd been on a month-long foreign exchange program. In Arad, I held the hand of a red-haired girl who cried when her work schedule at an ice-cream shop in a mall conflicted with my stay. Because Sivan wanted time to hang out with me. With *me*. She was sobs and apologies. I told her I would love to go to work with her, and she gave me scoops of whatever ice cream I wanted. There were few customers in the cooler temperatures of November, and Sivan and I chatted for three hours, watching mall-goers, noting the similarities and differences between our countries. The young people dressed in the same grunge look, and the mall played the same top-forty billboard hits that were in rotation on the radio back home.

One evening, we went out to eat at the Muza pub, all the Americans with their Israeli hosts, and I remember Ram, chin-length dreadlocks and acne, saying that it might be weird for us

Americans to see guys holding hands, kissing each other in hello and good-bye. *But we're not, you know, gay.* He communicated this with conversant English, with gestures to signal nuance, context—cultural practices he didn't have words for. Words that spoke to a way of being that made loving touch a basic part of their exchanges. And we got it. I understood, and appreciated reading a nation of bodies in this way. Suddenly I was no longer perceiving touch in terms of default heteronormativity.

Sivan and I spooned ourselves to sleep my last night there. She asked if we could, and she gifted me her Annie Lennox CD, because she saw that "Walking on Broken Glass" was my immediate jam. It was a good night.

I SHARED THIS WITH ONE of my closest friends, Delancey, upon my return from Arad. I was never sure why Delancey was in a public high school. He presented more like he should be at the Dalton School in the Upper East Side. Delancey lived in Harlem, in a brownstone near where Langston Hughes once resided, and had a flair for fashion. Shoes to hairline, he was too fly. Had genres for his outfits: preppy; Brooklyn; nautical Caribbean; seventies meets nineties, and hip-fine, a combination of hip-hop and fine menswear. All the while being so very straight. We became friends his freshman year when he came up to me on the first day of school, having recognized me from an MTV News episode on censorship and the Internet. Since my family didn't have cable and I hadn't seen it yet, I asked him to tell me about it. To my horrified surprise, they'd edited my thirty-minute interview to thirty seconds. Delancey said I was quoted saying something about a chatroom I belonged to, how someone had posted a picture of a baby with an adult penis superimposed on it. MTV didn't include the part about how the members of the chatroom put up a fuss, which resulted in the user being removed from the bulletin board service. My point in sharing that story was to illustrate that the government should not censor—instead give the community the space to regulate what it needs and doesn't need. I could have gotten mad about it, but instead Delancey and I got a good laugh out of the way the media can spin and twist your words.

Are you gay? Delancey asked me square. We were listening to a demo of my cousin before he got famous, in the downstairs parlor room of the brownstone my mom and aunt had bought on Greene Ave in BedStuy. My inhibitions about coming out weren't about my family's rejection. My brother, the one who is three years younger than me, made a valiant declaration one Saturday afternoon that he would love me if I was gay, and then ran up the stairs to his room so there could be no contestation. What I was concerned about was the general perception that my sexuality arose from a flaw in my upbringing, the result of an absent biological father and physically and emotionally abusive father figures—that my desire was led by such a linear cause-and-effect. This kind of thinking made me feel dim. I didn't feel in reaction to anything or anyone.

This most dapper of sophomores looked at me, waiting for my reply. His question seemed to miss the point. I came back with, *This is not about gay, it's about how I want to live in my body. Where is the space for that?* Neither one of us had an answer about space, about where there was space to be black and unconventional in our gender presentations, and so in that silence we listened to the vocalist alto out *Feelin it...Feelin it—if you feel it raise your L in the sky*, and agreed that was the perfect hook.

IT TOOK ME NEARLY A YEAR to answer Delancey's question directly. *Am I gay?* It wasn't a simple conversational response, but a series of personal inquiries and actions, which set me on a journey that would take me to a café, a community center, and dance parties in lofts, penthouse apartments, and eventually nightclubs, and to encounters with people who would help me articulate and define my desires.

In that near-year time, I was crushed out on a white guy name Tate from the Upper West Side and couldn't understand why he wouldn't give me play. So one night I made out with his best friend when we were at someone's house party in an apartment that gave expensive views of the city. Guy's mouth tasted like Olde English and discontent, and none of this was making Tate jealous. While they snorted coke through a fifty-dollar bill, I balanced on the arms of two couches and bopped to "Block Rockin Beats."

Around that time my best friend Kimberly came out of the closet. We were in Theater Club together. Once we did a minimalist rendition of *Hamlet*, all dressed in black, which got us an honorable mention at some high-school Shakespeare festival. Kim and I ate lunch together in our English teacher Ms. Griffin's room because we both had a crush on her. When Kim went from innocent schoolgirl crush on unavailable adult figure to publicly making out with sophomore Mariana, I was shocked. That most scandalous kiss in front of Burger King was all the talk to be heard in school the following day. And Kim had kept it all a secret from me, her feelings for Mariana. Supposedly the sparks sparked on afterschool train rides home; they both rode the A—Mariana got off in Brooklyn somewhere and Kim went way out to Far Rockaway. Kim said it just happened: "She was saying French fry and there was a grain of salt on her lip and a kiss felt like the right thing to do."

I forgave her for withholding her secrets from me, and then a month later she was dating Konstantin, who was in our year. Kim's bisexuality was a sweet spot of possibilities that intrigued me. *Was I bi?* I still remained in contact with Sivan, and would squeal each time I received a letter from Israel. I cut my hair to a short natural like Roshumba Williams, and people would stop me on the street, tell me I was beautiful, say I was brave. Then a cybercafé, the first of its kind owned and operated by black women, opened up in Fort Greene. I eyed Kokobar on a wintery afternoon, as the B52 bus waited at a red light. Just a week before, I'd been talking to my mom about wanting to open a cool café that sold books and had a cyberlounge. I remember thinking, as the bus drove past, *That place is my dream.*

Kokobar was owned by writers and activists Rebecca Walker and angel Kyodo Williams, who were known to be a couple at the time. It was good for me to see two black lesbians together. Kokobar opened its doors in January 1996, on Lafayette, where Lafayette meets Fulton Street and forms a vertex. Because angel had an appreciation for Japanese aesthetics, Kokobar translated to "the place to be." A café, espresso bar, and cyber lounge, it sold books by local writers of color too. The awning was pitch black, and the Kokobar logo, in calligraphic bright autumn red, like maple leaves fresh fallen, was centered in a rectangle. Sometimes I would sit at the front window, stare at passersby, occasionally seeing Spike Lee and his sister. I'd read a book and drink chocolate mocha lattes, which the baristas eventually knew to be my favorite. Farther back was the cyber lounge with its six Power Macintosh desktops, where folks were charged by ten-minute increments. They could login to New York Online, a bulletin-board service based in Carroll Gardens, Brooklyn. I interned with NYO from my sophomore to senior years, and sometimes I helped people troubleshoot when the baristas didn't know what to do. At the center of the café were chairs and tables and the most comfortable avocado-green couch, all of which would be moved around when Kokobar hosted events—readings by such writers as Paul Beatty, cabaret-style music concerts with Toshi Reagon, and dance parties.

I had a crush on one of the baristas, Tanisha. While ringing me up for a mocha latte, she asked me, *Are you a dyke?* Then handed me a flyer for a party. I took it and responded, *Thank you. Will you be there?* There were no more thoughts of Tate after Tanisha, especially after I kissed her at the Dyke Party in June. And so began my dyke summer. I interned at Citicorp in Tribeca, and during the orientation session, some girl who was working in my department said to me, while we snacked on dip, that I was checking out another girl. I didn't even know I was doing it—but I remember thinking, damn, Dip Girl was all in my grill. I read Audre Lorde's *Zami*, books about Stonewall, black gay and lesbian experiences here and abroad; I kissed more women in their houses, offices; and I danced. At house parties and parties thrown at local shops and cafés, where I didn't need an ID, but still lied about my age. Even when I said I was eighteen, they thought I was older, too cool and smart to be that young.

ONE NIGHT I DANCED so hard I lost sight of the crew that I came with. I couldn't resist the pull when we circled around dancing bodies, watching them exult, innovate to a rhythm within and outside of them. We created a ring to contain the energy, committed ourselves as witnesses. When the moment opened up, like that moment when the double-dutch ropes say *come*, I was ready. No longer hesitant, I entered and caught the beat like a heart. Moving limbs my mama gave me, putting myself in a Judith Jamison state of mind. My jeans heavy with sweat, our bodies' petrichor, made me feel like uncorked champagne.

The loft applauded when I bowed out of the cipher. A regular customer at the Kokobar had invited me to the house party, but she and her friends were nowhere to be found, and I was pissed they hadn't come to find me. Pissed. It was nearly two o'clock in the morning when I stepped out of the building by the Navy Yard. That part of the neighborhood at night triggers your primal instincts. The looming prison they called the Brig, poorly lit streets, the BQE overhead, and you pass through a section of Fort Greene Projects before you get back to Myrtle Ave, where a decent amount of cabs, or possibly just one, would be circulating during those night-a.m. hours. I may have appeared more mature than I was, but I feared for my life.

Fortunately, a cab stopped at a red light on Park Ave. I knocked on the driver's side and asked if he was still working. He gave me a fatherly look, in that critical, kind way Jamaican men can do, and asked me where I was going. "Greene between Bedford and Nostrand." It cost me ten dollars, and when I handed it to him, the bill was tinted blue from my jeans and wet from my dancing.

THE PEOPLE I MET that summer opened and broke my heart in varying degrees. Each instance of joy or pain was a moment where I could genuinely feel who I was. Tanisha eventually found out my real age, because I stupidly invited her to a family function, and thereafter she gave me the cold shoulder. After that the dishonesty was too much for me to contain. I was excited to be who I was, less and less comfortable with deceit. I started to tell some people my real age. Aliyyah, who was a former model and walked around in crazy-thick platforms, was smitten with me. She was five years older, and while we dry humped on her boss's chair, she said she would wait until I was legal. She called me the Kokobar's baby, and oddly it made me feel loved—the idea that this place I thought so a–mazing had spawned me. During the last party of the summer, I met Carolina. A self-proclaimed lyricist, she had recently moved to Brooklyn from Minnesota and was living in an apartment above Kokobar. I asked her to bust a rhyme for me, and she did so beneath the glow of streetlights. I never felt so thirsty for a kiss, watching her lips move. We danced until Kokobar told us to go home. A few days later after the start of my senior year, I ran into her again at the café, and she invited me to her apartment later that evening for dinner.

I was with Kim, about to walk her to the subway, and I told Carolina I would be back. Lit with excitement, I asked Kim, *What do you think is gonna happen?* She sassily said something in Tagalog that I didn't understand, but understood as "You foolish little girl." She gave me a hug and with a big smile on her face, said, You'll soon find out. What happened was that Carolina and I made love for the first time. My first time. I was so sprung. I began to worry when, after two weeks, she wasn't returning my phone calls. We met up one afternoon in Washington Square Park, and she told me she'd hooked back up with an ex and was now pregnant. Do you see me rolling my eyes?

THESE REJECTIONS SENT ME searching for the brochure I'd received from the guest speaker my freshman year. Even though Delancey and I didn't end up talking directly about whether I was gay or not, I opened the brochure in the privacy of my bedroom, and found my answer. I read about a group for LGBT and questioning youth. I felt like LGB, and was definitely questioning. It was a group for thirteen- to twenty-year-olds, and it met at the Gay and Lesbian Community Center on Fridays, after school.

It was exactly a year after returning from Israel that I went to my first meeting. The Center was another place where I could be my alphabet. I took the A train to Fourteenth Street in the West Village, and as I walked to the Center I felt the increased presence of gayness. I entered through a front metal door, and I remember feeling small, even though I was five foot ten at the time. A smallness like a toddler more than a feeling of diminishment. I asked the front-desk person, in a voice coming out of its own shell, where was the group meeting for young people. She told me a sequence of rights and lefts and through an area that reminded me of a closed-roof atrium, with amber lights. I passed through, found the room to my right, and there they were: some sitting in the circle of chairs, some milling about, light chatter. The ones who knew each other had more animated threads of conversation. I found a patch of empty chairs by the door, and acknowledged everyone with a hello that was genuine but not too enthusiastic, a head nod, and a lazy queenlike wave. I looked around but didn't stare, casting my eyes on a crack in the wall, on an AIDS awareness poster. I joined the group in waiting for the facilitator to come.

Our discussions were facilitated by a person trained in social work, or something—I never remembered their credentials. We would go around and check in, and eventually unload whatever was on our minds. I attended those meetings nearly every Friday until I graduated from high school, and although new people would come in and out, there was always a committed group who showed up. Milly, funny, lively and vocal—when she opened her mouth she had something to say. Cute too. Andy was an inch taller than me and *bea*utiful. That kind of beauty that made me pucker my lips on *beau*. But Milly and her were an item. Nadine was petite, with the most generous boobs, and lived on Staten Island. We always made sure she got the eleven o'clock boat home. When I started to read Alison Bechdel's *Dykes to Watch Out For* in my early twenties, the character Mo Testa reminded me so much of Dani. Dani's number-one concern in group: safe sex with women. And we were like, *Who you fucking, Dani?* Our after-group hangouts introduced me to Peaches and Khadijah, both of them aged out of the meeting. Peaches was in her junior year at Brooklyn College, and Khadijah was—I wasn't quite sure what Khadijah was up to, but I'm sure she was selling weed on the side.

One night we were at the Waverly Diner, sharing a plate of fries, when Andy suggested, "Let's go to the Clit Club next Friday." There were yeses all around, even from Abassi, who had started coming to group recently because her father kicked her out of the house when he found out she was gay. She was living at a shelter, where her mom came by to drop off clothes and give her pocket money for the week. Abassi was insisting on buying my dinner, and said order anything you want, when Khadijah reminded everyone, "Them bitches be carding folks, so have your IDs." I didn't have my ID yet, of course. I had no older sister or cousin or friend I somewhat resembled. I felt done with pretending, but I had to do something about this.

THE THING ABOUT MY ID, there was nothing official about it. No school logo, state insignia, no stickers or holograms. Nothing to give it institutional or governmental affiliation. It was a photo, typewriter-typed personal information, and the back of it was plain white plastic, no magnetic strip or barcode. A Blockbuster Video card was more official. It cost me twenty-five dollars. The ID maker had me fill out a form, no identification needed to verify the information provided. I sat for a photo and smiled like I was getting away with murder.

The Clit Club was the first place I used my fake ID. We stood outside in the brisk of a November night, and Peaches and Khadijah went on through. Peaches stopped to tell the bouncer, *Be good to my crew*, and made sure to emphasize that I was the last member in that crew. Milly and Andy in, Dani and Nadine in, Abassi didn't come out tonight, and then I handed my card to the butchie white chick, her hands nicely manicured and robust. She looked at me and it, turned it over, looked at me and it some more, and then asked, *What's your birthday?* I lied truthfully. She gave me a bullshit smile, with a twinkle in her eye, and the crew just in earshot, anticipating the outcome. The bouncer nodded her head, said, *All right, you're in.*

I loved those gurls. I was alive in their company. Astrologically, I am a fish, and what they gave me was a school. To be a part of something, and still individual, with the skill to act as a complete body that can disperse, go off in all directions, come back together again like we're magnetically pulled. A wonderful orchestration. In their company, I reached different freedoms, was in relationship with this part of myself without anxiety and fear, could know joy and love, curiosity and fun, beauty and acceptance, pleasure and possibility, and a more emotionally realized vision of myself. They help me see the multiplicity of our experiences.

I had an astrologer read my chart by phone the same fall I started going to the Center. I met him in a chatroom on New York Online, emailed him my birthdate, time, and location, and he sent my chart to me by postal mail. As he went over where planets are housed, and trine this, he asked, *Are you gay?* I asked if that was what the chart said. He explained that women and men were drawn to me and I'd do well either way. So that crew of friends confirmed the stars, and their lives equally smashed and reinforced stereotypes in combinations of being that assuaged my doubts. They allowed me to wake a part of myself and insist on her presence. I was in a relationship of love, through their friendship. I started to live the homointimacy I'd glimpsed back in Israel.

AFTER DANCING AMONG ALL THE LADIES—and me momentarily tied up with a chick from Florida in the corner with my hands down her pants—Andy, me, and Dani ended up in the bathroom sharing details of our conquests. For some reason, Dani felt my arm and then commented that I was real soft. She invited Andy to feel, and Andy agreed, *Baby soft*. I told them I exfoliated with a loofah, but they weren't convinced that this kind of softness came from rubbing off dead skin. They both had that freaked-out-pleasure look on their faces like they came across a favorite piece of candy at the height of a sweet-tooth craving. The light in the bathroom was the color of a cherry pop, or what it may look like standing inside a heart.

We went back to the dance floor with our laughter, and me with their touch. Andy passed around a cup of Long Island iced tea, and I took a sip and an ice cube. The bass was coming up from the floor. Our bodies securely puzzled together like a J.J. Evans painting. "Rhythm is a Dancer" getting us hyped. Our lean arms, the sinew of our groove uniting torso to torso, hips to hips. *It's a soul champion, you can feel it everywhere* was alive in our bodies—so close, as one, that a bullet could take us all.

HYPPÄÄ JÄRVEEN

Carrie Messenger

IMMERSION

Salolampi's camp song resembled a funeral dirge: no soprano notes, nothing allegro, nothing summery. I'd listened to my grandmother and great-aunts gossip in Finnish, with its blur of vowels, but this was the first time I'd heard people singing in the language. As we stood in a ring in the clearing, encircled by a grove of slender birches and towering pines that kept the weak morning light from warming us, the campers let out one long Finnish wail, a tragic song about a mysterious lake in the woods. I thought we were in mourning. At least, I was in mourning— for summer, for reading books in trees, painting the cat's portrait, sleeping late in my own bedroom instead of waking at dawn to the wispy breathing of the other campers. I shivered in my sweatshirt and rubbed my nose against the palm of my hand. I couldn't think of what everyone else might be mourning, except maybe the Finland we'd lost through immigration: our northern home bathed in darkness, drowning in vodka, snug in snow and reindeer herds. I'd never felt less Finnish.

But then that's why I was here. I'd been given a small scholarship from the Finnish-American Association after I wrote an essay about how I wanted to learn Finnish to discover who I was. My grandmother was the one who'd told me about the essay contest for teenage campers. She wanted me to go, and I wanted to know what I might have known if she hadn't been crazy for assimilation, if McCarthyism hadn't terrified her because of the dead communists banging away in our family closet. I wanted to know what I was besides white. Most of the people I knew growing up either weren't white in the first place, or claimed another identity if they were: Polish, Irish, Italian, Jewish, Catholic. I'd been telling people I was part Finnish, a branch of the family tree that had immigrated most recently and came from a non-English-speaking country, unlike the WASP parts. I was only one-fourth Finnish, a tenuous connection.

When Eino, the camp director, raised the Finnish flag, nobody said a word. Nobody. It was so quiet that I could hear, among the songbirds preening in the trees, mosquitoes buzzing at my ears. I slapped at them. I thought that when the flag reached the top of the pole and the blue cross on the white background waved across the pale Minnesota sky, the campers might cheer. They didn't. Nobody spoke until Eino announced, "For the next two weeks, Salolampi *is* Finland."

But I couldn't understand Eino, because he said it in Finnish. Ilse, who was in Kuopio Cabin with me, nonchalantly translated on the way to breakfast. Because Ilse's real name was Ilse, she didn't have a Finnish camp name. Her name marked her as 100 percent Finnish, camp royalty. She even spoke Finnish at home. Some kids had Finnish names without being Hundred Percenters, but Ilse was the real deal. Like me, she came from Evanston, outside Chicago, but I knew I shouldn't think of her as an ally among the Minnesotans. Her long, blond Barbie hair—really more Swedish than Finnish, with its sheer almost-white brightness—made her stand out. Unlike at home, where I would let the black girls play with my straight, thin Finnish hair if I could examine their cornrows, bead by bead, at Salolampi the range of differences was small. We all had relatively beady eyes. We tended to be stocky, but more solid than outright fat.

Ilse whispered to me, "God, I feel sorry for you, Erja. It's hard to be here without some Finnish. You can borrow *Purple Rain* as long as you don't get caught with it." It was August of 1986, I was fourteen, and since at Salolampi we weren't allowed to listen to non-Finnish music, Prince had become our most important contraband. Ilse had sized me up as the kind of camper who might somehow let it be confiscated.

Erja was my camp name. It hung on a wooden board around my neck and, when I walked, banged against my chest, an area I had been working for two years to hide at all costs. I liked *Erja* if I anglicized it: "Er-ja." It sounded like the name of a *Star Trek* villainess. But the Finnish pronunciation was "Eh-ri-ya." My Finnish name was a yawn. I was convinced that they gave the best names to the Hundred Percenters, then the Halves. The Fourths got leftovers. Who did we think we were, coming to Salolampi to muddle our way through a language that we didn't know, picking up customs that should have been taught to us by our lazy grandparents, eating food and learning songs that should have been ours already by birthright?

Although my grandmother had suggested Salolampi, nobody made me go. My non-Finnish father discouraged me, in fact, wondering why his child, the artistic introvert, wanted to spend two weeks in close quarters with other children, let alone while trying to learn an isolated language like Finnish. I did it because I wanted to please my grandmother. There were few ways to do it. She didn't like what other grandmothers liked. She didn't display the art projects we made, wouldn't let us win at cards, was more likely to pinch us than hug us, and tried to end phone conversations as fast as possible once the barest pleasantries had been exchanged. I was her only grandchild who tried to learn Finnish. I singled myself out in my cultural devotion, the same way that, later on, I'd be the one to buy her lingonberry jam from the Swedish delis in Chicago's Andersonville neighborhood. She'd make it last until the next time I visited, which was how I knew how much she liked it, not because of anything she ever said.

So I'd signed up willingly for these two weeks at Finnish camp, which was one of Concordia College's newest Language Villages in the north woods of Minnesota. There was a ring of them up here, placed too far apart to walk between but within easy driving distance. They ranged from the obvious French, German, and Spanish camps to the exotic—for the eighties—Chinese. It being Minnesota, the Scandinavians were overrepresented, with Danish, Swedish, and Norwegian camps in addition to Salolampi. When I tell people now that I went to "Finnish camp," they think I'm saying "finish camp," as if I hadn't gotten through it all in other years; I was a camp dropout, a runaway. Or some people have heard "finishing camp," and imagined long white gloves and tea-pouring practice in a rustic setting, an all-American mix of finishing schools and summer camps. What could be more aspirationally white, both rugged and classy at once? Had I read Susan Sontag then, I might have thought that Salolampi was teaching us Finnish as camp: the campiness of performing Finnish.

But Ilse didn't have to perform. She *was* Finnish. It was her essence. I filed into the camp canteen behind her for my breakfast. Although the kitchen workers were not Finnish, they wouldn't put anything on your tray unless you said *please* in the language. They enjoyed their power. My grandmother's cooking consisted largely of white blobs: mashed potatoes, farina, rolls, cauliflower, fillets of the palest fish. But *viili*, the stringy yogurt in my bowl, was whiter than anything I'd ever seen before. It was white with the blue glimmer of skim milk. It jiggled from side to side with the moves of a small animal.

I considered making jokes about the viili, but the other girls had already moved on to amply buttering their toast. Need I say that it was white bread? And that the butter was paler than Ilse's hair?

When Ilse asked me who I liked, I looked at her blankly and answered, "Prince. And Bruce Springsteen."

"No, stupid," said her sidekick, Kaisa. "She means if you like someone."

"Oh," I said. Ilse started talking about Matti, Salolampi's youngest counselor, straight from Finland. He was, I understood, someone to like.

Kaisa was the only other girl camper my age, and my bunk-mate. She'd taken the top bunk without asking, even though I was scared of heights and would have taken the bottom anyway. Kaisa was a Half. She wouldn't let anyone call her by her real name, Kim. She was little, more beady-eyed than you'd expect a Half to be, stocky, not blond. Her hair was short and brown, and she tanned brown too, so that she looked like a small bear in a T-shirt and shorts. Kaisa never forgot to wear her name tag. She was from Edina, she announced to me, but she wished she could live at Salolampi year-round. At the time, I didn't know Edina was the most affluent of all of the Twin Cities suburbs and so didn't understand what Kaisa was trying to tell me about her own importance.

Morning Activity was *pesapallo*, the Finnish baseball game. Kaisa and Ilse were team captains. Nobody explained the rules to the handful of new campers, so I sat on the bench watching with the veterans of Helsinki Cabin. Almost everyone in Helsinki was seventeen and eighteen. I couldn't figure out what they were still doing at camp. I'd been hoping there would be more glamourous, useful, or financially rewarding summer activities available once I entered high school. So I asked them. Immediately I knew I'd marked myself as a Fourth. I could hear my grandmother saying, "Why do you need to be nosy?"

I was at Salolampi to please a woman who didn't like to talk. The problem was, I myself was only one-fourth non-talker. Years later this would come home to me in a Scandinavian literature class I took in college. It was like being back at Salolampi. The most talkative student in the class couldn't understand why so many of the characters committed suicide and why there was so little dialogue in the novels. "Why do they just stare at each other and move from room to room?" she asked me. (She had apparently not seen any Bergman films.) She was Jewish, with a family back in Shaker Heights, Ohio, which she described as a hand-waving, shouting bunch half out of a Woody Allen film, half out of a Philip Roth novel, and she thought we were all crazy. I was the second-most-talkative person in the class, since I was only a fourth Scandinavian. Everybody else besides our talker was half or full, except for the Japanese-American student who understood quite well about silence and suicide. The professor himself was Swedish, although he'd specialized in Finnish-Swedish literature, the literature of the Swedes who had moved to Finland to run the country and, over time, had found themselves neither Finnish nor Swedish but something else altogether. He'd won awards for translation, something he shrugged off by saying it wasn't hard to translate writers who were constantly in the act of translating themselves even as they wrote. He was quite shy. Sometimes he could barely bring himself to ask us a question. He apologized to us before every lecture.

The Helsinki Cabin campers reluctantly talked to me. They told me they'd always gone to Salolampi. Salolampi's oldest camper didn't look Finnish. Meeri was stunningly beautiful, with dark tight curls that framed her face, smooth brown skin, and big eyes that made her look scared all the time. When she moved, it was like she was pouring herself through the air. Meeri was only a Fourth, like me, but she was fluent. Her Finnish grandmother lived with her, teaching her how to play the *kantele*, how to bake little cakes, and telling her stories from the *Kalevala*, the epic poem of Finland. Meeri was going to give a kantele concert on International Day, at the end of camp. I didn't want to become friends with Meeri; I wanted to steal her life. I wasn't allowed to touch my grandmother's kantele, though when I was little I had hidden under the table as she played it. The kantele is a kind of table harp, although it looks more like what you might imagine the insides of a miniature piano to be. The plucking of the strings sounds to me like tuning, a constant warming up.

Meeri's best friend, Tuija, was reading *Dune* in Finnish. That was beyond fluency, and indeed Tuija, with her heavy braids, was a Hundred Percenter. I was beyond jealous. My only book, tucked safely away in my sleeping bag, was a paperback edition of *Amadeus*—contraband, like the Prince album, since it was in

English—which my father had insisted I smuggle in. I didn't just read books, I digested them, and he didn't think I had a chance of making it through without something to read. But I think he also liked the idea of my smuggling something in, something that wasn't Finnish, something that meant I wasn't so invested in my mother's side of the family and was willing to break rules that struck him as arbitrary.

When I watched the pesapallo game, for the first time I understood why the Jamaican kids in Evanston looked lost when they had to play baseball, so close to cricket but not cricket. When Matti, the counselor, pitched a high, looping ball and Kaisa whacked a line drive to the exact spot between outfielders, she ran to first base, which was at baseball's third base. Second was in right field, third in left. Fly balls weren't outs. The innings went on forever.

The Helsinki girls eventually ditched me to talk in Finnish, and I went to lunch alone. I sat at a table of the littlest kids. They didn't like the food, either. They didn't want to practice Finnish, because they didn't have any Finnish to practice. I asked them solemn questions about cartoons. They didn't care who was better, Scooby Doo or Bugs Bunny. They blinked back tears when I asked them where they were from.

Afternoon Activity was language lessons, where I discovered that there were two other girls from Kuopio Cabin in beginning Finnish as well. Hannele waved at me shyly. "Hey, Er-*ja*," Maria said, chomping on her gum. She blew a bubble past her nose, almost up to her eyes. It spattered; she smacked it back in and started over. Maria nudged me in the shoulder. "The baby class. Effing awful, right? Did you hear that that bitch Ilse gets private sessions with Matti?" I nodded, trying to keep my eyes on Sini, the oldest counselor and the mother of two campers herself. Sini was asking us, in Finnish, to hop, first with our right leg, then our left. Down, up, forward, back, turn. We did a Finnish hokey-pokey. As Sini jumped, her armpit hair swayed and her breasts jiggled freely. She seemed so European.

Maria wasn't Finnish. She was an Italian-American from Philadelphia, and at Salolampi by mistake. Her parents had checked the wrong box; she was supposed to be up the road at the French camp, Lac du Bois, to recover from her near-failing French grade sophomore year. Her parents had decided that rather than receive a refund, they'd still like to send her off to Minnesota for two weeks. Nobody ever called her by her camp name; I don't even remember what it was.

Hannele lived on a Minnesota farm. She missed her cows—Clover, Millicent, and Happy—and she recited their names like Santa's reindeer. She also missed her boyfriend, who was in 4-H with her, but she thought the oldest boys in Tampere Cabin were cute, not to mention Matti, who was the most gorgeous boy she'd ever seen. Hannele was a Half. She thought her camp name was pretty. Where she was from only grandmothers had Scandinavian names. She kept flipping her name tag up to read it again.

When I first met them, I didn't want to be friends with Hannele and Maria any more than I did with Ilse or Kaisa. It was the oldest girls that appealed to me, the fluent Meeri and Tuija. Maria and Hannele were sixteen and boy-crazy, and didn't speak Finnish, so how could language immersion work? In the math of Finnishness, Ilse and Kaisa equaled one and one-half, Meeri and Tuija one and one-fourth, and Hannele, Maria, and me together three-fourths. We weren't going to be even culturally Finnish.

But Maria and Hannele were willing to be friends with me, so I went along to dinner with them. Maria offered me some gum. Hannele recited the names of her cows again. We whispered so the counselors wouldn't hear us speaking English, until Sini sat with us. Then we stared at our plates. Dinner was white, salt the only spice.

The Tampere Cabin boys began banging forks and knives on the table, chanting "*Hyppää järveen!*" Some weird *Oliver Twist* ritual? Please, Eino, can I have some more? The clatter grew as more and more tables picked it up. Hannele and Maria started too, Maria shouting "Blah Finnish blah," so I picked up my fork. I banged once. I stopped. Group behavior made me nervous. In high school, I would ditch all the pep rallies. I never wanted to cheer for anything just because other people were doing it.

As the clamor grew louder, Sini grinned and folded her napkin neatly. Eino stiffly nodded. Matti kicked open the door. The counselors followed him along the path, down the rickety pier, and into the lake, jumping in one by one. The little campers raced to the water; the older campers draped themselves around the porch. The counselors held their breath underwater to scare the little ones, then burst out of the water, splashing. Sini bobbed up and down like a seal. Once on land, Matti shook the water out of his golden hair with the flourish of a Labrador too cute for his own good. While I bused my tray, Tuija grudgingly told me that *hyppää järveen* meant "Go jump in the lake."

At the evening bonfire, we sat on logs while Eino and Matti built the fire, which sent up sparks as tall as the pines. We kept our hands in our pockets to warm them. Maria wanted to start a game of telephone until Meeri did a solo. Her voice was pure alto, and the notes floated out to the constellations above. I was used to the hazy pink sky over Chicago, and the void of space over our heads unnerved me. Finns, even the urban ones who lived in Helsinki, were always heading out to cabins in the woods to cross-country ski or go ice fishing. It made me wonder what part of me wanted to get back to Chicago so badly. The quarter German? The quarter English? The eighth Scottish, eighth French-Canadian?

Before bed, on our way to the toilets, a five-minute walk in the dark along a path dense with tree roots, Kaisa sang, "One, two, Freddy's coming for you. Three, four, better lock the door."

"Shut up, Kaisa. The little campers will hear," scolded Ilse.

"Five, six, get out your crucifix. Seven, eight, better stay up late."

When Kaisa whispered in Maria's ear, Maria leaned over to say to her, "What the fuck? You don't mess with crucifixes, you don't mess with Freddy. You don't mess with anything you don't understand, *Kim*." Kaisa winced at the sound of her real name. Maria fingered the filigreed cross at her neck. I'd thought she was just a Madonna fan, but I realized it was real to her, that she was Catholic like the kids back home who went to Saint Athanasius. Maria wasn't just Italian, she got to be Catholic, too.

There is something Gothic enough about summer camps without adding on maniacal killers amok in the woods. As we walked back to Kuopio, the camp was dark, the woods were darker, the deep cold lake darker still. Our young society was fragile, the rule of the counselors tentative because there were so many more of us than them. For two weeks, we were all provisional orphans. It was, perhaps, the best way for me to think about camp, as entering into the world of children's literature: *Anne of Green Gables*, *The Adventures of Huckleberry Finn*, *Pippi Longstocking*, *Lord of the Flies*. Assimilation into a society of children. Each night, the dark walk from the cabins to the toilets, from the coziness of sleeping bags to the rows of sinks and our daily ablutions, was an in-between space that was wild. Did I want to join the darkness? Or did I want to stay with the campers?

Neither. I wanted to be somewhere else all together. After lights-out, I dived into the far corner of my sleeping bag and read *Amadeus* by flashlight. They were eating a dessert called Nipples of Venus, which sounded decadent, well beyond *The Lion, the Witch and the Wardrobe*'s Turkish delight. The fact that it sounded dirty made it all the more delicious, something Prince would sing about. Salieri's jockeying for position with Mozart was like the behavior of the girls at Salolampi, except that being fluent in Finnish didn't seem as much a gift from God. But above all, *Amadeus* was a play. I eavesdropped on its conversations to make up for Salolampi's silences.

INTERNATIONAL DAY

On International Day, the last day of the camp session, the Concordia Language Villages gathered together at the German camp of Waldsee in a fake United Nations. It was the only time the camps came together. We were supposed to show off what we'd learned and celebrate our international cultural heritages with food, music, and games. The night before International Day, to give us one last gasp of Finnishness before we were diluted by other ethnic groups, Salolampi held an extra-long bonfire and we were allowed to stay up late, midnight for the oldest cabins. The counselors called it the Midsummer Night, even though Midsummer had happened weeks before camp started. Because camp was almost over, rules were lax. We were permitted to whisper in English, take off our name tags, and eat contraband candy.

Maria pulled out packs of bubble gum from her pockets. She plopped down between Hannele and me, wrapping her arms around our necks. We popped our bubbles whenever the choruses came around. We didn't know the songs. They were all in Finnish, about Midsummer, and the beginners' language group had barely made it past table manners, counting, and the days of the week. I didn't know much about Midsummer. My grandmother didn't celebrate it. It didn't sound like her kind of holiday, staying up all night in the woods, dancing and drinking on the longest day of the year to make up for winter's endless nights. Tuija, over on the Helsinki bench, made a joke about all the Finnish children conceived at Midsummer, and Hannele giggled so hard she swallowed her gum. I choked on mine, the thick pink blob like some alien second tongue. As the logs crackled and the sparks flew off higher and higher, first Maria and then Hannele peeled off to go meet boys in the woods. Ilse and Kaisa had already disappeared, Ilse after boys, Kaisa after her.

I scooted down to the Helsinki girls. Leaning in as close to the fire as Eino would let her, Tuija belted out song after song from her perch on the bench. I was worried she was going to singe her braids as she thrashed around. Meeri sang softly, breathily, each note true. Her eyes were closed. She was in the memory of a real Midsummer Night.

What could they be talking about, these Finnish boys and girls, as they went off together? I knew instinctively that they wouldn't be talking, because these weren't people who talked much. Whatever they were doing was quiet, without whispered endearments, without inside jokes. It must be wordless, without much more sound than it took to slurp up viili. They would be making less noise than the crickets, the hoot owls, the mysterious splashing in the lake, the rustling of the leaves as the wind raced through the birches, the roar of the bonfire. Pressed together, their bodies would build a hollow in which they would be absolutely alone. It seemed like a desperately lonely activity to be involved in, and I knew when my time came, I would fill up the space between with awkward chatter until I missed the moment where it was possible for that space to vanish.

None of the boys from Tampere Cabin were left at the bonfire, but there were some pimply-faced blonds. They weren't in the beginner-language class, didn't go to arts and crafts, and played pickup games of pesapallo, which I still hadn't managed to learn. I didn't want someone like Matti, either, Matti so blond, muscular, and unfailingly kind to small children. I wanted Prince. Because he was brown, neither black nor white. Because he was skinny and short and wiry. Because he wasn't afraid to wear purple. He seemed comfortable in his skin, in his clothes, wielding his guitar. Because he was a musical genius, like Amadeus, with a gift he didn't have to work at.

When Kaisa spotted Matti and Maria making out behind the sauna after lights-out, Ilse and Kaisa vowed revenge. Ilse had been with a Tampere boy, but that wasn't good enough for her. She deserved Matti. Although counselor-camper relationships weren't officially allowed, when the campers and counselors were the same age, which was often the case with the counselors, like Matti, imported directly from Finland, they were briefly tolerated if the couple was discreet.

In the clearing the next morning, Eino pulled up the flag as we sang the Salolampi song for the last time. I caught a flash of color below the flag, but thought at first it was simply a bird on the wing, or glare from the sun. As I saw the billowing bit of red, I knew what it was: Maria's lacy panties.

The counselors gasped. The little kids whispered, "Underpants!" The Tampere Cabin boys whistled. Ilse and Kaisa shuffled their feet, staring at the ground.

Maria was beaming. She called out, "That's not even my best pair!" My grandmother's worst fear, the fear of dirty laundry being aired in public, had literally happened to Maria, and it didn't faze her. She thought it was funny. She was proud of her underwear. Maria wasn't Finnish. Even Eino stifled a laugh in relief as it became clear that Maria didn't mind if we laughed, and in fact approved.

I thought the underpants flag would mean that Maria would be marked as the ultimate outsider, impossibly beyond the boundaries of normal Finnish behavior, that Hannele and I, as her friends, would be ostracized too. But suddenly it didn't matter. Already I was thinking about what would happen after International Day, how my dad and brother would be there waiting for me in the parking lot of the Mall of America. I would get off the Salolampi bus, and, as we leisurely wended our way back to Chicago, be whisked to a world of motels with cable and Ping-Pong tables, late-night diners and mini-golf with their blinking neon lights, that weird, transient America that Nabokov so loved in *Lolita*, that Edward Hopper painted in garish and velvety light, that Clark Gable and Claudette Colbert journeyed through in *It Happened One Night*, that killed off Janet Leigh at the Bates Motel in *Psycho*.

The Helsinki girls approved of Maria, though. "*Sisu*," Tuija said.

Sisu! My grandmother hadn't told me about this word, because my grandmother so rarely told me anything at all, but my mother had once used it when she was trying to describe what Finns were like. *Sisu*, that untranslatable Finnish word that meant something like "spunk" or "gumption," but was nothing like the behavior of perky cheerleaders or the mouthing off of rebellious adolescents. It was closer to the stoic grit of Minnesota pioneers, who had reached a windy wilderness and found beauty in the freezing lakes and streams, who had learned to see warmth as a luxury that could be looked forward to but wasn't necessary. The determination of the Finnish peasantry to keep speaking their weird, isolated language in spite of being ruled by Sweden, then Russia. The wild radicalism of Finns in North America, their commitment to unions and socialism, a legacy from their resistance against kings and czars. The utopian vision of my great-grandfather, who had fled poverty, political oppression, and the czar's wars in Finland to make his way into the United States from Canada without papers. Draft dodger. Illegal immigrant. Communist. All facts my grandmother wanted to keep from us, so we wouldn't slip and tell anyone else, to let us be good Americans instead of Finns, to lose our sisu and gain spunk instead.

My grandmother had secret reserves of sisu. What was sisu, if it wasn't her pluck as she left the coziness of her Finnish-American world in the Upper Peninsula for Detroit's car industry because of the Depression? She grew up on a farm within a forest much like the land around Salolampi; she ended up in suburban Dearborn, where all the houses looked the same, where the police escorted black men back to Inkster if they crossed the border, where Ford built his model town according to his vision of a mechanized America. In spite of her sisu, I thought she'd gotten the short end of the deal. Dearborn's little pink brick houses and relentless car culture made me cringe. If I went to camp to please her, I also did it to rebel against her, to remind her what she'd given up to remake herself.

It was easy for me to think that, though. I was born in the seventies. My grandmother didn't even get her kantele until the seventies, when she took lessons on it and began finally to speak Finnish again with her sisters and cousins. Piano lessons were what she'd insisted on for my mother and her sisters when they were children. I hadn't lived through the Depression or World War II, events that made conformity in the fifties—the power of being a white person who got to live in Dearborn—desirable to my grandmother. Suddenly, in the eighties, it had become cool, admirable even, to be ethnic, a kind of white instead of just white. It was commendable to know about things like sisu. As a Fourth, I could know about it, but wasn't ever going to be it. It wasn't a matter of blood so much as culture—of all the campers, Meeri was the one who'd lived Finnishness. To get what I was after, two weeks wouldn't do it. I'd have to live my grandmother's life, and she wasn't going to let me. She'd fought too hard to keep everybody out, first for protection, then as an instinctive reflex.

Before our last sauna, Salolampi's twice-a-week treat, we jumped in the lake. The sky was clear, so the water was too, a rich dark blue warmed by the morning sun. The insects were gone, and instead of their buzzing I listened to the sound of the lily pads turning over as we flapped our arms through them. The icy cold water stabbed at everything below my armpits. Salolampi's pier, a shabby gateway into our sapphire world of water, listed to one side.

As I turned to wade back to shore, I imagined we were raiding Norsemen approaching villages. Burn the dock, capture campers as our slaves. But Finns weren't Vikings. The Norse became the Swedes, Danes, Norwegians. Over time, the Swedes and Danes took turns conquering everyone else. No one bothered much with Finland. Bad farmland. Not much more there than mangy reindeer and the people who ate them. The Finns spoke their own language, kept their own counsel. Not that they weren't murderous themselves, killing off some of the missionaries sent to them during the Middle Ages.

Sini draped us in our towels one by one as we came out of the water, and pushed us into the cocoon of the sauna, so we could sit together and steam as if we were root vegetables. Meeri, Tuija, Ilse, and everyone else extremely Finnish, as well as Maria, were naked, but Kaisa, like me, wore her suit. Maybe saunas were something you appreciated with age? The extremes in temperature were supposed to be relaxing, to push you until you couldn't stand it and had to roll around in the snow, until you had to stoke the fire high and beat yourself silly with a birch branch. I found that I couldn't turn discomfort into pleasure. Was that ability a definition of sisu? When someone tells you to go jump in a freezing lake, you not only do it, but enjoy it?

"This is the best part about being Finnish," said Maria dreamily. Ilse gave her a blurry nod. Kaisa leaned her head on Ilse's shoulder, her short hair in her eyes, impossibly puppylike. For the first time, I gave in to the sauna. It didn't matter who was a Hundred Percenter, a Half, a Fourth, or nothing at all. The sauna turned twelve girls into one sleepy organism, breathing in and out at the same time slowly, rhythmically, a slumbering beast that would mean payback for Sweden come International Day. I let the warm, damp steam enter my lungs. I was completely part of the group, not an interloper, a reporter, performer, spy. If I closed my eyes, I could orchestrate our breathing into the piano chords at the end of "Purple Rain": no need for lyrics, just Prince wailing, the chords slowing down, a drama petering out into a light summer rain.

Finnified, rosy clean from the sauna, united in our Salolampi T-shirts, we got on the bus for International Day. We drove past the gingerbread world of the Norwegian village. It was richer than Salolampi. They owned their own camp and ran all summer long. Salolampi rented from a church camp for only that one August session. Proof that the other Scandinavians were wealthier in America than we were? Or that they were wealthier back in Europe in the first place? At Waldsee, the German campers had cabins that looked like ski lodges as designed by *Dallas* or *Dynasty*, and I couldn't believe that campers slept in them. They were chalets with running water and electricity. You could have dumped them wholesale into Edina or the snootiest Chicago suburbs and they would have fit right in. Whole societies of birds could have perched in their eaves. The design of the planned French Lac du Bois was supposed to be even nicer.

Waldsee's massive chalets formed a village square, and within the square each camp set up tables for the international marketplace. It was a dazzling display of stereotypes of many lands. What could you quickly learn about a culture in two weeks? What could you learn even faster during the span of International Day? How much would campers from other villages pay to eat viili? Who was going to line up to listen to the kantele, to buy a birch-bark candelabra, or play pesapallo? How were we going to make a splash when the buttery smells from the French pastry table wafted across the square? I was already counting the coins in my pocket. Who would watch anything else when the Chinese camp did their dragon dance? The dragon, stuffed to the gills with campers of varied height, was already meandering through the square. It was such a relief to see faces that weren't Finnish, or trying to be, that I had to keep myself from staring. Some of the German campers were walking around in lederhosen. The only villages we could compete with were the Scandinavian ones, with their tackily painted Dala horses and lutefisk.

While I was trying to choose a marzipan pig at the Waldsee table, Ilse pulled me into the cadre of Kuopio Cabin. Next came Helsinki Cabin, Meeri still running her fingers through kantele scales, then Tampere. We shouted "Hyppää järveen!" at everyone we met. "Bonjour," "Guten tag," "Buenos días"—it was all met with "Hyppää järveen!" When the Waldsee campers looked confused, Maria pointed to the Finnish flag and shrugged. What could you expect from such a strange language? Of course we wouldn't sound like a Germanic or Romance language. We weren't *bon* or *Gut*, but *hyppää*.

We whirled our Finnish chain of campers about, trying to locate Swedes. "God dag," they trilled, arrayed before us like a battalion of Dala horses. "Hyppää järveen!" we sang out, smiling beatifically.

We were sticking it to the Swedes. The only problem was, they didn't understand a word we said. They never did. They thought we were saying hello. How to talk to such unruly colonials, how to talk to the Finn who farmed your estate, who fished for your dinner, who made the clothes you wore—this wasn't part of the curriculum at Swedish camp. We had longer memories. They saw us as blondes, like them. They saw us as allies against the effete French, marauding Germans, inscrutable Chinese. They were letting us in under the umbrella of Scandinavianism, but we didn't want to belong. We wanted them to jump in the lake, even if their lake was nicer than ours.

I was tempted to pull some Swedish campers aside and tell them we were insulting them to their faces, but I couldn't talk about it. Translating, communicating, would destroy our small victory. It was our sisu, the secret insult. For the first time, I was beginning to learn Finnish.

And of every living thing of all flesh, two of every sort
shalt thou bring into the ark, to keep them alive with thee.

MEMORANDUM TO THE ANIMALS

Amy Leach

U nfortunately, Animals, we are not going to be able to bring all
   of you with us this time. Last time there were eight humans
on board and at least two of each of you; but that was a sentimental
era and God was a sentimental fellow, like the old pack rat up the
road who won't give up any of his whim-whams. Bringing two of
every sort of creature onto the ark meant bringing all two thousand species of scorpions, and all the blotchy toads and testy wasps
and malevolent snakes and countless other creatures as unneces-
sary as insanity. This time around we are in charge: producing our
own cataclysm, designing our own boat, making our own guest
list, which does not include Every Living Thing.

That first, ancient boat we have retrospectively christened
the *Fantasy*; today we sail in a boat called *Reality*. Realistically,

logistically, it would be too complex to try to save every single kind of you multitudinous miscellaneous creatures. Dormitory assignments would be a nightmare, because we don't know who might eat whom or who might die of social stress. We'd have to go nectar-collecting beforehand for sustenance for the sugarbirds and gather angelica blossoms for the hoverflies, and if little blue poison frogs were going to maintain their poison, we'd have to bring along extra oribatid mites for them to ingest, and special leaf litter for the oribatid mites to ingest.

Anyway, we need the space for *our* works and wonders. Many of you are being superannuated because we must give priority to our machinery, our televisions and computers and refrigerators and cars, trucks, airplanes, combination microwave/convection ovens with auto–time zone adjusters. We will still bring a few of you with us, especially those of you with rumps and ribs (please refer to the Keep-Alive List). But we are not going to waste time holloing for the bush babies, waiting for the mayflies to drift in and the kiwis to materialize. We are certainly not going to stand around until the tortoises figure out what's going on.

If you are concerned about the devastation of your genetic type and you do not see your name on the Keep-Alive List, you might think about clumping some vegetation together into rafts on which to rescue yourselves. You animals (slugs, bats) who cannot assemble your own rafts, or whose spindly legs (dromedaries, moose) are liable to poke through a grassy vessel, or who are graminivorous and oblivious (sheep) and would nibble through the rescue raft: know that the extinction of your type is not necessarily the extinction of your glory. You can live on in the imagination, like the angels—although like the angels, you are likely to be simplified.

To *properly* live on in the imagination you should have someone who really knows you, who knows the pitch of your buzz, the rufous hue of your throat, your fondness for comfrey—who has watched two of you golden frogs, separated by a loudly gushing stream, waving your hands in semaphore fashion. As the Holocene is winding down, don't be foolish like the okapis, who use their acute hearing to detect and avoid human beings; they have sabotaged their chance to survive in anyone's mind.

But even the most knowledgeable imaginer is a fallible vessel—like an iceberg, liable to get carried away, to melt, to be at bottom very very blue. Don't you know, Animals, nothing lasts forever. The Holocene was the Age of Miscellany, the Age of Pandemonium, the Age of which Noah's Ark was a microcosm: of thirty million passengers, only eight were human. It was a noisy, dirty, dangerous, eccentric, anarchic, inefficient, rowdy ride. The co-passengers knocked us over a lot and sometimes we fell over laughing. But now we are proceeding into the Age of Efficiency, the Age of Sanity, the Age of Refinement. We salute you, Animals, as we salute the unruly Holocene; but the future belongs to us.

THE JOURNEY HOME

Shuchi Saraswat

At the center of a temple, a dark room. The blinds are half open, and dust floats in the slats of light. The room is a library in name—glass-doored bookcases line the walls—but it is mostly a closet in function. In here are the objects belonging to a life forever in transit: two metal lockers, a doctor's scale used to weigh luggage, and stacks of not-yet-unpacked cardboard boxes, old and soft, the weathered flaps not sealed with tape but tucked into each other for easy access. Among these objects, on gray folding tables, occupying most of the room, stand row upon row of statues of the Hindu god Ganesha. Some are nearly a foot tall; others, no larger than a thumb. Hundreds of crescent-crowned elephant heads with sleepy trunks resting on swollen boy bellies, hundreds of painted eyes looking forward, hundreds of right palms up, asking you to stop for a second. To be still.

I stood among those statues, or murtis, on a late afternoon in September 2012, trying to photograph the feeling of being in that room: the eerie company of all those copies of a single deity, each one believed to actually be the god himself. Each had been brought to life by a *pran pratishtha*, a ceremony whose name literally translates to "enlivening the resting." In four days, these statues would no longer exist—at least, not in this state. I was here, with the heavy, semiprofessional Cannon DSLR that I'd borrowed from a generous uncle, to document their end, when the statues' owners would drop them over a ship's railing and into the San Francisco Bay. In the bay, their clay bodies would dissolve, releasing the god from his earthly shackles.

Ganesha is a benign god; he is a hopeful god. He is known for being an exemplary son, the god of beginnings, the god of the arts. The stories of Ganesha—of how he won a race around the world by sitting on his mouse and circling his parents, his universe; how, when he was tasked with transcribing the *Mahabarata*, he broke off the tip of his tusk so that he could finish—are symbolized by the mouse at his feet and his jagged half-tusk. These stories are what make him the most beloved of all the Hindu gods.

But the best-known story, the one that brought me to the temple in California, is of how his father, Lord Shiva, the destroyer, decapitated him in a rage and then brought him back to life with an elephant head. This is the story of Ganesha's birth, of his rebirth, and of his rebirth-day, which his followers celebrate every year. They invite the god, temporarily embodied as a statue, to their homes, where, for ten days, they treat him like an out-of-town guest. They hold dinner parties in his honor. They offer him sweets on a silver platter at the end of each meal. When the celebration, the Ganesha Chaturthi, ends, his devotees return him to his home on Mount Kailasha, in Tibet—the path to which is the water. But because Ganesha is the god of good luck, the god of auspicious beginnings, this ceremony of immersion, or visarjan, also serves as a cleansing for his devotees. Into the ocean he goes, carrying with him all of his worshippers' misfortunes.

The photos I'd seen of visarjans were surreal. A Ganesha murti three stories tall, photographed from up high and so far away that the thousands of bodies carrying him down the streets of Mumbai turn into one body, a thick river of people carrying the statue down to the sea. Another image: the enormous murti being escorted into the water on the shoulders of men, each individual now clearly visible—some capped, all fully clothed and soaked. Now you see their faces, pained and joyous, and all the people behind them, watching from the beach against the backdrop of lush trees and South Mumbai's Victorian skyline. And there's Ganesha, larger than all of them, dwarfing even the buildings, animating the landscape into something out of fantasy. I wanted to witness that. I wanted to recreate that image in a landscape I knew.

This is how I found myself at the Vedic Dharma Samaj Fremont Hindu Temple—the temple of my childhood—which also hosts one of the largest Ganesha visarjans in the country. The temple is located in Fremont, a sprawling city that makes up the southern part of the East Bay. Tucked in the valley of the Mission Hills, Fremont is as reliably bright as San Francisco is foggy. The sunshine bounces off the bleached hills, off the concrete, off the unkempt fields that line the highway. In my memory, Fremont has a golden hue. But as I approached the temple—my first time visiting in years—I was reminded that it is not, in fact, a beautiful city. The Auto Mall Parkway cuts through South Fremont and stretches across four lanes in either direction, surrounded by Targets, Best Buys, Walmarts, and Ikeas, their bright signs' desperate electric flames designed to lure people like moths. Driving north on this highway, though, you get a glimpse of what first brought people here: those beautiful sandy hills that seem so close that you swear you could touch them, that if you keep driving on that road you'll drive right into their blanched bellies.

Fremont—named after the "great pathfinder," explorer John C. Frémont, who found a passage through the hills and created maps that led European colonists to its sun-baked lands—has always sat in the shadow of larger cities; Oakland up north, and San Francisco across the bay. Throughout Fremont's history, it has been the city in which settlers have made their homes. Those settlers in the colonial era were, first, the Spanish, who built Mission San Jose and swept up the Ohlone Indians in their Catholic fervor. Then the Mexicans, who pushed out the Spanish, neutralizing the Mission. Then those who followed John C. Frémont's maps during the Gold Rush, cutting through Fremont on their way to Mission San Jose for supplies. And, a little over a century later, the rush of immigrant software engineers, who could buy affordable homes for their young families and commute to Silicon Valley. That was when my family arrived, in 1987—and the Fremont Hindu Temple, built just two years before, became our temple.

The surge of immigrants in the 1980s, many arriving directly from engineering schools in India, led to the need for a communal space. Temples in India are numerous; on city streets, in the form of shrines on highway medians; on large plots of land, warrens of white marbled obelisk structures offering shelter for each god. But in the United States, temples are few, and calmer, visited most often on weekends, or on special holidays, when they may fill to overflowing. Within the walls of a Hindu temple in the States, you will hear Tamil and Telugu, the languages of south India; Marathi, the language of the west; Punjabi, the language of the north; Gujarati, the language of the capital; and Hindi, the Indian government's official language. You will detect the sweet South Indian flavor in the cafeteria lentils. Skin color ranges from the cream color of those who descend from Himalayan dwellers to the south Indians' deep plum. Hindu temples in the United States are more than a place of worship. They are a substitute home country.

As of 2010, more Asian Indians live in California than in any other U.S. state. The Bay Area is richly diverse and densely populated, and Fremont is second only to Cupertino, twenty-five miles away, the home of more Indians than any other city in California. The Fremont Hindu temple, in offering a grand sendoff for Ganesha under the Golden Gate Bridge, attracts thousands of Indians from all over the area.

THE DAY AFTER I LANDED in California from Boston, I drove to the temple to get to know the people I'd be photographing. The temple is on a normally peaceful neighborhood cul-de-sac at the foot of the Mission Hills. But by the time I arrived midday on a Saturday, in the middle of the ten-day Ganesha Chaturthi celebrations and on the weekend of the associated cultural program, the place had erupted into messy, crowded, free-flowing chaos. Children and teenagers performed classical Indian moves to Bollywood songs and Indian classical music performances. They read from religious texts and acted in skits illustrating the stories of Ganesha. Cars filled the temple lot and lined any vacant stretch of sidewalk. Thousands of pairs of shoes spilled from the entrances, and conversations shrieked in many directions, so that it was near impossible to pick up on just one. There were no indications of where one should be, of what events were going on, no directional order, no apparent authority. I was overwhelmed. I felt as I had so often felt when arriving in India: that I was intruding on a chaos that was not mine. I kept my hand on the camera. Through the lens I was able to digest my surroundings in rectangular moments: the heavily made-up girls waiting by a side entrance for their turn on the stage; two boys practicing their lines under the shade of a palm; a cardboard elephant, face to the sky, stashed behind a bench.

Trying to escape the chaos, I walked away from the program and through the rest of the temple. I was searching for a private place to gather my thoughts when I walked past a grandmother with her two young granddaughters sitting on a cement ledge. The grandmother spotted my camera, and asked me in Hindi if I'd take their picture. I was surprised. I was aware of the camera around my neck, but it hadn't occurred to me that I would appear to someone else as a professional. The grandmother put her arm around the youngest. I tried to be conscious of the angle, tried to look at where the light was coming from, fiddled with the manual adjustments. And then I gave up. All she wanted was a picture with her grandchildren. I took a couple of photos and showed her the screen, and she gave me her husband's email address so I could send one.

I continued on my walk, eventually spotting a slightly open door at the end of a long hallway. I peeked in to see a few children squirming in metal chairs, waiting while family members took turns using the single bathroom in the hallway. Around these children were about a hundred Ganesha murtis. I knew then that I would come back here when it was quiet to photograph these statues.

Three days later, I did, feeling more welcomed by the empty parking lot and by the young man behind the front desk, who was eager to have something to do as he unlocked the library door for me. In front of me were the tables of statues, so many more than were there the weekend before. They nearly filled the room. By the time of the visarjan, the number of idols would triple, and nearly seven hundred would be packed away into rubber crates and brought onto a boat aptly named the *San Francisco Spirit*. But for now, a few hundred sat here at rest. I set up my tripod and kept the lights off. For two hours I took pictures of the idols of Ganesha in the ghostly light. Later that day, I uploaded all of my photos to my computer, and found the one of the grandmother with her grandchildren. I sent them to the email address, and received the response: *Namaskars, Grateful thanks for your kind gesture. You have really elevated Moods of the Tiny Children & their Grand Maa. Regards, Mohan.* I smiled when I read the email. Finally, I felt like I was doing what I had flown three thousand miles to do: photographing this god's journey home.

MY PARENTS LEFT INDIA IN 1982. Their first home was an attic apartment in Pittsburgh, where they lived on my father's meager graduate-school stipend, and where they quickly had two children, first me, and then my brother. We moved from Pittsburgh to Mountain View, California, so that my father could begin his first job out of school, as a computer programmer at XEROX PARC's campus in the Los Altos hills. Our small family moved together, continuing my parents' westward migration. We grew alongside Silicon Valley, the Bay Area a place of firsts for my family. When my parents bought their first new car, a 1989 gray Honda Accord with a sloped nose and boxy top, the plush inside felt so soft that I often ran my hands across it, watching the fibers flick from light to dark. We took our car to the Fremont Hindu Temple to be blessed. A pandit walked out to the parking lot and performed a vahana puja, circling a tray in front of the car. He placed a red dot on the hood, between the headlights, before putting a dot on each of our foreheads, between our eyes, marking the car as our fifth family member.

The four of us spent our weekends in that car, just going for a drive, as my mother would say. Aimless trips took us down the coastline to wade at a Half Moon Bay beach, or up north to stand among the redwoods. Soon we spent those weekends looking for our first house. House hunting during the early nineties, in the Bay Area, for an immigrant family, meant traveling to large areas of undeveloped land owned by housing associations. We'd drive up to a razed space and see four different homes side by side, the flat concrete foundations for new houses next to them. These four styles were what we could choose from. To me, our house-hunting felt like a game. In the fully furnished model homes, I peeked into refrigerators and closets, stuffed my pockets with sample candies. I claimed rooms for myself. I'd slip off my shoes, push my stockinged feet into the carpet. I'd sit on the bed, and if no one was around I'd lie on it, imagining it was my own, pretending myself, weekend after weekend, into these houses. In the leasing offices, I felt the power of choice, looking at neighborhoods under display cases, pins pushed into the roofs of the claimed properties. We had a god's-eye view of a possible future—we could pick the one we wanted as our own. That was what it meant to be a family starting out at the start of a boom. We determined what was built, and we were built, together.

The neighborhood we settled on was in Fremont. In the evenings we piled into our Honda and drove from our rental home five miles away to watch our new home slowly sprout from a rectangular plot of mud. Watching my house grow made me feel like I was there for its birth. It gave me a claim to a place.

Children of immigrants are of at least two homes. One home is told to them through stories. The homes my parents spoke of—the house in Jaipur where my mother was born, in which my grandparents still lived, the flat my father designed for his family in Delhi—were so far away, I never felt as though they were my own. But California, the Bay Area, Fremont—this was my place, the place I belonged to, and I felt bound to it, part of its history.

I lived in California from age four to thirteen. After I told my eighth-grade history teacher that I would be leaving, she pulled down a map of the country and pointed out the small state of New Jersey to the rest of the class, since no one knew where it was. Someone said, "It looks like the opposite of California!" And it did, with the swell of its bow shape jutting into another vast ocean and toward another continent, the inward curve an open arm to the rest of the country. So New Jersey became the inverse of California. From now on the two places I lived with my family would be in constant opposition to each other, the warm wild place we fled for the small town in the suburbs of Manhattan.

Our first six months in New Jersey, I childishly referred to California as "home." My parents laughed at first, and then grew increasingly annoyed. They could not understand my insistence. They had left the landscapes of their childhood long ago and had since moved, and moved, and moved again, creating a space for themselves in each new place. Our move was not done out of necessity, but out of the luxury of choice. Years later, I'm embarrassed by my teenage insistence. And yet, when asked where I'm from, I still answer with California.

When I moved into my second apartment in Boston, my mother sent me an idol of Ganesha, a four-inch white soapstone statue. She'd bought him in India. He came to me with instructions: clean your apartment and then leave him in there overnight, before you move in. So there he slept, upright on the cold multicolored kitchen-counter tile of an empty one-bedroom apartment in downtown Boston. Remember his story: Ganesha, before he was given the head of an elephant, was a boy who guarded his mother's home. By sleeping in my home first, he would bless it, forming a cosmic shield that would protect my boyfriend and me from outside dangers. Though it was hardly sacred, we never moved him from that spot, the kitchen counter that became the place for mail and magazines and unpacked groceries. Since then, I have carried him with me from apartment to apartment. His soapstone no longer sparkles, but he still wears the vermillion blessing that my mother placed on him before giving him to me, the red stain on the cone of his crown and at his feet, startling, like spattered dried blood. He now sits on a box covered with an orange scarf, on top of my bookshelf—the god of scribes, watching me as I write this. He is not my religion, but he is the physical reminder of my childhood, of my beginnings, of home.

THE MORNING OF THE IMMERSION CEREMONY, I took the BART to the stop nearest the temple. I spent my time looking out the window, at how the occasional tree or house popped out from the blurred landscape, perfectly clear, but just for a second. As we neared Fremont, the BART rode above a vista of matching roofs, crests of slate, the peaks and valleys of housing developments. Here again was my god's-eye view, but this time, everything had already been built.

When I arrived at the temple, Deepak, the event's coordinator, greeted me. The Ganesha Chaturthi was one of the largest the organization put on, and Deepak was like the director of this elaborate performance. Before the temple expanded its celebrations, members released Ganesha from his temporal body by submerging their idols in inflatable kiddie pools. Taking a ship out to the bay certainly had a more official, even poetic, feel. This year, 465 people had paid the price of fifty-one dollars for the cruise ride into the bay. Even more had paid half of that to leave their idols with the temple, whose staff would submerge them on the families' behalf.

Deepak accompanied me throughout the ceremony, motioning me to the front of the crowd so that I could get a better shot of the pandit and of the temple's Ganesha murti. Make way for the photographer, his arms seemed to say, ranking me above all those bearing similarly expensive cameras. During the parade around the lot, the temple's Ganesha rode in a chariot held high above the staff's heads. Deepak let go of the side of the chariot and reached out to my camera, offering to photograph me with the god. But I waved him off, preferring to remain an observer.

On the VIP bus to San Francisco, I realized no one wanted to sit next to me. No one was certain that I, the non-VIP girl in jeans, actually belonged among them. People who had been standing and couldn't find a seat would sit in the vacant spot beside me but keep their backs turned, talking to their friends across the aisle, before someone cleared a spot for them so they could move. The women on the bus had the air of wives of important men, people I had understood, as a child, not to have much power outside of their social circles. But here, they were arguing, gossiping, making snide comments about our lateness, making others chuckle. After a while, though, I felt all right with my one-seat buffer. I leaned against the window, looking out over the gray highway, thinking about how highways looked the same everywhere.

Deepak walked up and down the bus, handing out deep-fried bread with chutney, offering up a bunch of bananas, then ripping one free and handing it over. Bananas, why always bananas? I thought, recalling the peels that would lie in my family's Honda, blackened by hotboxed sun. He remained standing when the bus started, and as it picked up speed going down the highway, he finally sat in the empty seat next to me. He mopped his brow with a handkerchief. Like nearly everyone else on the temple staff, he was a volunteer. He worked a full-time job, had a wife, two children. Earlier that week, he had returned from a trip to India, and he had brought his parents back with him. He looked tired. I slowly began to ask him questions, basic ones, the ones I knew the answers to, and again he told me how he had spent six months obtaining permits for this visarjan. Finally, I asked him if he was trying to replicate the celebrations he had seen in Delhi when he was a child. He smiled at me sheepishly and shook his head. He had never been to a Ganesha visarjan in Delhi, he admitted. "We took the idea of going to temple more lightly in India," he said. "But here, you hold on to everything you can."

The buses parked along the sidewalk to the pier, and we emptied out, flooding the streets in a calm, slow trickle. Gone was the confidence everyone had within the temple walls, within the bus. Now we were in the city, en masse, drawing questioning glances. The temple's chairman, in his gold kurtha and aviator sunglasses, his head wrapped in a spice-colored scarf, proudly lifted the three-foot-tall marble statue to his head, and led all four hundred of us down to the dock.

When we boarded the *San Francisco Spirit* and I saw the

wall-sized photo of the Golden Gate nestled in fog, I felt that familiar childhood excitement. That bridge, with its own mythology: the story of the painters who keep its color orange—how, once a year, they paint the bridge from one end to the other. How, on the rare clear day, you can see the hole in one of the safety nets, allegedly made when a bridgeman fell right through. That bridge, which my mother couldn't pass without taking a photo, my brothers and I posed in front of it, my hair whipping their faces.

I walked around the decks with my camera, surprised by just how many wanted their photo taken. I found a group of women leaning over the railing, their golden-ringed, fingernail-painted hands clutching their Ganeshas. I took photos of the statues, and then they exclaimed, Hey, what about them, so I took a photo of them with their arms wrapped around Ganesha, as though he was their stoic infant.

I met a man named Surya, who was standing alone against a railing and looking out toward the Golden Gate. He told me of how he had grown up celebrating the festival in Hyderabad, in all-night celebrations that drew devotees from all over Uttar Pradesh and concluded in an immersion in Thangam Lake. He spoke of the festival fondly, but without nostalgia, as if it were part of another world, another life. Since he'd moved to the United States four years ago to work as a web developer, he had celebrated at home, but he had eventually donated his idol to the temple. This was the first time he'd had the chance to participate in a visarjan in the States. I asked him what he thought of it, and he laughed. "Oh, this is nothing in comparison," he said, but then he added, "They've done as best as possible."

The boat suddenly stalled. We bobbed, sandwiched between the Oakland Bay Bridge and the Golden Gate. Even on that clear, bright day, the bay was too choppy. We would not be able to make the trip out to Kirby Cove. Instead, this in-between place was where everyone would release their statues. We could see the Golden Gate, but it was so far away I could barely distinguish its color. But I didn't have time to be disappointed. There was a frantic rush as people went to retrieve their murtis. The temple's Ganesha had been seated on a table on the main deck, while the devotees gathered around him performing the final prayers, sitting cross-legged on tapestries laid over a wooden surface meant to be a dance floor. As the chairman carried him up the stairs, people reached out to touch the statue's feet before he was sent off. I ran to the front and leaned far over the ship's railing parallel to the god, so I could photograph his vertical descent. One man shouted "*Ganapati-bappa!*" and everyone else responded "*Morya!*" A familiar good-bye chant in the form of a see-you-later, a request by the god's devotees—calling him by his Marathi name—that he come back soon next year. For a split second, after the chairman released the temple's Ganesha into the bay, you could look out to the horizon and see dozens of rainbow-colored statues diving into the water. Some launched their idols out as far as they could, as if giving him a head start toward home. Others, aware that the figure they held was an embodiment of a celestial being who'd been the central guest in their home all week, hung out over the railing and gently dropped him. Children anxiously waited for their parents' signal before they threw their miniature idols into the bay. And nearly everyone had a moment of calm, looking out at the floating statues long after they hit the water.

Ganesha was now on his way home around the globe to Mount Kailasha. The water is Ganesha's train, his time machine. Through the bay he'd make the perilous journey through the Pacific to the Indian Ocean and the Arabian Sea, then into the mouth of the Indus River, and back to his mountain in Tibet. No one has ever climbed Mount Kailasha; it is off limits to thrill seekers, out of deference for religion. He comes down from this mountain, a place we can see but can never reach, for his people. And so the world of the gods hovers slightly above our own, in an invisible realm. Imagine the demon god, Ravana, shaking this mountain, then being trapped beneath it by Shiva. Imagine Ravana abducting Sita and taking her to an island far from mainland India, called Lanka. The gods, with their human emotions, interact with our landscape in superhuman ways. This is why Hindu mythology is so appealing. The myths have their own puritanical purpose, but it is their backdrop—a world once removed from our own—that makes them memorable.

In a similar way, memories hover over the places we've been.

After that quiet midweek trip to photograph the gods, a few days before the Ganesha visarjan, I drove to the first house my family owned, the four-bedroom in California Meadows. It was a hot day; the sun appeared heavy and low, a hazy orb above the horizon, larger than I could ever remember. I turned off the rental car's navigation system as I exited the highway, at once recognizing the lush pasture of Ardenwood Farm right off the ramp. I knew to take a right, I knew to go straight. I could not pass places and see them for what they were. The Little Caesar's pizza parlor with the bullet lodged in the window. Deep Creek Road, the road my grade school was on, the one I'd helped break ground on in a ceremony twenty years ago. I found my house—the faux Italian lines, the pale stucco siding, the pink trim, the terra cotta–tiled roof. The twin triangular peaks of the room, their own domestic mountains, half moons topping the square windows. It looked the same as one-fourth of the other houses in the development. I parked and stared at it, unimpressive as it was, but I could not see it. I could not take in the trees without thinking of my mother's love for gardening, the length of road without thinking of how I'd once fractured my elbow there while playing baseball. I stayed for no longer than a few minutes. I had expected I would photograph the house, but I didn't. I didn't even take out my camera. I gave the house a small wave and drove off.

ON THE SHIP, just after I'd photographed a group of young men, a man my height, with cherry cheeks and a broad forehead, asked if I had sent a statue off. He gestured toward the bucket of statues belonging to those who could not come for the trip. I said I hadn't, hesitating, knowing the question to come. I added, no, it's all right, and he added, "But you must."

He was right. I couldn't come all this way, photograph this ceremony, and not participate when asked. Though I looked like the other participants, I had felt different this whole time, and perhaps that's why I had come. We had all abandoned one home for another, and we were all trying to reconnect with a place we had left, a place that we had once considered home. We all were, as Deepak had said, trying to hold on to a past life in this new one.

Someone handed me a statue, and another man offered to take my picture, but when I handed him the camera, he seemed frightened. I gave him my phone instead. He took two photos—the only ones I have of myself from that trip. Only looking at the photos now do I notice: my statue is missing his left ear, the thin piece of clay snapped right off, likely lying at the bottom of a rubber tub. This ear faces my ear as I hold him next to me. We are cheek to cheek, and my smile is big, as if I've been reunited with a beloved friend. The other photo is of the one-eared Ganesha in midair. His back is toward me, and my back is toward the camera, both of us looking out into the bay. My arm is still outstretched from having just tossed him, as if in salute, as if in wave, as if asking him to pause and take me with him on his journey home.

Women are words.
—THOMAS HOWELL, DEVISES (1581)

A DISTURBANCE OF BIRDS

Terry Tempest Williams

How strange the way change comes, without warning, and never the way we think. Like a flash flood in the desert, it doesn't have to be raining before the water hits. I always believed my mortality would arrive on wings of grace, not through a numbing of my body that would prevent me from walking or finding my way toward words.

I close my eyes.

Let me run this scene through my mind once again. I was at the movie theater in Ellsworth, Maine. *Inglourious Basterds*. The film ended. The violence stayed with me. As I stood up to exit, the right side of my body went numb. I was having trouble walking. Once outside, I called my husband, Brooke, and I could hear that whatever was happening was affecting my speech, as well. It was dark. I was in my car, being guided to the emergency room through online directions delivered to me by Brooke from our home in Utah. I pulled into the parking lot and told my worried husband I would call him as soon as I knew anything.

Once inside the Maine Coast Memorial Hospital, primarily used by injured lobstermen, I apologized. For what? I can only remember thinking I was overreacting. Sitting in a bright white room where I waited after my symptoms had been described, blood pressure noted, and temperature taken, I watched a fifteen-year-old boy walk into the hospital screaming in pain. He was accompanied by a policeman who by law had to place him in handcuffs. "I'm not a criminal! I didn't kill anybody," the boy cried. "I just wanted to kill myself."

After several hours of tests, including a CAT scan and an EKG, a physician's assistant finally came into my room. Without a preamble, she said, "There is a soft-tissue density on the left side of your brain measuring 11.8 by 8.6 millimeters in maximal dimensions."

I asked her to speak to me in a language I could understand.

"I don't know exactly how to say this," she said. "But it appears you have a brain tumor and you're in the middle of a stroke."

I started to laugh, unable to take in what I had just heard. By then the doctor had walked into the room. Overhearing the conversation and the edges of my humor, she interrupted, "How about this: on a scale of one to ten, you are at an eight."

That got my attention.

I called Brooke and told him what I knew. He listened and said little. Between the long silences, I shared medical terms like *meningioma* and *aneurysm*. He said he would do some research and call me back. He also told me that our home in Castle Valley, Utah, was flooding. Friends and neighbors were sandbagging the banks of Placer Creek even in the middle of the night. He took the phone outside and I could hear what sounded like thunder as the rising river roared through the arroyo past our house.

We hung up and for the next seven hours I lay in the dark hospital room alone.

My mind became a falcon following its prey, darting through canyons above a turbulent river with the velocity of a bird flying blind around each sandstone curve. I recalled the afternoon when Brooke and I were running Westwater Canyon, a narrowing of the Colorado River known for its intensity, especially during high water. If you paddle poorly through a set of rapids called Skull, named for a set of boulders resembling bones, you end up in the Room of Doom, helpless to escape the violence of a whirlpool where the only way out is by helicopter. I was in that room now, caught in the circling terror of my own thoughts.

I kept thinking, *This is not my story, this is not my story, this is not my story*, until out of utter exhaustion I surrendered to the comfort of fatigue and the reality of the cold, hard gurney I was lying on covered by a thin cotton blanket. So this is where I am, I thought. How surprising. And the strength of gravity returned to me.

As if the falcon had settled on a ledge, my mind calmed, able to grasp a different vantage point. *What if I do have a brain tumor? How shall I live? What if I am in the middle of a stroke? How shall I live? What if I am fine and this is all a mistake?* And then I realized, in the darkness of my inquiry, the outcome didn't matter, the question remains the same.

The nurse came in to take my temperature. She flipped on the lights. I sat up, squinted and looked at the clock. The two black hands on the white face began to rotate wildly. Twenty-four hours circled in seconds.

"No, it's not your brain," said the nurse matter-of-factly, seeing my confusion. "The hands are circling the clock. And I can't tell you why this is happening."

After being taken by ambulance to Eastern Maine Medical Center, in Bangor, for more tests and meetings with doctors who wanted to operate immediately, I said after five days that I needed to go home to Utah. Brooke was with me and agreed.

Back in Salt Lake City, I am given a definitive diagnosis: I have a cavernous hemangioma located in what doctors call the "eloquent" part of my brain, or Wernicke's area, the home of language comprehension, where metaphor and the patterned mind live. It is a small tangle of vessels, likely benign, resembling a raspberry, with pockets of pooled blood bunched together. In simple terms, I had a bleed, and therefore went numb. It could happen again, at any time. Prior bleeds predict future bleeds. Treatment comes in two forms: brain surgery or wait and watch.

The conversation with the neurosurgeon went like this: "I will cut a ring of bone from your skull. We will enter the brain and, while you are conscious, run some tests of comprehension to see where the 'no-fly zones' are, the areas we need to avoid to make sure there is as little risk to your language center as possible. After that, we'll put you under, we'll remove the malformation, put the circle of bone back in place, cover it with a six-inch plate of titanium with screws, put back your skin flap, stitch it closed, and wait and see how you recover."

"Meaning?" I asked.

"Meaning we'll have to wait and see if you can understand what I say or can speak."

I couldn't find my words to ask the next question.

Uncomfortable with the silence, he continued. "Worst-case scenario, you will hear the words but not be able to make any association with the sounds. You will speak but nothing will be comprehended." He paused. "And then there's always the possibility the hemangioma could burst. I had one patient…"

I stopped listening.

I asked him if I could see the image of my brain one more time. With a click on the computer, my cavernoma appeared back on the X-ray screen. I stared at the black-and-white image. It was unclear whether I was looking at a bullet hole or a window of light.

Doctors delivering second and third and fourth opinions, from the University of Utah to the Columbia School of Neurology, all ask the same question, "How well do you live with uncertainty?"

"What else is there?" I say.

I opt to do nothing.

For weeks, months, after my diagnosis, I dreamed of birds. White birds. White peacocks. White owls. White doves and crows. These white birds inhabited a frozen landscape accompanied by white bears and wolves and I wondered what was frozen in me, what had rendered me numb in a world I thought I was so open to feeling.

The body doesn't lie.

ON JANUARY 23, 2010, I was in Maine attending the memorial service of a beautiful young woman. Gifted with words, she was a promising writer who had just graduated from college. From time to time, we exchanged essays and stories. She was smart, irreverent, and undone by the pull of her own perfection. She starved herself. It made no sense. The suicides of our children never do. And as a community gathered around her parents and brother, we all bore the burden of responsibility and regrets.

Inside the church, all the ushers were fathers, and it was the mothers who brought offerings of food throughout the week to the bereaved house, serving the family as they became guests in their own home, comforted. And I thought about how we parent each other through grief in gestures large and small. My eyes focused on the small, tender box—made by the hands of a neighbor—now holding her ashes, *ashes, we all fall down*. The woods she ran through as a child hold her in memories of maple, birch, and balsam fir. Pink tulips soften the edges of the altar. Emily's favorite flower. Yes, I will speak her name, her beautiful name, *Emily*, for in a year when health care reform was debated and the question "Who pays?" was frequently asked, those of us sitting on the hard pews of a January day knew the answer. She had sought professional help. She had wanted her life to be different. But she lost her job, like so many in this country, and fell through the cracks of our institutional care. She made a choice. I, too, am making a choice. Do any of us ever fully understand the consequences of our actions?

Winter's searing light burned through the stained-glass windows of the white-steepled church as we listened to the pastor read, unapologetically, from "The Judgment of the Birds," by Loren Eiseley:

> The sun was warm there, and the murmurs of forest life blurred softly away into my sleep. When I awoke, dimly aware of some commotion and outcry in the clearing, the light was slanting down through the pines in such a way that the glade was lit like some vast cathedral. I could see the dust motes of wood pollen in

the long shaft of light, and there on the extended branch sat an enormous raven with a red and squirming nestling in his beak.

The sound that awoke me was the outraged cries of the nestling's parents, who flew helplessly in circles about the clearing. The sleek black monster was indifferent to them. He gulped, whetted his beak on the dead branch a moment and sat still. Up to that point the little tragedy had followed the usual pattern. But suddenly, out of all that area of woodland, a soft sound of complaint began to rise. Into the glade fluttered small birds of half a dozen varieties drawn by the anguished outcries of the tiny parents.

No one dared to attack the raven. But they cried there in some instinctive common misery, the bereaved and the unbereaved. The glade filled with their soft rustling and their cries. They fluttered as though to point their wings at the murderer. There was a dim intangible ethic he had violated, that they knew. He was a bird of death.

And he, the murderer, the black bird at the heart of life, sat on there, glistening in the common light, formidable, unmoving, unperturbed, untouchable.

The sighing died. It was then I saw the judgment. It was the judgment of life against death. I will never see it again so forcefully presented. I will never hear it again in notes so tragically prolonged. For in the midst of protest, they forgot the violence. There, in that clearing, the crystal note of a song sparrow lifted hesitantly in the hush. And finally, after painful fluttering, another took the song, and then another, the song passing from one bird to another, doubtfully at first, as though some evil thing were being slowly forgotten. Till suddenly they took heart and sang from many throats joyously together as birds are known to sing. They sang because life is sweet and sunlight beautiful. They sang under the brooding shadow of the raven. In simple truth they had forgotten the raven, for they were the singers of life, and not of death.

I walked out of the church into the bitter cold. A friend had told me that a painted bunting, normally not seen north of the Carolinas, had flown in on the tail of a blizzard, blown off course, and stayed. I needed to see that bird. I made a house call to the man whose feeder it was frequenting. Turns out he was the pastor to all the islands in Penobscot Bay.

"Come back at 6:45 tomorrow morning," he said. "He's been pretty punctual."

And so I kept my date with the painted bunting, driving in the dark down a snow-packed road in coastal Maine. I knocked on the door. The pastor opened it and invited me inside. His wife had three cups of coffee brewing. The only light in their home emanated from the woodstove in the kitchen, where a large picture window framed the feeder outside. It was 6:30 a.m. We made small talk in whispers and long pauses. Mainers are never ones to say too much. At 6:43 a.m., the painted bunting arrived like a dream between the crease of shadow and light. His silhouette grew toward color for the seven short minutes he stayed. And when dawn struck his tiny feathered back, he ignited like a flame: red, blue, and green. There were no other birds around him. He was alone with his singular tapping on the lip of the feeder, eating one sunflower seed at a time, and then he flew—

I have not dreamed of white birds since.

A MONTH LATER, another accidental appointment. I step into the Spheris Gallery in Hanover, New Hampshire. I find myself standing in front of a spiral of birds—black, black-gray, gray-white, red—in the cutout shapes of swallows and swifts. These birds gain momentum against a white wall. Each bird flutters and flies according to the length of the pin that keeps it in place.

Black-white; black; black-gray; red; red-gray; blue; these birds create an unexpected velocity even in the gallery. *Red Swirl* is an installation created by Julia Barello, an artist who lives in New Mexico. She understands swifts and swallows, how they toy with tawdry heat waves playing off red-rock walls.

The gallery is empty. I pull up a chair. The spiral of birds registers as a joyous familiarity alive in the desert, alive in me. And yet something is not quite right. I feel a disturbance, a quiet wounding. I am holding a question like a trapped bird that is fluttering inside my cupped hands.

Each bird bears the burden of text on its wings. Small white sentences, fragments too small to read from afar. I did not notice this peculiarity until now. I stand up and walk toward them for a closer examination. My hair stands on end. These birds are made from the X-ray films of MRIs, magnetic resonance images like the one that exposed the cavernoma in my brain six months earlier.

I pinch the skin on my right hand to see if I am numb.

Each bird is an image is a presence is a person and I wonder if the people represented here are alive or dead. The partial scans of their brains, their bones, their organs, with letters of their identity here or there, are now revisioned and reconstructed, but the evidence of a person in peril remains. Like me, an image becomes the diagnosis, determined and named. What cannot be named is a disturbance.

No wonder I have been disturbed by Barello's *Red Swirl*. It is the creation of flight born from the place of private reckonings. The art of living as we are dying is a terrifying beauty.

To be numb to the world is another form of suicide.

I feel myself separating from the sentence written on my own wings. How do we move beyond our own diagnosis? I turn to the birds, the ember of painted bunting is burning in my hands. Of course. Off-course. The bunting got caught in a storm and stayed. I have been seized in a storm of my own making. Whirlwind. World-wind. Distracted and displaced. In the wounding of becoming lost, I can correct myself. We can take flight from our lives in a form other than denial and return to our authentic selves through the art of retreat. Accidental sightings, whether witnessed in a brain or during a winter dawn, remind us there is no such thing as certainty. Tulips dance even after their lives have been cut short.

And so we embrace the surprise.

I was drawn to these transparent swallows and swifts because of their familiarity of form. But that's not what kept me here. I stayed with the birds in this room because of an increasing discomfort, caught in the clutch of wonder. These birds were calling me to a different point of view. Usually, with swallows and swifts, I am looking up. Here in my chair at the Spheris, I am looking down, watching the swallows' backs, not bellies, seeing the X-ray birds from a place of omnipotence, the vantage point of the gods and the dead brought back to life.

The red bird at the center of this spiral accumulates its own velocity (yes, I will use this word again and again), a velocity that invites and attracts other birds to gather in motion, creating a cluster which must be similar to the shape of my own cavernous hemangioma—only this is a cluster of blood, blood in my brain, congealed blood, stagnant blood that oozes and seeps, bleeding into the folds of my own gray matter, perhaps one day flooding my capacity to speak or comprehend the world I love. I am a woman of words. Take away my words and what is left of me? The gift of my patterned mind begins to flatten and take flight, leaving me—leaving those close—with no memories of how to apprehend a word like *bird*.

I bleed. I become numb. This frightens me.

EACH YEAR SIXTY MILLION OF US around the world are ordered to slide into MRI chambers like prisoners. What if we viewed this as ceremony instead of incarceration? Trusting that something like a symptom is prompting us to take a closer look inside. Out of panic or pain or instinct, we examine ourselves in the name of survival. What if we were open to receiving revelations rather than restrictions? What if fear was transformed into awareness? And what if a team of doctors was to be joined by another kind of authority, grounded in the imagination, where white gowns became robes of feathers?

I entered the world of Magnetic Resonance Imaging. As the hammering inside the enclosed walls of the MRI began pounding and I had no way to get out, I was told by the technician through headphones to relax, which I was trying to do, but failing miserably, as the terror of claustrophobia enveloped me. I closed my eyes and began breathing slowly, deliberately, until suddenly, I found myself sitting with a Council of Birds reminiscent of those living inside Hieronymus Bosch's *Garden of Earthly Delights*.

Great blue heron appeared. Yellow warbler and house wren perched on my shoulders. Sapsucker began tapping on my brain. The hammering now had a purpose of taking down walls, the walls of thought I had constructed. Ruby-throated humming-bird pierced my skull and removed the calcifications I had been shown earlier on the CAT scan and replaced them with nectar. Ivory-billed woodpecker presided over the internal workings of my brain, assuring me that the invisible is real. Ivory-billed wood-peckers are still on the planet.

All this in the hammering and drumming of the MRI that became the rhythmic drumming of ceremony. I was simply breath-ing, reimagining my existence in the healing of birds.

To shut our eyes is Travel. Emily Dickinson.

It was all so natural, the drumming, the dancing, the speaking of birds—how they circled me with sound. And then the commo-tion stopped. In the stillness of my own mind, hermit thrush was singing between intervals of thunder.

Inside the walls of technology, there can be breakthroughs.

NOW, IN A SHIFT OF LIGHT, the shadows of birds are more pro-nounced on the gallery's white wall. The shadow of each bird is speaking to me. Each shadow doubles the velocity, ferocity of forms. The shadow, my shadow, now merges with theirs. Descension. As-cension. The velocity of wings creates the whisper to awaken.

How shall I live?

I want to feel both the beauty and the pain of the age we are living in. I want to survive my life without becoming numb. I want to speak and comprehend words of wounding without having these words become the landscape where I dwell. I want to possess a light touch that can elevate darkness to the realm of stars.

This vascular malformation could bleed and burst. Or I may simply go on living, guided by the songs of birds. What is time, sacred time, but the acceleration of consciousness? There are so many ways to change the sentences we have been given.

And we cannot do it alone.

The human mind always makes progress, but it is a progress in spirals. Madame de Staël.

How shall we live?

Once upon a time, when women were birds, there was the simple understanding that to sing at dawn and to sing at dusk was to heal the world through joy. The birds still remember what we have forgotten, that the world is meant to be celebrated.

SUMMER, 1959

Carolyn Ferrell

M y mother and her sister push the old green VW Beetle from
the shed down the cobblestone drive. This is their chance
to escape the drudgery of Mutti's home, the endless polishing of
wood and washing of wool and cooking of dust. The sun is high
and behind them, the house stands empty. Maike, newly out of the
Pädagogische Hochschule, wears a pantsuit and sandals; my mother
wears a dress, a gift from Maike, one of the first store-bought outfits she has ever owned (*You can have this and more, if you work
hard enough!* Maike promised, as my mother modeled the butter-
yellow shift in the mirror at Karstadt.) The women maneuver
the car into the street while clouds overhead drift smoothly out
toward the Baltic. Though this is midsummer, the air reels with
autumn crispness. The engine refuses to start, and so the women

get back out and push the VW toward the street's decline. There is something inelegant about this labor, but my mother and her sister don't care. They don't care how they look or what the neighbors think, most of whom have always been deeply suspicious of Mutti's daughters. My mother and aunt know that the neighbors know that Mutti doesn't approve of this VW—she often calls it a piece of junk while chatting in the garden with Frau Mortorf. But what does that matter? Maike drives it with obvious pride. Mutti herself drives a used Karmann Ghia, a reckless car that barely gets her to and from the center of the Heikendorf, where she teaches elementary school. She earned that Karmann Ghia, just as Maike earned the VW—but there is something awful, of course, about a daughter claiming the prize in much less time than it took the mother. (*Will Maike and Elke ever know what a struggle my life was?* Mutti asks Frau Mortorf as they shake their heads in the twilight.)

At the decline, my mother and Maike give the VW a final push, jump back in, and descend the hill. Frau Mortorf opens her curtains and shakes her head. *Look at that—the one girl merely seventeen and her sister no more than twenty-two, and a teacher at that! The height of* Unverschaemtheit!

My mother and Maike wave at Frau Mortorf's window as their car zips by, its motor finally engaged. *Auf wiedersehen, Frau Mortorf!*

They brake at the bottom of the hill to embrace each other and to apply lipstick in the rearview mirror. They can't stop laughing. But after a minute or so they drive off. My mother and her sister have to make good time if they want to make the festival at Flensburg, which will be starting in a matter of hours.

LONG ISLAND
NOVEMBER 2006

This was in the late 1950s. I was a student at the Pedagogic College where they trained teachers. To be honest, I was pretty mediocre. My teachers often let me slide when I mentioned that Maike Schmidt was my sister. She was the shining star, and the teachers expected me to do well because of her. And I did do well in Germanistik. But basically, I slid.

Maike had received her degree and was already teaching in a school. She was not married. My sister was not like other women. Germany in the 1950s, you have to understand.

I wanted to quit school. I wanted a job. I wanted to move out so badly. My parents had just gotten a divorce and Mutti used me as a sounding board. She complained all the time about Papa and his women—I couldn't take it.

I came out of a generation where there were no choices for women. There were no choices for girls. I wanted to work. I wanted to have my own money. There weren't even choices for boys. My brother, the highest in his class, was taken out of school to work on the farm. He did all the work Maike had done as a young girl.

After the war, we had mostly food from the farm, but not much. We owned no clothes except that which we sewed. Our sewing was lousy. The seams in our dresses were all off.

Sometimes refugees showed up at our door, begging for something to eat. Sometimes a small group of Jewish girls would appear at the door and simply sing for food. They wouldn't say a word, they would just stand in front of you and sing together for something to eat.

There was always hunger, deprivation. Old men like my father singing American pop songs, only using Nazi words instead of the English lyrics. People all around saying: Why can't we just forget?

After she divorced Papa, Mutti moved us all to Heikendorf. A small brick house. She moved the kitchen into the basement because she needed the space for six children. She did that by herself.

I was never good in school. But she insisted.

But then, in the summer of 1959, I met an American GI and we began writing letters to each other.

Mutti at first knew nothing.

IN THE 1950S, everyone is a hitchhiker. My mother's two sisters have traveled across the continent using only their thumbs: Switzerland, France, Italy. Now that Maike has the VW, she and my mother can travel in style.

One hour after they depart the sleepy village, the women take a detour through the streets of nearby Kiel—a foolish thing, considering how expensive gasoline has become. They have been through these streets dozens of times—ever since Mutti moved them to the small brick house in Heikendorf from the large farm in Muessen which, to her chagrin, Papa had gambled away. For my mother and her sister, there is nothing like the freedom of Kiel, and especially on a day like today, when something indefinable is in the air. The trip is an extravagance; it will cost Maike and Elke their lunch money.

But what does it matter? They are free. They will make it to Flensburg.

Sometime later—after more singing and laughing and getting lost—they stop the car outside of Rendsburg; Maike jumps out to use the bushes for a bathroom. At first they think they are alone on this stretch of highway, but then my mother notices a tall dark hitchhiker standing under a large road sign which shades him almost completely. My mother whistles a signal to Maike, who laughs in embarrassment, then runs back to the car while adjusting her pants (and new girdle underneath). Behind her, fields of yellow flowers, *Rapsfelder*, bend in the roadside breeze. The hitchhiker emerges from the shadow and smiles. The women see he is black.

But his face is so sympathetic. My mother goes for the lipstick.

The stranger waves awkwardly, then removes a military jacket from the duffel bag slung across his shoulders.

So, Maike says thoughtfully, *an American soldier*.

But a handsome one, my mother adds, rolling down the window.

You have to understand. I was ambivalent for so long—I had such mixed feelings. There was no one thing. Finally I just up and ran away to the airport. While I was there I sent Mutti a postcard telling her how sorry I was. My handwriting was a mess. A woman befriended me, took me to the jet. And then a stewardess placed me in my seat. I couldn't stop crying. But in spite of that, all the time I was thinking: What would my friends say if they could see me now?

After Mutti discovered the letters I had been receiving from Bob, she went down to the post and insisted they not give me my mail anymore, which they did. I realized I would have to get Bob to send his letters to my friends. So they got his letters and passed them on to me, but Mutti found out about that as well. My friends left me in the lurch.

I used to call him collect. Before Mutti made that fuss at the post, he used to send me letters with money—the first money I ever had. I bought a striped dress. I bought a pair of high-heeled shoes. I remember thinking: I never had high heels before.

I kept on spending the money he sent when in reality I was supposed to use it for a ticket. Finally he got mad and accused me of using him. But it was the first time I'd had any money. You have to understand.

I had to get away from Germany. We had no food in the house. I remembered when Bob and I met, how we wound up dancing at the music festival in Flensburg—it was heaven. There was no one thing that made me leave, only that I wanted more of that day in Flensburg.

After that festival, Maike and I wound up taking him with us to meet Mutti. She liked him well enough. Then he returned to his base and stayed about six more months in Germany. It was only after he returned to America that Mutti interfered with his letters to me. She stopped thinking of them as harmless.

I took the plane all by myself to America. He met me at the airport in New York. I remember thinking how disheveled he looked. He was tired. I'd been crying on the entire journey. His was a cool reception.

I remember thinking: But what of our letters? Nearly two years of letters, from Germany to America. There was so much romance. In them he said he couldn't live without me.

THE SOLDIER APOLOGIZES, telling them he knows it's unusual to pick up a complete stranger—back home he would never do such a thing—but would they consider taking him along? They don't know him from Adam, he admits, but really. He wouldn't hurt a fly.

My mother, fluttering, is unable to say a coherent word and simply holds the car door open for him.

They introduce themselves—another awkward moment—and immediately Maike starts the VW without any trouble.

My mother tries not to look at him, and he tries not to look at my mother. The trip to Flensburg goes by incredibly fast; the old car is on wings. The whole time, Maike is the only one talking, practicing the English she'd perfected from student trips to England. My mother, on the other hand, is embarrassed by her English and thus contents herself with stealing glances at the handsome soldier. *Why would he think we would be afraid of him? He looks as gentle as a lamb.*

They arrive at the festival by afternoon and park at a beach where musicians are busy setting up their equipment. A phonograph plays through ancient loudspeakers, Peter Alexander and his syrupy songs on eternal love; all around, young people mill about distributing fliers, talking, smoking, singing. The air is warm. The soldier asks my mother to follow him farther down the beach, where they can be alone and maybe find a spot to dance. Maike laughs, a little out of jealousy, but urges my mother to go. The soldier promises to bring Maike back something to drink, a soda pop perhaps, whatever they drink over here in Germany. Maike grins dourly and waves them on.

My mother follows the soldier along the crowded stretch of beach, where at every step, newer, flightier throngs of teenage girls and boys dance and laugh and chuck the fliers to the ground. In the distance, yachts glide in and out of the harbor. Closer by, gulls dive in and out of garbage bins. Eventually the soldier finds a somewhat secluded dune—only one other couple there, lips to lips—and pulls my mother into a makeshift sort of dance.

My mother wants to ask for a *Limonade* but wonders if it is the right moment. With the music playing, his eyes sparkling. This is, after all, love at first sight.

The soldier whispers in my mother's ear, tells her how lovely she looks, that she is the loveliest in all the land—he whispers under the drone of the loudspeakers, Peter Alexander crooning, *Ich weiss, was Dir fehlt.* The soldier's breath on my mother's cheek is like a miniature fire, a roasting anticipation of love, and just when my mother thinks she can handle no more, when she feels she is about to combust with happiness, the soldier steadies her with his hands, looks her in the eye and says, *All I'm doing is trying to find a way out.*

My mother nods, not understanding.

He is, of course, talking about the Army, the subject foremost on his mind, but my mother can't really know that. She doesn't understand most of his words, though what she has comprehended thus far has electrified her. She wants to hear more—no one has ever before told her that she was the loveliest of them all. *Ich weiss, was Dir fehlt*—my mother swoons to the music and to the eyes of the handsome soldier and suddenly loses track of the world—of Maike, of Flensburg, of Heikendorf, of Mutti. She wants to be in a fairy tale for the rest of her life.

He whispers again, *I need a way out. That's all I'm fighting for.*

My mother gazes dreamily into the eyes of this glorious stranger and sings along with the song on the loudspeaker: *I know what you are missing.*

You have to remember. This was the fifties. Someone once said the word orgasm *in Mutti's presence and she went berserk. This, after nine pregnancies.*

Bob took me from the airport to a hotel in Brooklyn, a true fleabag hotel. My first impression of America. When I pulled back the sheets, bedbugs scurried everywhere. He left immediately for work, and I was alone. The subway was next to our window. Everywhere you heard women and children screaming. We stayed for a week. I was so lonely, I didn't dare venture out. I cried every day out of loneliness. Soon I told him, We can't live like this.

We went to his mother's apartment in Brooklyn, which was stuffed with furniture and roaches. She was married to Bill, a drunken philanderer. After the births of my first three children, in 1962, 1963, and 1965, Bill always found a way to tell Bob that their skin was too light, that I must have had an affair. And Bob actually asked me whether that was true.

But when could I have found the time for an affair?

After I arrived in America I was immediately pregnant. It was taken for granted that we would have a family, though at first Bob didn't want to get married. He wanted to live together and raise children. He didn't consider marriage necessary, but I insisted.

So. 1961. We rented an apartment on Avenue I. Roaches everywhere. We had nothing, no furniture. Bob controlled all the money, and what he liked to do, for fun, to keep me from crying, was go for long drives. I always wanted to stop somewhere and walk. But he never stopped.

Mutti's letters came all the time. I was so unhappy—I couldn't speak the language, I had no one besides him. And he didn't want to hear about Mutti. All that was left behind.

Going back to Germany was no longer an option. I told myself, I did this to myself, I have to stick it out. I had fought for my freedom so ferociously. There was no turning back. You have to understand. There really was no choice back then.

I had given up opportunities—the Pädagogische Hochschule, the chance I would be a teacher like Maike. Having my own money. I was totally dependent on him, for everything. It was just like being in Germany with Mutti.

One day Bob said to me, It's time for you to go to work.

What do you mean? *I asked.* I have a home now, I can do whatever I want.

That's how I had always imagined it. That was what was always told to me: marriage, home, and children.

But soon Bob took me to fill out an application as a nurse's aide.

DANCING BAREFOOT IN THE SAND, my mother and father concentrate on the lovely racket of their own breathing. *Would they know, as evening slowly came on, and as the wind picked up heft across the water, and as some of the ships furled their sails in the purple dusk— would they know that I was not far away, following their every step?*

Before my mother left Germany, Mutti had warned her, *If you ever have children, we won't acknowledge them.* By *we* she meant herself, and my mother's brothers, and my mother's father who, though not directly in the picture, nearly died when he learned that his favorite daughter had run away to be with a black man.

After my mother became a mother, Mutti would send endless reel-to-reel tapes to the apartment in Brooklyn and then to the house on Long Island. Every inch of her voice burst with the hard nails of her tears. Mutti would narrate her suffering in great detail, how there was nothing left for Mutti to live for, how my mother had destroyed the hopes of the entire family. What had she worked all her life for, she wailed into the tape, if all she got in return was a selfish, selfish daughter?

Would my parents know I was there already, on that day in Flensburg, looking back toward the future?

That first year, before you were born, was the worst.

EIGHTEEN YEARS LATER, in a mall parking lot in Massapequa, Long Island, in the middle of a pitiful afternoon, I'm supposed to be in love.

I'm sitting in the front seat of Rob Richman's souped-up Chevy, listening to his boyish tears, feeling guilt sweat from my skin. Rob is spoiled, self-indulgent, but I can no sooner walk away from him than I can fly to the moon. In his most urgent voice he tells me that he wants a baby, that he wants us to marry, that he can't live without me. He does not apologize for punching me in the ribs just the day before, in front of my mother's house, the one she bought after her divorce. He does not say he's sorry because today is different from yesterday, and with Rob, the wisdom has always been: *don't look back.*

I'm supposed to be in love; indeed, everyone thinks I should love him, especially a few of the popular girls at school who've never taken an interest in me until now. How often do you get a guy who is clearly so crazy about you that he'll follow your every move? *I wish I could be loved like that,* one of them—until recently an arch enemy—tells me as we sit in the library, flipping through college guides.

AND ROB DOES FOLLOW ME: throughout the hallways at high school, to the library, to the door of my best friend's house. To orchestra rehearsal, to concerts, to classes. To parties, to practice rooms, to corners where I think I'm alone. There he is, in love. The only choice I have is to reciprocate.

And until this afternoon, I have done a good enough job. But today, something made me jump in his car, the way I usually do after every single school day, rain or shine, and borrow his wisdom. Right in his face I announce that I'm leaving and not looking back.

Because until this afternoon, it doesn't seem to matter much that his parents hate me. A month or two before this, his father politely let me in their house, led me to the closed door of Rob's bedroom, and then quietly ordered Rob to *get this nigger the hell out of here.*

Until this afternoon it doesn't seem to matter much that I know that Rob's own mother has stood crying every day at her cash register at the Grand Union Supermarket, bemoaning the fate of her beloved boy, the straight-B student. To her everything has always been plain as day.

A girl like Carolyn? With a German mother, no less! What else could she be after but a home and a husband?

I will use him, she believes. I will get pregnant and ruin his name.

I am trouble, his father tells him. That's what their kind is like.

Now all that is moot because I'm leaving and never looking back.

The rest of the afternoon is spent driving in circles around the shopping mall parking lot, where Rob continues to cry and beg and wheedle; he attempts to crash into a huge trash bin, but he loves his souped-up car too much to actually carry out such a threat. After an hour he drives over to Marjorie Post Park in Massapequa, the place where all the indiscreet high school couples make out. He puts his arms around my neck and wails. He tells me his parents never loved him, that they never expected anything great from him. Sadly, his older brother Mike is the success. Married at twenty, with a child on the way at twenty-one, and a scholarship to Nassau Community College in hand, Mike is his parents' golden dream.

Rob grabs me by the shoulders. *Why can't you expect something from me?*

A little while later he drives me back to my old neighborhood, to the house where I lived for fourteen years with my parents and siblings. I barely recognize the place. *We could move back here*, Rob suggests timidly. The house and lawn are neatly manicured but shabby all the same. Someone has told me that since we moved out two years ago, it has been burglarized five times. This neighborhood, full of black people who stand at their curtains and watch for the next thing, frightens Rob to death.

He takes off for the other side of town, the white part. At the gates of Amity Beach, early evening stars pave the sky like brilliant bricks. *I would be the best husband, I promise. I'd never make you cry.*

I roll down the window and stick out my head in the chill air. I swear I can hear the sound of laughter somewhere far away.

You can go to the community college. We can go together. Why do you need to go away to college?

He knows I won't wait for him. The college I have chosen is an hour away, in Rob's words a "sleepaway" college; he knows I won't look back. I won't visit, I won't write. I won't dream of his fairy tales, the future he imagines for us. When he suggests, as he does that afternoon at the beach, that we move in with his parents and give our love time, I almost vomit.

Rob will not stop his tears—he expects them to get the job done, despite my stony face, despite the fact that I have opened my door and am already out on the sand. This whole afternoon isn't what he has bargained for. People at school tell Rob he resembles John Travolta from *Saturday Night Fever*, and he loves hearing that. He loves hearing he is a catch, that he would be voted Most Attractive Male if it weren't for all those black fool boys who turn the teachers' heads. He loves worshipping me until I can't take it anymore, me, his first dark-skinned girlfriend. On days when he isn't crying, Rob plays drums and smokes pot and lines his bedroom walls— much to his mother's chagrin—with *Playboy* centerfolds.

You don't love me! You've always used me! My parents were right!

He is the first white boy I have ever dated.

A man and a woman walking nearby stop and stare at us, perhaps taken aback by the screaming. *Don't go, please don't go! I'll kill myself if you go!*

But I do move on, closer to the water's edge, where I look up once more at the clouds drifting across the brickway of stars. I can just make out the studded silhouettes of my parents as they touch each other's hair with their hands. A gentle gesture, one that will rarely come again.

Rob comes charging after me, not caring if this couple will try and stop him. But they do nothing but stare. *A baby would make everything all right! Why don't you love me?*

Once I begged Bob for a pair of nail scissors, then another time a tube of sunburn cream. We had gone to Coney Island and I was so burnt. I was homesick. But nothing. He refused to buy me those things. It took months before my personal effects were shipped—via boat—from Germany. Mostly books, some clothes. I read Goethe when I wasn't crying.

FOR A FEW WEEKS AFTER THAT DAY, I will not know how to leave Rob. Eventually June rolls around, and on my graduation day I see him, to my great shame, standing in the bleachers on the school lawn, cheering me on. My teachers have pretty much given up on me—this in spite of the fact that I've been accepted to Sarah Lawrence College on a full scholarship. They see how Rob tails me. They notice my textbooks scarred with his name in every corner.

But when my teachers ask, I don't talk about Rob. I tell them I am planning on becoming a writer, that I've dreamt of becoming a writer since I was a little girl, when my mother handed me a brown marbled notebook and told me to put my poems in it.

In reality, it would take that evening, and another boy—a tall, muscular thug who crashes my best friend's graduation party—to finally drive Rob away. At the party, this thug will get a little drunk and hurl insults at Rob; later on, he will dispose of my boyfriend in a good old-fashioned black boy–white boy fistfight. My best friend's father—who has been on the phone with his mistress and has gotten sick of our interruptions—will eventually come outside from the basement bar and kick the three of us out.

Rob walks to a local Carvel, where he calls his mother to pick him up. The next time I see him is in the middle of a later night, when the police are called to escort him from my mother's house, where he is weeping on the steps.

But for now, I am saved. As I drive the thug home, he kisses me on the neck; I am now his. He doesn't cry or wheedle. He simply states the facts in that kiss. He fought for me. I should be his. It is only fair.

Luckily the thug is not interested in marrying or having babies. *There are places you can go*, he will whisper in my ear, as we sit on the couch in the den of his house and listen to his parents scream in drunken rages. His fingers will twirl the lock of hair just behind my ear. *If I gave you a baby, you wouldn't have to keep it.*

In the background, oblivious to everything else, his parents travel up and down the stairs, throwing glasses, bottles, car keys at each other, cursing the day they ever met. His mother has just lost her job of eighteen years at Grumman Aerospace, where she worked as a secretary. His father's landscaping business flourishes, despite his nonstop boozing.

But the thug's fingers will remain in that caress, his eyes will remain on me, almost until the day I leave for Sarah Lawrence. *Trust me, baby. There are places you can go to get a baby taken care of. If that's ever the case.*

I worked as a nurse's aide until I was five months pregnant. Only after David's birth in 1965 was I finally diagnosed with severe anemia. I kept fainting with each pregnancy and was told I was simply tired. One doctor told me everyone fainted, that I was not special.

At the hospital, I met doctors who hated me. One of them, from Poland originally, called me a Nazi. He got the other doctors to dislike me as well.

I stayed on, working with a kind nurse, a woman from the West Indies, Mrs. Henry. She helped me because I still couldn't speak the language well. When I got home, I gave all my earnings to Bob. He then gave me ten dollars a week for expenses. Food. Clothing. Medicine.

Bob moved us out to Long Island after the roaches became too much. They were actually crawling in your crib at Avenue I.

We got the house in spring of 1963. The real estate agent told me, This development is just for colored people. *But the house was like a dream come true.*

Even though I had no money for plants, I found seeds, and started a garden.

I had one baby after the other. I had to rise each morning to make him breakfast at four o'clock. Even when I came home from the hospital with a baby. Breakfast at four was just one of my jobs.

On North Ronald Drive I was the only mother who stayed home. Mostly the other women on the block—all black women—were nice to me. But they all had jobs and they needed a babysitter. I would say yes, and then some would leave their kids with me for days. They took advantage, but they were never mean.

*Sometimes I would get a note in the mailbox—*YOU THINK YOU'RE SO SPECIAL. *People would lose their houses in the blink of an eye. But* *many of them saw me as lucky, because Bob was the provider. And not everyone on the block was married.*

Once a relative of Bob's came out from the projects in Brooklyn and called me Cinderella.

But if you had to name my story, it would have to be called, "No Choices."

EVERYONE COULD HAVE ONE. Every cheerleader, every home-coming queen, every honor student, every plain old average girl. All you had to do was look in the phone book. The 1977 yellow pages of Suffolk or Nassau County—it was all the same. If you didn't look in the phone book—if you were too country to do so, or too poor to know better, or so utterly uneducated that you actually believed you should keep the baby, then that was your own damn fault.

But everyone had an escape hatch. Everyone had an opportunity. This is what made us different from our mothers. We could escape a lifetime of bitterness just by lying on a doctor's table in the space of a lonely gray afternoon.

Three children with bottles. Three children in diapers. I used to go into the bedroom and cry. Bob would come in—What's the matter?

I would say I didn't know, then I would say, I need a break!

From what? You don't do anything around here.

All around me women went to work. I wanted to as well, and soon filled out an application at a local factory. They wouldn't hire me because of my language.

A friend from back in Brooklyn once asked me, Why don't you get a tubal ligation? But I had no idea what that was. One of the neighbor women on Long Island advised me to use a douche after sex. That way I could stop the babies. But I was afraid to try.

Things changed when my fourth baby was born in 1969. Bob got sick with the mumps and had to leave work. We had no money for a while. Then he took me to the local community college and signed me up. I didn't even know my own social security number. But in 1971, I went back to school. And that was the real beginning of my emancipation.

MY MOTHER AND MY FATHER didn't notice Maike approach them on the sand. The light was nearly gone. They both sat up and giggled, completely giddy. My mother's dress was ruined with wrinkles. There was not a trace of lipstick on her lips.

Maike worried about making it back home that night. They could not afford a hotel. And what of this GI? After she was so nice to him, a perfect stranger? He hadn't even bothered to buy her a Limonade.

Time to go, she whispered to her sister, turning in the direction of the car.

One professor raved over the first essay I handed in. I'd written it about my brother Uwe, who'd just died in an equestrian accident. The professor told me I was such a good writer. I couldn't believe my ears!

Though he had put me in school, Bob made sure to tell me: You can't make it without me. *He was beginning to have regrets.*

But then. I got a one hundred in Anatomy Lab, and a ninety-eight in Physiology.

It was so hard for me. I would put the last baby on my bed with a lot of toys and close the door. Then I would open the dictionary and write words down. It was so hard for me, the education. But I would go to bed at night and think about formulas in chemistry.

I remembered Mrs. Henry. How I used to admire her. But becoming a nurse was like a dream to me back then.

I was realizing how you grow when you get schooling. I thought: my God! The world is opening up!

It's not that I didn't enjoy having my babies. I did. But I suddenly saw myself as a nurse.

There is nothing like emancipation.

ANOTHER EIGHTEEN YEARS GO BY. I am driving my small son out to Long Island to Grandma's backyard, where he will kiss her many times and read many books in her lap and sing along to all the German songs she remembers from her childhood.

In another few years I bring out my new daughter to join in. By then I am a little over forty years old—twice the age my mother was when she first had me. I am a writer, a professor of creative writing at my alma mater, and married—happily—to someone I met in graduate school.

What if my parents had seen me back then? What if they could've heard me cry out, like some sort of heady savior? If I'd reached my arms toward the stars where they most certainly sat, and shook them hard? What then?

The children help Grandma tend her garden; this is her day off from the hospital, where she works full time in the ICU. She has worked as a nurse for more than twenty years, and now dreams of teaching nursing to others. She has even gone back to school to earn credits toward a bachelor's degree, though the grandchildren are taking up more and more of her time.

Ben gets a small patch to call his own, a circular area of earth around the sour cherry tree where he and Grandma plant a few petunias. Later, he helps his baby sister, Karina, slide down an old plastic slide to get into the wading pool, where they both shed the morning dirt in water that cascades over the edge and into the grass.

And even later, after lunch and baths and early pajamas, my mother takes out her book of German children's songs and points to the pictures and begins to sing, the kids curled up in her lap on the chaise longue. And there is no sweeter sound, no sweeter picture—but all I want to do is interrupt her. I want to ask my mother if she remembers that large cherry tree in Mutti's back-yard. I once climbed it when I was visiting Mutti for the summer. I remember experiencing the worst stomachache after a day in its limbs, indulging in the fruit, attempting to talk to the crows that were eyeing me from the gooseberry bushes. The tree was a true majesty, looking out over rooftops at the Baltic Sea, at the very beach where Mutti used to make the girls swim every morning before school, rain or shine.

She believed it would build character. She believed it would save them from something she refused to define in terms the girls would truly grasp. *Women just needed to be saved*, she would say. Not only from men, but from the world. Leave it at that. (To which her daughters would laugh and call their mother hopelessly old-fashioned.)

But what did that laughter matter? Mutti brought her daughters out to the rolling surf each morning before school and ordered them to swim in and out at least two times. Despite their complaints, their constant begging to be allowed back home, to sleep in, just this once.

She was so terribly old-fashioned, the girls moaned, stepping into the icy water. *Why didn't she listen to them, why didn't she forget the past, why didn't she just let them live their lives—just this once?*

SIGN HERE IF YOU EXIST

Jill Sisson Quinn

The female giant ichneumon wasp flies, impressively for her near-eight-inch length, with the light buoyancy of cotton-wood fluff, seemingly without direction, simply aloft. Despite her remarkable size, she is not bulky. Her three-part body makes up only about three inches of her total length, and is disproportionately slender; her thorax is connected to her abdomen by a Victorian-thin waist. Most of her maximum eight-inch span consists of an ovipositor half that length which extends from the tip of her abdomen and trails behind her like a thread loose from a pant hem. Fully extended, she can be nearly as long as your *Peterson's Field Guide to Insects*.

Her overall appearance of fragility—the corseted middle, the filamentous tail—portrays in flight a facade of drifting. But each time I have seen a giant ichneumon wasp she was on a mission, in search of something very specific: one member of a single species among the 1,017,018 described species of insects in the world (91,000 in the United States, 18,000 in Wisconsin, where I observed my second giant ichneumon). To comprehend this statistic, there are many things one needs to know: the definition of an insect, Linnaean taxonomy, the function of zero, the imaginary borders of states and countries. The female ichneumon wasp knows none of this. Yet she can locate a larva of the pigeon horntail—a type of wood wasp whose living body will nourish her developing young—hidden two inches deep in the wood of a dead tree, in the middle of a forest.

Charles Darwin himself, it turns out, studied the ichneumon wasp. He mentions it specifically in an 1860 letter to biologist Asa Gray, a proponent of the idea that nature reveals God's benevolence. Darwin, on the other hand, swayed no doubt by the rather macabre details of this parasitic insect's life, writes: "I cannot persuade myself that a beneficent and omnipotent God would have designedly created the ichneumonidae with the express intention of their feeding within the living bodies of Caterpillars"—and then, as if to reach the layman, he adds, "or that a cat should play with mice." The tabby that curls in your lap and licks your temple, after all, has likely batted a live mouse between its paws until its brain swelled and burst. And the larvae of the giant ichneumon wasp eat, from the inside out and over the course of an entire season, the living bodies of the larvae of a fellow insect.

Like Darwin, I think I have put to rest my belief in a beneficent and omnipotent God, in any God really. Contrary to what I once believed, it is easy to let go of God, whose essence has never been more than ethereal anyway, expanding like an escaping gas into the corners of whatever church you happened to attend, into the breath of whatever frightened, gracious, or insomnious prayer you found yourself emitting. But it is much more difficult to truly put to rest the belief in an afterlife, the kind where you might get to visit with all your dead friends and relatives. It will not be easy to let go of your deceased mother, who stands in her kitchen slicing potatoes and roast, who hacks ice from the sidewalk with shovels;

she is marrow and bone, a kernel of morals, values, and lessons compacted like some astronomical amount of matter into tablespoons, one with sugar for your cereal, another, for your fever, with a crushed aspirin and orange juice. You love her. You mark time and space by her: she is someone you are always either near to or very far from.

Can people live without the comfort of a creator? I think so. But relinquishing God—the Christian God, at least—does not leave everything else intact. A lack of the divine probably means that when you die what you consider your essence will cease to exist. You will no longer be able to commune with the people you love. Choosing to live without the assurance of an afterlife, therefore, feels like a kind of suicide, or murder.

MOST PARASITES DO NOT KILL their hosts. You—your living, breathing self—are evidence of this, as you host an array of parasitic microbes. Only about 10 percent of the hundred trillion cells in your body are really your own; the rest are bacteria, fungi, and other "bugs." The majority of these microbes are mutualistic, meaning both you and the microbe benefit from your relationship. A whopping 3.3 pounds of bacteria, representing five hundred separate species, live inside your intestines. You provide them a suitable environment—the right moisture, temperature, and pH—and feed them the carbohydrates that you take in. They shoot you a solid supply of vitamins K and B12, and other nutrients. But some microbes, like the fungi Trichophyton and Epidermophyton, which might take up residence beneath your toenail as you shower at the gym, are parasitic—they benefit from you, but you are harmed in some way by them. If you were the host of either of these two fungi, you would experience itching, burning, and dry skin. But you've probably never heard of anyone dying from athlete's foot, because it has never happened. Successful parasites—parasites that want to stay alive and reproduce—in general do not kill their hosts.

The giant ichneumon wasp is one of a few parasites that break this rule. Actually, it is not a parasite at all; it is more correctly called a parasitoid, because its parasitism results in the death of the host. This is not to say the ichneumon wasp is not successful. It can afford to kill its host because its host has a very fast reproduction rate. If we did not have the ichneumon wasp, we also might not be living in wooden houses, because the wood-boring insects that these wasps parasitize would probably have killed all the trees. The wasp might look formidable, but in terms of its ecological role, it is a friend to humans.

This is what it does: a new giant ichneumon wasp hatches from its egg in a dark, paneled crib deep inside a dead or dying tree where the pregnant female placed it. Nearby, or sometimes directly beneath the egg just deposited, lies an unsuspecting horntail larva that has been chewing its cylindrical channels in the wood, sometimes for as long as two years. The wasp baby latches on to the exterior of the caterpillar and feeds on its fat and unvital organs until both are ready to metamorphose into adults. Then, when the host has chewed the pair nearly to the surface of the tree, and the giant ichneumon wasp larva, which cannot chew wood, has a clear exit, the ichneumon kills and consumes its host. The wasp metamorphoses, possibly over the course of an entire winter, then emerges. Often before the newly metamorphosed females have even passed through their exit holes, they will mate with one of the plethora of males that have alighted on the bark for just this purpose. It's a kind of ichneumon *quinceañera*, a spontaneous debutante ball.

THE PROBLEM OF WHERE I WOULD GO after I died began with simple arithmetic. In our family there were five—my mother, my father, my two older sisters, and me. Yet the world never seemed to divide by fives or threes as easily as it did by twos: I stood between the double sink my sisters occupied when we brushed our teeth; the chair where I sat for breakfast, lunch, and dinner was pulled up to our oval table just for meals, positioned at a point not opposite anyone, and then pushed away when we were done—it didn't even match our first dining room set; I sat in the middle of the backseat of the car, while my sisters each got a window; and when we bought a dozen donuts, the last two always had to be divided, somehow, into five equal pieces—or three, which was no easier, if my parents were dieting. At some point in my childhood, for some unknown reason—I have asked them, and they still can't say why—my parents bought four burial plots. I couldn't make any sense of this. I worried. Where would the last one of us who died—probably me—be laid to rest? All I could foresee was my parents and sisters lined up neatly next to one another for eternity. All I could do was fear my impending, everlasting physical absence from the people I loved the most. Now that my sisters and I have married and they have had children and I have moved away, I realize the accounting error was not in buying too few but in buying too many: there will likely be two empty plots next to my parents. I've become accustomed to physical distance from my nuclear family, after settling eight hundred miles from where I grew up, but the problem of where I will go after I die, what I will be like, and who will be with me has not gone away. It has only magnified.

MEGARHYSSA, the Latin name for the genus to which the giant ichneumon wasp belongs, translates to "large-tailed." The species that I saw was likely the most common of the eighteen species of this genus, *Megarhyssa macrurus*, which translates to "large-tailed, long-tailed." These genus and species names, then, provide no information that an observer couldn't pick up in a single, fleeting interaction with the insect itself. The tail is more precisely called an ovipositor, an appendage used by many female insects—and some fish and other creatures—to place their eggs in a required location. That place might be soil, leaf, wood, or the body (inside or out) of another species.

The ichneumon's process of depositing eggs with her long ovipositor goes from mystical to complicated to bizarre. First, she locates her host by sensing vibrations made by its chewing beneath the wood. Her antennae stretch out before her like dowsing rods, occasionally tapping the bark, and she divines the presence of the horntail, catches it snacking like a child beneath the bed sheets who has made a midnight trip to the kitchen. She "listens" for the subsurface mastication of an individual caterpillar encapsulated in old wood.

Now the pregnant female begins the increasingly complex actions that will transport the eggs from her body through as much as two inches of woody tissue to the horntail's empty channel. Keeping her head and thorax parallel to the wood, which she grips with her legs, she first curves her abdomen under, into a circle, touching its tip to her thin waist. Her ovipositor, as if its outrageous length were not surreal enough, now performs a magician's feat: it separates into three long threads. The center one is the true ovipositor; the other two are protective sheaths that will help steady the insect's abdomen and guide the ovipositor as it enters the wood. (When she is finished laying and flies off, you will sometimes see these three threads trailing separately behind her.) The two sheaths, one on each side, fold back and follow the curve of her abdomen, then come together again at the very tip of her thorax and head straight for the wood, sandwiching her body in two broadly looped capital *P*s. The ovipositor extends directly into the two sheaths where they join, and disappears between them. In order to allow the ovipositor's acrobatics, the exoskeleton at the tip of the abdomen splits somewhat and pulls back. At this stage in her laying, with her ovipositors perpendicular to the tree, her wings flat and still, and her legs spread-eagle, the ichneumon looks as if she has pinned herself to the wood as an entomologist might pin her to a cork for observation.

BEFORE WE HANG UP from our once-weekly phone call, my mother says she has one more little story to tell. This one is about Kristen, my niece, at age five my mother's youngest granddaughter.

The week before Easter, she and Kristen drove to the church where my grandparents and my mother's little brother, who died when he was a baby, are buried. My mother wanted to put flowers on the headstones. Before they got out of the car, Kristen began talking about her own mother and her older sister, Katie.

"Mommy and Katie want the same," Kristen said, "but I want to be different."

"What do you mean?" my mother asked.

"I want to be buried," Kristen replied. "But Mommy and Katie want their bones..." She paused for a minute, thinking, then continued. "They want their bones burned." Kristen paused again, then concluded, "But, really, I don't want to die."

My mother said she had to stifle a laugh. And I laughed, too, when she related Kristen's words. Yet I can't help but think our laughter was cover for some deeply rooted disquiet. It's merely the brain's best method for dealing with this cruel yet basic fact of life—that it ends—stated here so rationally by a little person just in the process of recognizing it.

My mother, always prepared for the teachable moment, put forward to Kristen, "Well, Jesus is going to give you your body back, you know."

Kristen was not appeased. "That's weird," she replied.

THE VERY INTRICACY—and weirdness—of the ichneumon's egg laying makes it difficult for most of us not to wonder who came up with the complex series of steps involved. Part of that is because humans seem to be, as professor of psychology Paul Bloom puts it, "natural-born creationists." His essay "In Science We Trust," from the May 2009 issue of *Natural History*, posits that where humans see order—anything that is not random—we immediately assume that an intelligent being has created that order. Bloom sums up the research beautifully: children aged three to six who were shown pictures of both neat and messy piles of toys, along with a picture of a teenage girl and a picture of an open window with curtains blowing, reported that both the sister and the wind could have caused the messy pile, but only the sister could have stacked the toys neatly; likewise, shown a cartoon of a neat pile of toys created by a rolling ball, babies as young as one year old stared longer than normal, which, according to developmental psychologists, indicates surprise.

I once found, at the mouth of a sizable hole along a favorite trail, a mashed garter snake, a flattened mole, and a deceased opossum. They were each uneaten and—I knew intuitively—could not possibly have all died there coincidentally. Rather, I soon found out, they were a stack of "toys," planted neatly by a mother and father fox at the den entrance, to occupy their kits in the dusk and dawn while the parents hunted and scavenged for food. (When the family moves to a new den, which they frequently do, the parents will actually move the toys as well.) A pile of sticks pointed on both ends, with the bark removed to reveal the white wood underneath, mortared together with mud and lined up across a stream, has never been the work of the wind in the entire history of the earth, but always the work of an intelligent being—*Castor canadensis*, the American beaver.

But being "created" does not inherently imply the existence of a creator, as evidenced in Darwin's work on natural selection. Bloom explains, "Darwin showed how a nonintelligent process driven by random variation and differential selection can create complex structure—design without a designer." So we can say this instinctive assumption that complexity is the work of an intelligent being is true *most*, but not *all*, of the time.

Natural selection, though, in itself, does not inherently negate the existence of a creator. It is possible to imagine that a creator put into motion several set laws—the laws of Newton, for instance, and the laws of natural selection—then, without interfering, let creation unspool itself.

But even this belief prompts a question. I asked my mother this question once, when I was seven or eight. We were in the car, on the way home from my organ lesson. "What was there before God?" I asked. "Who created him?"

"There was nothing," my mother said, and her hands left the steering wheel for a moment. Her fingers spread, like the fingers of an illusionist, as if she were scattering something, everything in the known world, I guess. These religious discussions of ours were delicate and infrequent. Almost, like discussions of sex in our family, too intimate to occur between parent and child. When we did have them, it felt as if we were too close to uncovering something—for her, something too hallowed to be near; for me, something possibly too tragic. "I know," she conceded, "it's hard to imagine."

But I did imagine it, using the only sequencing skill I had then: a two-frame comic strip. In the right frame there was a profile of a cartoon God, and in the left frame, just blackness.

MEGARHYSSA MACRURUS is a mixture of mustard yellow and auburn, with chestnut brown accents. From a distance, the wasp may look just dark, but pinned as the female is during egg laying, and patient as the male is when waiting for the virgins to emerge, you can easily get close enough to notice the mostly yellow legs, yellow and auburn striped abdomen, and brown antennae and wing veins.

When the female is well into her egg laying, and possibly at the point of no return, she becomes even more colorful and, at the same time, more bizarre. We left her with her three tails separate and in position, and her abdomen curled in a downward circle. Once it is time to deposit the eggs, she uncurls and raises her abdomen so that it is nearly perpendicular to the tree and her body. Her tails remain in their same positions. But two of the segments near the tip of her abdomen open wide, like the first cut in an impromptu self–Cesarean section, revealing a thin yellow membrane. The membrane, taut like the surface of a balloon, is about two centimeters in diameter. It pumps gently. It is as attention-getting as a peacock's display, but wetter, more intimate. Within that membrane you can see what look like portions of the ichneumon's three tails as they exist *inside* her body. Though the ovipositor appears to begin at the tip of her abdomen, as an appendage—like an arm or a leg or a tail—it must in fact be more tonguelike, and extend into her inner recesses. It's as if you're witnessing an X-ray, but even so, it's very difficult to figure out exactly what is going on. There are too many parts, too many steps, too much intertwining. Watching the ichneumon lay her eggs is like trying to decipher one of those visual-spatial problems on an IQ test: if the following object is rotated once to the left, and twice vertically, will it look like option A, B, or C? Give me the 3.5 billion years that natural selection has had—whether here or in the afterlife—and I just might figure it out.

BELIEF IN AN AFTERLIFE, and the manner of behavior, prayers, rituals, and burial practices necessary for navigating one's way to it, can be considered a universal in human cultures. But belief in an afterlife cannot be considered the essence of all religions. Certainly there were cultures obsessed with it—the Egyptians, for instance, who took part in elaborate processes of mummification in order to preserve the dead and aid them in making the physical journey to the Elysian fields. But, hard as it may be for Christians, for whom a belief in resurrection and the afterlife takes center stage, to understand, many other cultures and religions either simply didn't address the afterlife, or had a less-than-attractive view of it. Those who originally penned the Hebrew Bible, for example, did not conceive of any type of survival after death; God harshly punished those who did not listen to his Word in this life with plagues, fevers, famine, and exile, and rewarded those who did with immortality only through their physical descendants. Were natural selection an option for the early Hebrews, I believe they would have been more accepting of the theory than today's Americans.

Other cultures did conceive of an afterlife, but not the type that came as a reward for moral behavior or religious faith or acceptance of a certain savior. For the Babylonians and the ancient Greeks, immortality was reserved for the gods alone. Death for mortals meant a sort of eternal, shadelike, underground existence, where food and water would be merely sufficient. Incidentally, the Babylonian afterlife was so unappealing that it actually became the paradigm for hell in Christianity.

The concept that an afterlife is a reward for, or at least related to, moral acts carried out in this life was made popular by Plato and later by Judaism, Hinduism, Buddhism, Christianity, and Islam. In Hinduism and Buddhism, one can achieve immortality only by breaking the cycle of rebirth, something I am not sure, were I Hindu or Buddhist, I would even want to do. (The only thing more comforting to me than a religion with an afterlife would be the ability to exist on earth forever; returning even as a dung beetle could be quite exhilarating for someone who'd already had thrills at observing eight-inch wasps in this life.)

An appendix to *How Different Religions View Death and Afterlife*, by Christopher Jay Johnson and Marsha G. McGee, contains my entire former worldview. In response to the question "Will we know friends and relatives after death?" the spokesman surveyed on behalf of the United Methodist Church says: "We will know friends and relatives in the afterlife and may know and love them more perfectly than on earth." This was a belief I picked up during

sixteen years of weekly thirty-minute lessons in a tiny, basement
Sunday school room at Patapsco United Methodist Church,
where my mother was organist and my parents purchased their
bewildering number of burial plots. The church was high on a hill
above a creek and across from a junkyard, whose collage of rusted
colors I viewed every week through the window during Sunday
services: old cars tethered to the earth by kudzu and honeysuckle,
seemingly inert, but easily unfettered when a father or brother
came in search of a hubcap, a passenger's door. Belief in an afterlife has been the grounding expectation of my existence, the hope
I find so hard to give up even after giving up the Father, the Son,
and the Holy Ghost.

BEFORE AND EVEN THROUGHOUT my adolescence I was a believer.
I'd always held a sort of patient expectation for the second coming
or some other miracle. As soon as I learned to write, at age six or
seven, I tried to speed things up a bit. SIGN HERE IF YOU EXIST, I
wrote to God on lined white paper, in a collage of yellow capital and
lowercase letters. The color, which made the note barely legible,
was not chosen for its symbolic connotation—enlightenment—
but, rather, never even considered, in the way that children,
caught up in the greatness of an act, overlook the details necessary
to achieve it. I slid the note under my dresser, and checked it every
day. One morning, I found that God had answered.

There came a moment of astonishment, then almost assurance,
when I pulled the note from its hiding place. But too soon I recognized the blue Bic pen, the neat, curvy letters, the same arcs
from the thank-you notes Santa wrote for the cookies we'd left
him. Perhaps I would have believed it was God who'd answered if
my mother had simply done what the letter requested. Instead she
wrote me a note about love and faith, which I think was followed
by a series of *x*'s and *o*'s, like she put in our Valentine's cards. She
was, and is, a believer; she would not forge his name.

TIM LEWENS, AUTHOR OF *DARWIN*, a book that deals with the
impact Darwin's thinking has had on philosophy during the last
one hundred fifty years, has discussed the very same question I

asked my mother in the car as a child on the way home from my organ lesson. Although the question applies to any type of creator, in Lewens's interview for the Darwin Correspondence Project, he specifically addresses the idea of the laissez-faire God who sets up the laws of physics and of natural selection and then lets them do their own work, the kind of God who might appeal to most scientists, the God that Darwin himself, Lewens says, likely believed in.

To deal with this question, Lewens draws from the rationale of philosopher David Hume. If you subscribe to this type of God, you are still left with the question of who or what was responsible for God, and who or what was responsible for whoever or whatever was responsible for God, and so on down the line, endlessly. At some point, Lewens says, if you want to be a theist you have to stop asking the question of what came before God or created him and just accept his existence as—in Lewens's own words—a sort of "brute, inexplicable fact." And if you allow for the existence of brute, inexplicable facts, then you might as well just accept the brute, inexplicable laws of physics and natural selection. If the only purpose for a creator is to set into motion the laws of science, Lewens asks, then why on earth do you need one? According to Hume and Lewens, whether God exists or not doesn't solve anything.

When the question of a creator's existence became for me just a matter of semantics and personification, it was easy enough to put the idea of that creator to rest. Would the ichneumon become any less immanent if it were created not by some*one* called God but by some*thing* called Natural Selection? Both may warrant capitalization as text, and both require faith of a sort. This part of the equation is easy, but I find it much harder to let go of the one thing God gave me that I coveted: an afterlife, and a clear path to it. I blame nature for this.

ABOUT A WEEK AFTER my second sighting of an ichneumon, I encounter another on the same path, on the same tree, in what I have come to call the pinned position. I wait for her to curve her abdomen up, split it open, and reveal its inner workings, but I see no movement. I poke at her gently with a twig. She barely stirs. (I have read that occasionally during the drilling process, which can take half an hour, a wasp's ovipositor will become stuck in the wood, and she will be left there, a snack for some predator that will pluck her body from her tail as if detaching a bean from its thin tendril. The ovipositor is left protruding from the wood like a porcupine quill.)

A week later she is gone, and yet another ichneumon is performing her ancient task, already flexing the yellow circle. She is close to the ground, and the leaf of a small plant is obstructing my view. When I attempt to move it, my thumb and forefinger coming at the wasp like a set of pincers, she bats at me with her front legs, then takes off, detaching herself fully from the wood. Her membrane looks like a tiny kite. Her ovipositor and its sheaths, as well as her body, still warped into laying position, are like distorted and cumbersome tails, yet she flies, unimpeded, up and up, as if to another world.

ONCE, WHEN I WAS NINE OR TEN, I opened the screen door to share with my dog, who was lying on the back porch, the remnants of a grilled-cheese sandwich that I couldn't finish. The family parakeet, Sweetie, was perched on my head. The scene must have looked very Garden of Eden–esque: a primate accompanied by a parrot feeding a canine. But I'd forgotten about the bird in my hair, and when I opened the door he escaped to a high branch on one of the oaks that grew behind the clothesline. A crow landed next to him, looking huge and superheroish. But nothing could coax him to return, not even his open cage, which for the next several days we stood next to in the yard, calling his name. Immediately after his escape, I ran into the forest in tears and was gone for the afternoon. Later, on the porch steps, I asked my mother if Sweetie would go to heaven.

Like many years before, she could not lie.

"The Bible tells us that animals don't have souls," she replied. Perhaps seeing my devastation, she added, "But it also says that God knows when even the smallest sparrow falls."

✳

MY POSITION IS NOT UNIQUE: more Americans believe in an afterlife than in God himself, according to the National Opinion Research Center's General Social Survey. As Alan F. Segal notes in *Life after Death*, that survey shows that Jewish belief in an afterlife has jumped from 17 percent (as recorded by those born between 1900 and 1910) to 74 percent (as recorded by those born after 1970). Segal's hypothesis, which is that a culture's conception of the afterlife reveals what that culture most values as a society, fits right in with these statistics. Americans define themselves as defenders of freedom and individual rights. We believe we should be happy, wealthy, and healthy all the time. Why, then, even after giving up God himself, or even when subscribing to a religion that doesn't pay much attention to the afterlife, would we consent to imprison ourselves with mortality? Why would we give up our individual right to eternal life?

Paul Bloom would attribute my tendency to believe in life after death simply to being human. Humans, Bloom maintains, seem to be born already believing in an afterlife. In his essay "Is God an Accident?," published in the *Atlantic* in December 2005, he argues that humans are natural dualists. He does not mean that we are born with a Zoroastrian belief in the opposing forces of good and evil, but that we hold two operating systems in our minds— one with expectations for physical objects (things fall down, not up) and another with expectations for psychological and/or social beings (people make friends with people who help them, not people who hurt them). These expectations are not learned, but built in, and can be observed in babies as young as six months old. The two distinct, implicit systems cause us to conceptualize two possible states of being in the universe: soulless bodies and, no less possible, just the opposite—bodiless souls. The two systems are separate. Therefore, when a human's body dies, humans are predisposed to believe that the soul does not, necessarily, die with it. Bloom cites a supporting study by psychologists Jesse Bering and David Bjorklund, in which children who were told a story about a mouse that was eaten by an alligator rightfully believed that the mouse's ears no longer worked after death and that the mouse would never need to use the bathroom again. But more than half of them believed the mouse would still feel hungry, think thoughts, and desire things. Children, moreso even than adults, seem to perceive psychological properties as existing in a realm outside the body, and therefore believe these properties exempt from death. According to Bloom, "The notion that life after death is possible is not learned at all. It is a byproduct of how we naturally think about the world."

I want my mother to read Bloom's essay. I'm not sure why. Throughout her childhood my mother walked of her own volition up the hill from her house to go to the little church across from the junkyard. Her mother and sister went; her father and much younger brother did not. When she was nine or ten she was chosen by Mrs. Myrtle, the church organist, to receive free piano lessons. My mother had an old upright piano in her family's unheated front room. Some of the keys did not play, so the ramshackle instrument was eventually chopped up for firewood. Then she had to practice at Mrs. Myrtle's, and was sometimes politely sent home when she played too long. My mother has been the volunteer organist at Patapsco United Methodist Church for more than thirty years.

She is sixty-two years old. Why, at this late stage, do I want to push Bloom's essay into the face of her contentment? Why does it feel slightly cruel, as though I am a bully, and why do I want to do it anyway?

I bring "Is God an Accident?" with me during a summer visit. The first page has been somehow lost on the plane and I have to make a special trip to the local library to download and print out another copy. I'm hesitant to give my mother the essay, but when I find her one afternoon on the couch preparing for her Bible study—they've reread the entire book of Genesis, she says—it feels like an open invitation. She puts the essay to the side to read later, and the discussion that ensues between us is as unfulfilling, as inconclusive, as this discussion is everywhere—in high school biology classrooms; in rural, local papers' letters to the editor. It ends only with her decreeing, exasperated, "Your faith is stronger than mine." She does not mean my faith in natural selection, but my faith in God. She believes, perhaps counterintuitively, that all of my research and questions indicate some sort of allegiance to the religion I was raised with, or, at the very least, an inability to simply cast it aside.

My mother could live for forty more years, another entire life, longer than my own life has been so far. Or she could be dead in just eight years, at seventy, before her youngest grandchild reaches high school, possibly before she meets any child of mine. The current life expectancy for American women lies somewhere in the middle of that. Of course I know I could die in the next fifteen minutes from a brain aneurysm, or be murdered by the man tuning my own piano, but those are exceptions, and each would be a shock. If I am certain of the afterlife, what should not be a shock, what should be normal, is this: our mothers are going to die, and for a while we are going to have to live without them. But if I abandon my belief in life after death, am I putting my mother to rest before I really have to?

MY MOTHER TELLS ME about an email she sent to another of my nieces, Julie, who is seventeen. Julie had just lost her guinea pig, Charlie, a faithful pet for seven years. Twice in the last month she had found him lying in his cage, with his neck askew, unable to move. The second time, he died the next morning.

My mother wrote to Julie that she would never forget her cutting up vegetables for Charlie, making his daily salad. *He had a good life*, she wrote, *and you just might see him again one day.*

I can't help but notice the difference between my mother's unsolicited response to the death of Charlie and her answer to my direct question years ago of whether my escaped and presumed-dead parakeet would eventually make it to heaven. Perhaps, with age, my mother's views have softened a bit. Honesty has become less important than comfort. What she would like to believe has superseded what she once took as fact. We come to see that death is less about losing the self than about losing what was built between selves when they were alive. When she dies, my mother will be in a casket on the hill outside Patapsco United Methodist Church. The question I would like to ask is: Will we find each other again? But that is not it at all. Rather, I must find a way to live now knowing that one day we will no longer be mother and daughter.

NOW THAT I HAVE DISCOVERED the ichneumon nursery standing in my woods, I will revisit it often. In spring I want to see the newly metamorphosed wasps born from the horntail's tunnels, these burrows that double as grave and womb. I'd like to see how many will emerge, how big they are, how long they rest on the dying tree before their first, seraphic flight. I'd like to search for whether there is any evidence of the horntail larva that nourished them—an exoskeleton, perhaps—or whether the larva is now present somehow only in the new body it has helped to form. All winter I will anticipate the decaying oak's promise: the giant ichneumon wasps' emergence.

There is life, it seems, after death—but it may be only here on earth. Nature provides too many metaphors for us to so easily give up on this idea. It pummels us with them season after season, and has done the same to others, I suppose, for thousands of years, playing on the human mind's ability to compare unlike things in its search for truth. I once shook a nuthatch from torpor on the side of a red pine, where it had stood unmoving, facedown—as only its kind can—all through my breakfast after a night of below-zero weather. I lifted a mourning dove, seemingly frozen into my cross-country ski trail during a surprise snow squall, in my own two palms, from which it flapped as if from Noah's hands. In my parents' woods, where my mother pitched a flower left from her mother's funeral, a patch of daffodils came up the next year—and has come up every year since—on its own, through a foot of dry leaf litter, shaded and unwatered. And there is the freezing and thawing of wood frogs in northern climes; the hibernation of chipmunks and groundhogs and jumping mice; the estivation of turtles in summer; metamorphoses of all kinds, but in particular the monarch butterfly (what Sunday school classroom has not used this metaphor at Easter?); the dormancy of winter trees; the phases of the moon; the seasons themselves; sleeping and waking; monthly bleeding; and, though it is too early to remember, probably birth, even.

This is what it comes down to. My mother, in giving me life after birth, also engendered in me the idea of God, and the unstoppable desire for life after death. We live on an earth where it seems nearly impossible for humans to have ever avoided inventing heaven, an earth that throws things back at us so reliably it is hard not to imagine that one day we will be resurrected, too, and that we will live forever. *Sign here if you exist*, I once wrote, but the question of whether God exists is really a question of whether we do. Without God and the promise of resurrection, you become extremely short-lived. Or the other option: you live forever, but what you currently perceive as yourself is a mere phase, a single facet: once oak, now horntail, soon-to-be ichneumon.

What type of afterlife do I need to survive—not so much in the next life, I realize now, but to get me through this one? I got my elements from stars: mass from water, muscles from beans, thoughts from fish and olives. When Edward Abbey died, his body was buried in nothing more than an old sleeping bag in the southern Arizona desert. He said, "If my decomposing carcass helps nourish the roots of a juniper tree or the wings of a vulture—that is immortality enough for me. And as much as anyone deserves." Abbey is right. Your trillions of cells—only 10 percent of which, remember, were yours anyway—will become parts of trillions of things. And even the 10 percent wasn't really yours to begin with. You were only borrowed. We've had it backward all along. The body is immortal—it is the soul that dies.

A HOUSE IN KARACHI

Rafia Zakaria

I t sits on a hill—a fact that does not, in most places, distinguish
a house as anything beyond ordinary. But it does in Karachi,
which is in large part a flat city, squat and sprawling and a bit surly
on the edge of the Indian Ocean. There are so few hills here that a
house on a hill can only been found in two or three locales. But this
is a special house for more than just the gradient of its setting—it
is the home of my grandparents, the site of more laughter and
the cause of more tears than any other my life. When the house
was built, two similar but not identical others were built on either
side, the homes of two of my grandfather's brothers. Three out of
seven sons of my great grandparents, all living on the same street,
the same hill.

To get to the house, one has to ascend a steep driveway, a feat as odd for drivers in this flat city as encountering a snowstorm in the desert. When my mother drove, she relished the moment and our gasping delight. Would we make it? Would the car slip back, the blunder of a lower gear? We always got to the top, and from the head of the driveway we raced through the back entrance and past the large wooden cage of parakeets and up the kitchen stairs and into the arms of an aunt and then another aunt and then my grandmother. Up we climbed, to lunch, which we ate early and they ate late, or to tea, which my grandmother sweetened with generous teaspoons of condensed milk. If we were good, and sometimes even if we weren't, we got to lick the spoons.

The house was midcentury modern with three floors and wrap-around decks. It was very nearly palatial, an adjective that was apt for unusual reasons. My grandmother had, quite literally, grown up in a palace. It was a palace in exile, but still...a palace. Her parents had been part of the retinue of the Aga Khan, the last of the Iranian Qajar dynasty, which had to flee Iran for Bombay in the 1920s when she was a child. In a story that was top-secret, and which I only pieced together many years later, she had eloped to marry my grandfather, an ordinary man from an equally ordinary straitlaced and middle-class Indian Muslim family. Before this house, my grandparents had lived in many others, all of them cramped or in distant suburbs, or old and crumbling, or all of the above. This house was the fulfillment of a young bridegroom's promise, the return to his bride of the life she had left for him. On either side lived her brothers-in-law, men who had for a very long time refused to accept her into the family, now unable to turn their faces away from the woman they had blamed for "stealing" their brother.

The bond between my grandparents, their love marriage, would set the course for the marriages of all their daughters and at least one of their granddaughters, me. Because my mother had run off, the shadow of moral laxity—of headstrong independence, of an errant nature—hung over the house. My own story would be a bit different, but its opening scenes would also play out in the house on the hill.

Behind and to the side of the house was a terraced garden,

which began with a plush lawn bordered by rose and jasmine bushes. The blooms, whose heady scent punctuates my earliest memories, were resplendent, two or even three shades in a single flower's petals, pink and yellow and cream and burgundy. If you climbed up the stone steps hewn in the hillside you came to a vegetable garden: rows of the hottest peppers, okra, and the curry leaves whose fronds we picked and whose strong and spicy smells emanated from nearly everything my grandmother cooked. The higher terraces beyond were off-limits to us, unless an adult accompanied us. If we were allowed to dig in the yard, we found tiny shells, which we collected with wonder. The sea, in the limited mental geography of our childhood, was very far away, though in reality only a distance of ten or twelve kilometers.

Behind us, farther up and on the other side of the hill, was a Sufi shrine. As children, we never knew about the shrine; we did know of the mysterious black-clad men who would sometimes clamber down in the craggy path beyond the house. If we weren't good, if we didn't eat our food or drink our milk or were naughty, we were told that they would come for us.

My grandparents had four children, all of them daughters, a predicament that had defined much already and would define so much more. By the time I was born, three of the four sisters were married, my mother's older sister and her twin sister, both to brothers. My brother and I were still the first grandchildren, though, because my mom's older sister had no children. She was often the first to greet us when we got to the house. After running through the kitchen and up a short flight of stairs, eight exactly—we counted them often when we were learning to count—you came to what was then called the TV lounge, the room from which all the bedrooms branched out.

It was in this room that my mother was sitting when her water broke. Pregnant with twins, she had come to stay with her parents through the last trimester. Bed rest in her husband's house was hard; she had not been married very long and she missed her sisters and parents, even though they lived only ten minutes away. My childless aunt had not been able to tolerate the chaotic and cramped apartment her husband's family lived in. Thus, flouting all conventions, she and her husband moved in to the palatial house and installed themselves in the second-largest bedroom. That evening all of them, my mother, her oldest sister, and her brother-in-law, who had recently returned from London, sat laughing and joking on the armchairs.

It was eight in the evening when her water broke, and nearly everyone was home, and nearly everyone accompanied my mother to the hospital. She had to be helped down the eight steps to the main floor and then down another ten to a walkout basement that abutted the garage. She was scared and moved slowly, step after step on the metal and wood staircase. Her brother-in-law, whom I would grow up calling Uncle J, drove the car. Someone, I assume, called my father. Everyone was eager for the babies to be born and even more eager for them to be boys.

They were not boys, not at least both of them, but that wouldn't be known for a while. The two grandfathers who had now joined the crowd in the waiting room paced and made polite conversation. When my arrival was announced, only one of them celebrated. My maternal grandfather was crestfallen. He had always hoped for a son, but the twins my grandmother had borne were my mother and her sister. Now he felt the familiar force of fate, bent on denying him a grandson.

My brother, born a long fourteen minutes after me, saved the day. Suddenly, the mood in the waiting room, only hesitantly joyous, erupted with celebration and congratulation and prayer. Sweets were ordered and distributed excitedly among friends and neighbors and relatives, charitable gifts among the city's poor, beaming smiles among strangers.

Over a week later, when my mother was discharged from the hospital, she returned not to her husband's house but, as was the custom then, to her own parents' house. There she would remain for the first forty days after giving birth, to get accustomed to being a mother without the scrutiny of her in-laws. The house on the hill was the very first house we knew. Our cradles, specially ordered, had been set up in one of the bedrooms off the lounge with the cream couches. It was the third largest bedroom, a pink room with two walls of half-windows that looked into the garden. The smell of jasmine wafted in at night and the incessant cawing of crows at all other times. Against one wall stood a low-slung bureau full of my grandmother's romance novels. This was the room of my best childhood naps, awakenings made euphoric by the realization that I was in my grandmother's house, that mansion of delights, where all rules could be suspended.

AFTER FORTY DAYS my mother returned home, but in those early years she returned often to the house on the hill, spending entire days sleeping, the only time she felt she could do so with abandon. My aunts, ecstatic every time we visited, pampered the two of us. The eldest, Aunt J, would take care of me, and my mother's twin, back from London and pregnant herself, would look after my brother.

A few years after we were born, there was a wedding in the house. My mother's youngest sister, my Aunt N, was to marry her cousin, a not-uncommon practice among Indian and now Pakistani Muslims. This was not any cousin, however; it was a first cousin and a neighbor. My mother's new brother-in-law, whom I still call Uncle N, lived there and had long wished to marry the youngest sister; they had played together as children, laughed together as teenagers. My Aunt N was less keen on the match, on marrying this boyish-looking man whom she had always thought of as a brother. She put it off and put it off, and then she gave in. At least she would only be moving next door.

Except she never really moved. If garrulous laughter and wit and repartee filled the meals and moments at my grandparents' house, courtesy in no small part of my grandmother's familial lineage as a courtier (and the vast gaggle of relations that had followed her to Pakistan from Bombay), the house to the right was austere and severe. Aunt N's mother-in-law was frail and frugal, a gossip whose nosiness we were warned of even as small children. She and my grandmother had a polite nodding relationship, and it was the men, older brother and middle brother, setting up the match and informing everyone else. Aunt N never took to her new home or to the mother-in-law who measured the rice down to the grains and added no spice at all to the curries in her kitchen. Within days of being married, she began to spend all day, every day at her mother's place, returning only to sleep. For years and years, I believed she still lived there.

My grandfather was a rich man without sons. To compensate or perhaps to project the sort of strength he felt a man with sons would have, he auditioned sons-in-law for the role; or perhaps it was some of the sons-in-law who insisted on trying out for the part. My uncles not only lived in or next to his home, they worked alongside him as well. Every morning at nine, he presided over breakfast in the informal dining room on the bottom floor of the house, and both came to offer their morning greetings as he sat at the head of the table. Then, with one or both stand-in sons in tow, he got into his chauffeur-driven luxury car, a Chevy Impala, and drove to the executive office of the industrial parts company that he ran, leaving a house full of daughters behind him.

AND THEN, SUDDENLY, HE DIED. It happened after a short illness, the entire length of which was spent abroad in London, where my grandparents had gone for a vacation. Nine years old at the time, my brother and I had noticed our mother red-nosed and crying and praying for several days. There were hushed and anxious conversations, worried glances, muffled tears. The house was full of people. Neighbors and relatives and friends, all women in the upper lounge off the bedrooms, all men in the formal sitting room off the garden. My mother and her youngest sister were hosts to the mourners; my oldest aunt had left for London, to bring my grandmother and her father's coffin back home. It took five days. So it was that my grandfather's funeral was held, nearly a week after he had passed away, a long time in a culture where most people who passed were buried before sundown on the same day.

On the day of the burial, my grandfather's body was laid out downstairs, just steps from the door through which he'd left for work every day. There he was, our tall and majestic grandfather, lying in a box, his face wooden and unmoving, his skin leathery, his eyes closed. The smell of camphor hung in the air, mingling with our shock and the prayers being chanted by the men standing around the coffin. Later, when the time came for his coffin to be carried out, we scurried to the windows that looked down over the driveway that led to the bottom of the hill. He was borne aloft, his body covered with a green cloth amid a sea of male mourners, all chanting "God is Great" and "Muhammad is his Prophet." It was a scene and a sound we would never forget, a crowd walking down the driveway we loved driving up, carrying the dead body of our grandfather.

But we recovered fast. We were kids, and staying at the house on the hill, as we would be for the next few weeks, was a treat even under the circumstances. We loved waking to lazy breakfasts with all our aunts and sleeping every night with our cousins on mattresses rolled out on the floor. The adults were distracted so our escapades expanded throughout the vast house. We hid in the bushes and spied on visitors, who continued to appear in an unrelenting stream.

UNTIL THEY LEFT FOR LONDON, my grandparents had occupied the largest and highest bedroom in the house. It stood on its own floor at the very top of everything and was reached by its own flight of stairs. A wide, breezy deck opened out from it, sporting spectacular views of the sprawling city all around it. As children, we had spent many hours at those windows, insisting that we could see the sea. The room and adjoining bathroom were modern for their time, an overhead shower and a custom-made bed ordered to fit my grandfather's six-foot-two frame. One closet was filled with my grandfather's suits, brown and black and gray, tweed and wool, hanging next to his starched and ironed white shirts, his boxes of cufflinks standing in a row on the shelf just below. Next to it, my grandmother's closet was full of elegant saris in every hue and fabric, chiffons and silks, embroidered with sequins or embellished with lace. It smelt of Jean Patou's Joy, her perfume, of which my grandfather made sure she had an ample supply.

My grandmother would live for decades more but she would never again climb up the stairs to that room she had shared with her husband. Her grief, unlike the grief of many Pakistani women resigned to marriages of compromise, was as passionate as her love for him. She had lost the man for whom she had left every-thing. At night, pretending to sleep, we heard her cry and we saw her smoke. She had not smoked for decades because he had hated cigarettes; now, she smoked for hours.

A FEW DAYS AFTER THE BURIAL, my grandmother decided she wanted to visit my grandfather's grave. She gathered her daughters and the grandchildren who belonged to them and said she would go on Friday, the first since he had been interred. We went in two cars, because we could not, all of us, fit into only one, even with the creative squashing that is so ordinary in a country of big fami-lies and lax traffic rules. Other than my grandfather's chauffeur, no men came with us. We stared out the window as we went through neighborhoods we didn't know, farther and farther away from the house on the hill, to the cemetery at the edge of the city. We made a stop for a blanket of roses, sold on the outskirts of all cemeteries in the subcontinent and laid over the newly filled graves. With our fragrant blanket in a plastic bag, we walked through rows and rows of graves, marble coffins raised above the ground.

My grandfather's grave was at the very back of the cemetery, in a plot reserved for his family. When the caretaker led my grand-mother to it and she found this out, it made her cry even more. His brothers had buried him there without asking her. Always considered an interloper by his family, she would likely never be buried with her husband, with the love of her life. When she set-tled down, we sat around the grave, its earth still wet and fresh, and we prayed from the small prayer books that we had brought with us. We children pretended to pray, chastened by the unfa-miliar surroundings, the oddity of being surrounded by the dead. We would be back here on many more Fridays, almost until a year after my grandfather's death, and the place would become a little more familiar, a little less macabre.

The location of the grave was perhaps the smallest, least con-sequential of exclusions that my grandmother would face. Others would sting much more. For a man who had been so fastidious in protecting his wife and daughter in life, my grandfather had left them utterly unprotected in death. There was no will, no written document that would protect the inheritance of his wife and daughters against the claims of his brothers, who, noting the absence of a male heir, would clamor for their part of his sizeable estate.

THE ISLAMIC RULES OF INHERITANCE provided a greater share for male relatives than for female ones, a greater share for his six living brothers than for a living wife and four married and living daughters. My grandmother was told all of this by one of the brothers. She had been flouting other Islamic rules as well in her grief, which had not, despite the circumstances, endeared her to her husband's brothers. They relished their power and prepared an indictment of sorts. Per Sharia law, they told her, she was required to observe the customary waiting period, or iddat, imposed on widows, a duration of three months and ten days spent inside the home and outside the presence of unrelated men. But she had chosen to visit the cemetery, again and again. In fact, the Sunni and Shafii school of Islamic law that they followed dictated that women were not permitted to visit cemeteries at all. Women, because they menstruate, were viewed as sources of impurity, impermissible in the realm of the dead as they were in mosques, the pure spaces of the living.

All the sisters were furious. The house belonged to their mother, they said, as they fumed over their uncles' treachery and thinly veiled threats. How convenient for them to hide their own greed in the jargon of Sharia and Islam, they remonstrated to each other deep into the night as their mother blew plumes of cigarette smoke. Were they lesser Muslims? Did they need these men to show and teach them about Sharia? All contact with the uncles and their families was cut off, but it could only be an incomplete severance. The youngest of them, after all, was married to the cousin next door, the son of the eldest of my grandfather's brothers.

OUR BANISHMENT AND EXILE from the house on the hill did not happen suddenly. There were small steps, a delicate architecture of exclusion that was built bit by bit until we looked back and it was a fortifying wall, us standing outside. It began with a truce. To ensure that her brothers-in-law did not usurp her share of her husband's inheritance, wrest from her the grand house, the life-style fueled by the company that her husband had partially owned, my grandmother brokered a deal, propped up by the marriages of her daughters—or at least three of them.

All the sisters except my mother were connected in a web of marriages that had taken place after my eldest aunt was married. Her younger sister, my mother's twin, was married to her husband's younger brother, two sisters married off to two brothers. My youngest aunt had married her cousin. This meant that my mother was the only one who was not, by virtue of marriage or blood, within the fold. Yes, all connected, all tangled, save for the one. After my grandfather's death, this difference became momentous, the basis of a collusion that determined who got a share of my grandfather's inheritance.

No one ever explained this to my mother. But the consequences of the new order were visible in the rearrangement of who occupied which room in the house on the hill. We arrived one Thursday afternoon to find Aunt J's husband descending the stairs from the highest bedroom, my grandparent's former room, the room my grandmother now refused to enter. "Mummy wanted us to move up there," my eldest aunt offered by way of explanation. Even as almost–ten year olds, my brother and I could not miss the shock on our mother's face. Her father's room now belonged to a man who was not even related to her. She asked questions—where are his things, his clothes—but her inquiries were tremulous, quaking and unsure. It had all been moved downstairs, my aunt told her. She had tired of walking up and down the stairs again and again to fetch this and that for her mother. Like all the arrangements that would be made regarding the things my grandfather had left behind, she made it seem unimportant, as if questioning her was making a big deal out of nothing, an impudence borne of malice.

Our visits to the house on the hill reflected the seeds of mistrust germinating between my mother and her sisters in the space left by their father's absence. The intimacy that had once been natural began to strain and wane—my mother seemed always like she was guessing at some drama, her sisters like they were avoiding some crucial truth.

On another day, it began as a silly argument among us children. We had been playing on the driveway when a shoving match began. "Go back to your own house," one of our cousins yelled. "This is our house too," we yelled back. "No, this is OUR house. Nani loves us and that is why we live here and not you," they yelled. This shut us up. We had not considered that such a thing was possible. Still in doubt that it could be, we took it up with our mother on the short drive home. We got nothing in response, but later that evening, after I was supposed to be asleep, I heard her sobbing as she spoke to my father. "Does she love me less?" she asked him through her tears. My father said nothing, but I felt my throat contract and my eyes well up. I had not known until then that love could be so closely related to pain.

After weeks and some months of these slow changes, one day the world of the house on the hill and our connection to it crumbled completely. It was a Friday morning, a holiday when the men as well as the women were all at home. On that day, my mother and father were summoned to the house for a meeting with my grandmother, with all of the sisters, with all of their husbands, and they fought. The two whose husbands worked at the company banded together. The shares of the company that had belonged to my grandfather secured their jobs, and they did not see why they should share them. My mother's twin vacillated, trying at first to stand by her twin, then falling in step with her husband, who was allied to his older brother. My mother, the only sister left out of the arrangement—the tacit distribution of my grandfather's inheritance, the occupation of his home—became the bad sister, an outsider. The uncles insisted they were guarding my grandmother against her own daughter, the shyest and quietest of the four.

The poisonous words that were said that Friday at the house on the hill would reverberate through our lives for days and months and years. In the immediate aftermath, there were many tears. I had never seen my mother so bereft, so lost in grief, so betrayed. If she had lost her father to death, she seemed to have lost everyone else to a worse sort of devastation. Their accusations echoed in her ears as she tried to resume the rhythm of her days, cooking and shopping, ironing our uniforms and helping with our homework, the minutiae from which there was no reprieve. When it was time to pray, she would lay out the prayer mat and sob, hiding her face with her hands and crying out for her mother and her father.

I don't know who uttered the words exactly, whether it was my mother who had vowed she would never enter the house on the hill again or my eldest aunt who, in her effort to protect my grandmother, ordered my mother to never come again. The result was the same: we did not go. The long afternoons and evenings we had spent laughing and drinking tea and cracking jokes with our aunts and cousins were no more. They stretched before us—at the end of the week, on days we did not have homework, on our birthday, on our cousins' birthdays, at the Persian New Year we had celebrated with our grandmother, and on so many other days.

AS DAYS BECAME MONTHS, though, others intervened. It happened the first time at the wedding of my mother's maternal cousin, the daughter of her own beloved aunt. My mother had wanted to avoid the occasion, the week of pre- and post-wedding feasts and revelry that were sure to include her sisters and mother. But her aunt had come to our house herself, to press her to attend. They had huddled and cried together. "You can fight with your sisters but you have to honor your mother," she had whispered. "You have to do this, my child, you have to come, you have to see your mother at my house."

My mother did. Even as her sisters turned their faces from her, pretending to look through her and through us, she sat down next to my grandmother and talked to her. It was not an intimate conversation—reserve restraining either side, a mother and daughter unsure of each other, conscious of an audience of relatives milling about them, watching, listening. "How are you, my love?" my grandmother said to my mother, holding her face in her hands. Both began to cry, quickly rubbing their noses with the dainty cotton handkerchiefs they carried. "Don't punish your mother, don't punish your mother who is a widow," my grandmother wept. "How am I punishing you, mummy? I love you," my mother whispered. I am not sure my grandmother heard her, but she had said what she wanted to. My grandmother believed she was the victim, not her daughter, not us. It was my mother who had misinterpreted everything, my mother who should apologize to her, to her sisters. She began to ask about my mother's health, complain about her own health. She kissed each of us, once on our cheeks.

The meeting resumed some traffic between the house on the hill and our home. Once or twice a year, on the two Eids, the big festivals on the Muslim calendar, we returned to pay our strained respects to our grandmother. On the short drive from our house to theirs, we were given strict instructions. We were not to laugh too much, to not go off somewhere out of earshot to play with our cousins, forcing our parents to stay longer than they wished. We were not to act as if things were just as they had used to be. It was hard—we were twelve by then, but we had spent more of our lives playing in the terraced garden with our cousins than we had not. And sometimes, even on those short visits, we did forgot. Sometimes, for a minute or two, our mother also seemed to forget.

My father never forgot. He accompanied us on all of the visits now, his face tight-lipped, a man present to protect his wife and children against people who might hurt them. We never went upstairs into the informal lounge where we had spent so many afternoons. We sat downstairs, in the formal sitting room where my grandmother received all her guests on special occasions. She tempted us with treats still, but we looked to our father to see if we could take them. On one of these visits, I said I needed to go bathroom and ventured upstairs. As I walked through the lounge, my eyes fell on the low shelf on which my grandmother had always kept photographs of her grandchildren. A huge double portrait of my brother and me as babies had always stood front and center. Now pictures of all my other cousins had been propped up in front of it.

OUR ULTIMATE RETURN to the house on the hill required a sacrifice. I learned what it would be on an ordinary afternoon in March. After picking me up from school, my mother told us we would be going over to our grandmother's. I was fifteen. Six long years had passed since my grandfather's death, and a strained four since the big fight between the sisters. We had, to some degree, all settled into the new and awkward status quo, where we depended only on my father's income. Those who lived in the house on the hill, now all three of the four sisters, lived on the proceeds of the estate they had divided between them. It was a weekday afternoon during the month of Ramzan, a time everyone passed indoors resting. My mother was religious about her naps and our schoolwork, so it made no sense for her to suggest such an outing. Even odder was the fact that my father, who always worked long hours, was home from work. My mother never left to go places without him when he was home.

In retrospect I could have noticed my mother's hushed telephone conversations, or the suddenly imposed silence when I walked into the room. But I was not particularly observant, and had little precedent to work from. So, oblivious, I showered and dressed and followed my mother and brother to the car.

More surprises awaited us when we got to the house on the hill. Despite the fact that it was Ramzan, a table for lunch had been laid out. Uncle J presided. He was a diabetic and did not fast, but that too was not the point. Next to him sat a man whose presence explained the meal. It was his nephew, visiting from the United States, in Karachi to complete a medical internship, and not fasting owing to a cold.

This was how I was introduced to the man I would marry. I had been shielded from young boys my own age, and certainly men, with a devotion that was shared by all my relations, who made sure to prevent even accidental exposures. Now, to be suddenly introduced to a male stranger from America could not, I knew, be a heedless mistake. I tried to swallow this knowledge, while keeping up the pretense, as I knew I was expected to, of not knowing. He asked me what I was studying and I answered, although what exactly I said I cannot remember. I remember wanting very much to prove that I was fluent in English, that we in Pakistan were not as provincial and backward as so many Westerners assumed. To that end, there was some talk about the weather in Karachi (already hot) and his impressions of Pakistan (so warm and hospitable). The sum was seven or eight sentences, more than the total I had exchanged with a man my whole life.

I did not see him again before he returned to the United States. I did, however, return to the house on the hill, with my mother and brother, more times in a month than we had in the previous four years. If there was something askew now, it was not my mother guessing at some secret, but a collective secret that all the sisters and my grandmother held together, tossed about in knowing looks. It felt wonderful to be together again with my cousins, to laugh and drink tea upstairs in the lounge off the bedrooms. The poison of veiled insults and opportunistic jabs, of alliances and betrayals, seemed suddenly to have sifted from between us. Ensconced once again between her mother and sisters, my mother seemed to bloom and beam, as if regaining a wholeness that had been denied her during the long years of conflict.

She was not the only one who rejoiced at the reunion. My childless aunt now called me her daughter; my husband to be, her son. Her niece and her husband's nephew would be united in marriage. My mother had felt that her sisters owed her an inheritance, and they felt they had repaid her by arranging my marriage to a wealthy man—an odd sort of quid pro quo, but one that makes a lot of sense in Pakistan, where girls' marriages are hard to arrange, and a good match represents a relief and a success.

In the late summer of that year, my eldest aunt and her husband traveled to the United States. Uncle J's older brother was a physician who lived in Connecticut, and they were going to visit him, see the sights. It was in the talk around the coming trip that I realized that their hosts were the parents of the man I had been introduced to in Ramzan. References to him were now peppered into all sorts of conversations, provoking laughter from my grandmother, who made the least effort of all of them to pretend that nothing at all was going on.

My aunt returned with many pictures of the nephew and of his parents and of their beautiful house. They had traveled all over America together; they had spent time with him where he lived and where he went to school. He had been to Harvard, I was told again and again, and was at medical school at Duke. He was the best in the richest country in the world, boasted Uncle J. He was such a caring boy, added my aunt. Their picture albums were left in places where I could easily find them, in case I was interested in looking.

Then that winter his parents arrived. If our visits to the house on the hill had become frequent in the months before, they became even more so now. My father, who usually goaded my mother to refuse invitations, now embraced them on our behalf, regardless of whether he could attend himself. Marrying a daughter off is a duty, a burden. The match, to an ivy league–educated doctor in the United States, would be a good one, he likely thought. We went to all the weddings that took place that winter (also odd for us) and my mother ensured I had beautiful outfits for each occasion. Garnet-colored velvet and gold for one, and rust-colored raw silk for another. I was allowed makeup, the subject of much wrangling before, and as much of my mother's jewelry as I wished to borrow. At each of these occasions, the visiting parents were there, eager to say hello, ask questions, sit at our table and be at our side.

The question came one unassuming evening. Sixteen now, I was in my bedroom wrapping up my homework for the next day. We had once again spent the afternoon at the house on the hill, and it had been, like the days before the fighting, a wonderful time. My mother sat next to me on my bed and said it plainly. There had been a proposal for my hand in marriage. "Do you want to marry him?" she asked. There was no pregnant pause, no dramatic interlude. I simply looked at her, just as I did when she asked me if I wanted jam on my toast or a cookie with my tea, and said, freely, "Yes, I do." With that, it was done. The man I had met at the house on the hill earlier in the year, the son of Uncle J's older brother and his wife, was to be my husband.

There was a lot that I did not say but understood. I did not know him, but I also knew that it was unlikely, given our family's conservative beliefs, that I would know the person I married. I knew that my father felt the burden of marrying me off acutely; it was something he agonized over, and I wanted him to be unburdened. I knew how happy my mother was at being reunited with her sisters. With my marriage into the family that included my two aunts, my mother would be less of an outsider. I had considered my gamble: a man who was highly educated, raised abroad, I decided, would be an open-minded man. Married to him, I would have to face fewer constrictions, fewer restrictions than the average Pakistani wife. I would, I convinced myself, be free.

WITHIN AN HOUR of my saying yes, we were all at the house on the hill. The mood there was jubilant, every room was lit up, every face full of delight. Garlands of flowers were put around my neck, and a box of sweets was passed around, everyone putting some in my mouth too instead of just their own. My grandmother sang wedding songs, and my cousins were full of glee. My parents were the center of the celebration even more than I was, the parents of the bride-to-be, the very first in the family to welcome a son-in-law. With this wedding, our family would be united in a new generation, cementing bonds for many more years. My mother would be part of the family circle that included her sisters and their husbands, no longer the odd one out. In arranging my marriage, my aunts and uncles had made amends, repaid all debts, made up for whatever had been usurped.

We stayed at the house on the hill deep into the night. We returned for more revelry and rejoicing over the following days and weeks and months, for wedding planning and for selecting the clothes I would wear on that day and for so many other reasons and for no reasons at all. The wedding, my wedding, had enabled our return.

But more important than our return to the house, I was restoring trust between our warring families. The same trust that had been extracted from our midst after my grandfather's death, and without whose tempering presence our anger, our recriminations, and our many, many qualms had bubbled over, tainted everything, separated everyone. In trusting this proposal, in entrusting my life and future to it, I told myself, there could be healing. That I would have to leave Pakistan as a consequence of it seemed incidental. When I visited the country in the years to come, I told myself, there would be laughter and good times with all of us together at the house on the hill.

IT HAS BEEN OVER TWENTY YEARS since I left the house on the hill. For many years after I did, it remained full of cousins and aunts and laughter. For many years, when I returned to Karachi, it felt like the old times. But then my cousins, as I had, began to leave. The girls were married, the boys left to study and then work abroad. My oldest aunt's husband, Uncle J, died. Then, years later, my grandmother died. Finally, my mother, although she was young, also died. My marriage ended as well, after some of the deaths and before the last ones, but that is a story of its own, connected to the house but not of it.

Only one person lives in the house on the hill now—my oldest aunt, who has no children, and whose bad knees make it hard for her to navigate all of its stairs. My mother's twin sister moved abroad to be with her children. My younger aunt has settled into the house next door, the one she refused to live in when she first married. Her son lives with her. All the other children of all the four sisters are gone, to England and America and elsewhere.

The neighborhood around the house has also changed. Climbing up the terraced garden, one can see the apartment complexes sprouting up everywhere. The devotees of the Sufi shrine on top of the hill do not come around as much—too many people and too little peace, too little space for the spirit, they may think. The terraced garden has dried up, the roses gone; there is not enough water for it in a city of many wants and many millions. Only the jasmine vine still blooms, hardy and determined, insistent on scenting the silent evenings of a mostly empty house.

I think all the time of returning to the house on the hill. I dream of it awake and asleep; I write about it and talk about it. But a whole life lies between us now: the life I made in a faraway land, the life I began because I wished to return. Or maybe it is fear, the ghostly wafting realization that it was never, perhaps, the house, but the people in it. They are gone, scattered or lost, and without them, there are only walls.

THE PONY, THE PIG, AND THE HORSE

Alison Hawthorne Deming

Someone at work told me about the Shetland pony. "My sister's little girl has outgrown it. You ought to get it for your daughter."

I didn't know then how to be a cultural animal. I was poor, living in the north and working for one social program or another during the War on Poverty. Planned Parenthood or maybe, after a wave of budget cuts, for a job-placement program in which I counseled poor people more desperate than I was and helped set up a drug intervention program for youth called People Who Care. My farmer neighbors, lucky to have land and cows and an appetite for hard work, used to laugh whenever I found a new job after a layoff. Other friends would sit around smoking weed, playing music, and complaining that there were no jobs. I would always find one.

Linotype operator at the small-town newspaper, dishwasher at the ski resort, calf feeder on the dairy farm, horse teamer on the maple sugar farm. It wasn't that I was so smart. And I certainly wasn't accomplished. I was just desperate. And, coming from a theater family, I felt pretty sure I could do a reasonable performance of a person who looked like she knew what she was doing.

My twenties were a decade of rural self-exile. I was trying to complete the project of growing up, raising a daughter on pennies and pipe dreams, performing the role of a grown-up as best I could, writing poems in the dark of night on a barn-board desk, shuddering alone in bed beneath the blackness of eternity. I still love her, that desolate version of me, stubborn Yankee, who never quit no matter how bleak the odds.

A pony. Yes, that sounded good. Something for my daughter to care for. That had to be good. That's what country people did. Gave their kids chores to do. An animal whose life depended on you—that wakes a kid up to what's real. Tenderness is necessary. Water and hay. Molasses and grain. Currying and combing. Shoveling the muck.

"We've got a truck. We can bring her over. We'll get the saddle and bridle."

"Okay. We'll come over and see on Saturday."

"I'M NOT EATING IT!" my daughter screamed in the fury of a five-year-old who knows injustice when she sees it. It was her birthday. 1970. East Enosburg, Vermont. Mud season. She had chicken pox. She lay in bed in our cold, dilapidated farmhouse listening to the sounds of the men who had arrived to slaughter the pigs. She heard the rifle shots. She heard the pigs scream. She tells me forty years later that it was the worst birthday of her life.

I was so poor in those years that the only people who paid attention to me were other poor people living in that derelict region. It was so cold in winter, a person could die from cold. Hardly anyone did. The poor looked after each other. I lived far from family, far from work, far from knowing who I was and how I was supposed to find my place in the world. Oh, the town had a dairy festival with bluegrass fiddling and horse-pulling contests. Exotic to me as a transplant most recently from the Harvard Square of the radical sixties. I'd left and come to the clarifying north, after being attacked by a group of meatheads wearing fake army helmets who yelled at me and a group of friends, "What'ya think you're doing? Protesting?" Well, no. We were just taking a walk at three in the morning after taking a trip together in someone's pharmaceutically enhanced apartment. Violent turmoil on the streets sent me packing. No one lived in rural Franklin County except family dairy farmers, brusque oddballs, and dreamers who'd left something behind that they didn't want to talk about. It was the perfect place to imagine as prophetic what a loopy, angel-faced acidhead had once advised me: "Revolution means move to a farm."

I was ashamed of being poor, as I had been ashamed of being a teenage mother. I did not regret the sex or the daughter. Both had catalyzed energies and direction in me that I loved. I was ashamed of what others thought of me, a taint I carried for decades after my parents' poisonous response to my digression from the script in which they imagined I would live. I saw with disdain their lapping after approval and praise. They seemed to care more about what others thought of them than about living by their own convictions. And here it was, this same weakness for seeking approval, for shrinking into defensiveness at the supposed judgments of others, in me—mine to suffer and hopefully to outgrow.

I've always had a need for independence, sometimes to my detriment. This trait has meant that I find it generally easier to live alone than in intimate partnership. In this case—the decade of my poverty and self-exile—the spirit of self-sufficiency saved me. There is a longer story here to tell, a story of pain and temporary alliances and slow forgiveness won only as my parents aged and grew close to their deaths. I came to understand how much is demanded of family and how rising to those demands is a service to one's own deepest self and to another's need—a strange simultaneity of I-and-thou in the hours of extremity. But my intention here is to remember what animals meant to me in those lonely, difficult years, how animals kept me and my daughter alive.

One day a neighbor who took care of my daughter after school said I should go on welfare. My old car was dying. I didn't have a penny extra or the profile for a loan. This neighbor was wise to surviving in poverty. She and her husband and three kids lived on a rented postage stamp of land where they milked one Jersey cow and canned beans and corn for the winter. The husband was disabled and mean and treated his wife with ridicule. But he had some good tricks, like pillaging through railroad cars parked near a grain elevator for animal feed that could be tapped out of the walls of the freight cars and stuffed into burlap sacks. She was savvy and Episcopalian. A sturdy woman, she held the whole show together with dignity. When I came to pick up my daughter, we'd sit over coffee for an hour and talk about whatever.

"You ought to go on welfare," she said. "That's what it's there for."

I cringed and thought, Why not?

So I went to the welfare office in St. Albans.

"I don't need welfare, but if you buy me a car I can go to work."

I could see the stifled laugh in the caseworker's face, the way she caught herself from cracking up at my childish pride. I hated feeling so transparent, but I was grateful for her discretion.

"We can't buy you a car, but we can get you some assistance and maybe you can use some of that to buy one."

That's what I did, working as a dishwasher at a ski resort that was too far away from home to make sense, then upgrading to waitress, then stumbling by luck into better work as the tail end of the sixties drifted north and back-to-the-land people came, setting up alternative schools, food co-ops, and social justice programs. I never got over feeling like an outlier, somehow less worthy and connected than these hip urban refugees. When they were partying and playing in bands and throwing together handmade houses from scratch, I was inventing motherhood out of sticks and stones, enduring visits from a social worker about whom another social worker had warned, "Yes he's very kind, but watch out. He's a kleptomaniac." It all seems crudely comic now, how inept I was at asking for help from anyone who cared. Underlying it all was the question, Who cared?

Another neighbor came by. A dairy farmer.

"What are you raising in that barn?"

"A few chickens," I said.

"Well, how about raising a couple of pigs?"

He could get a piglet for twenty-five bucks. One for himself. One for me. Maybe I could share mine with another neighbor. He'd bring me the grain, take care of butchering. I'd do the chores—water and slops and feed twice a day.

"Sure," I said, and the little squealers arrived, snouting around with glee in the fragrant hay of their bedding. They were cleaner than I thought they'd be, crapping in one corner of their pen far from their food. If I brought cornstalks from the garden, they routed through them, tunneling and tossing the leaves with exuberance. At first the piglets were so small they'd become lost burrowing down in the greenery. Weeks later, they had lengthened and fattened so they looked like torpedoes with legs and their tunneling looked like a cataclysm had befallen their home, a rubble of hay and shredded stalks heaved up like the aftermath of a bombing raid. Cute squeals became throaty grunts and nosy snorts. I became wary about climbing into their pen to shovel out the muck. Grim rural legends of farmers who'd been overwhelmed and eaten by their own pigs elbowed their way into my protective attentions. They greeted me with excited trilling snuffles when I entered the barn and they cooed over their food, their pleasure requiring quite a ruckus. In the last month, as my neighbor instructed, I sweetened them off by feeding them only pure cornmeal and water.

Meat was wealth in this cold part of the world. The only boastfulness I heard among my rural neighbors concerned how many quarts of green beans or tomatoes they had canned or frozen, how many gallons of cider pressed, and if they had a side of beef or a pig put up for winter. One could be sure, if one was poor, of nothing except the stores in one's cellar, freezer, and pantry. Security could be measured this way, built up jar by jar, freezer box by freezer box, like a house made of bricks.

The pig man straddled the shot pig, riding it around the pen as it faltered until he could slit the leathery throat to clean the meat of the animal's blood. The carcass was split open, the steaming, ropy, gray entrails with their sickening ripe scent were dumped into a grain sack, the hollow body hoisted and dipped into a barrel of steaming water mixed with pine tar, the formula used to loosen the pig's bristles. We laid the pig down on a makeshift plywood table and set to work with scrapers while the skin was scalded hot and the coarse fibers ready to slip from the follicles.

Finally four halves of two pigs, so cleanly parted, lay in the back of the pickup, pink flesh laced with white bones and fat—so inanimate, so surgical, the cuts. The animal was gone, on its way to becoming meat I would retrieve from the local meat locker, each cut wrapped and labeled—center chops, shoulder roast, and loins. The ham and bacon were sent out for curing and returned weeks later to be cooked up, carrying an allure every bit as enticing as the smell of animal fat crisping over a fire has been to human appetite for the millennia we have called ourselves civilized and well before. No meat was ever sweeter than the pig I raised by hand, the texture somehow more defined, flaky, tender, the flavor redolent with every sweet bite of corn the pig had savored, that alchemy of the flesh continuing in my cells.

For me this was a time made honest by hardship and work, a time when I had to learn that the price of living included many dependencies. So it is not only for the meat that I owe gratitude to the pig, but also for the web of connection to my neighbors. Bookish since childhood, I had brought my appetite for learning from the city to the boondocks, and I began to read with relish the good people of my neighborhood, savoring all they had learned about living through tough times, as if I'd been turned loose in a treasured and ancient library that held wisdom I had yet to understand.

My daughter's anger and disgust abated. Surely that birthday was a terrible one. I'm certain she felt unseen, unloved, neglected at a time of anguish. I must have run back and forth between the barn and the house, trying to keep two time frames in mind: what she needed in the moment and what she would need at our dining table for the oncoming cold winter. To little avail. It did not help that I followed one too many bits of advice from the pig man, who had sliced out the animal's tongue and told me to boil it with bay leaves and cloves. The house stank of entrails; the tongue turned out tough and repulsive. Perhaps the French would know what do with an animal tongue. I clearly did not. My poor sick child must have felt she had landed in a nightmare. Even I, committed to the cause of our subsistence, knew that this meal was an assault on good taste and possibly on motherhood. Shortly afterward, the bacon arrived from the smokehouse, and I earned at least provisional forgiveness.

My daughter had her own trials among the animals, and I believe they helped her too to survive those difficult years and cultivate a keen mind and a loving heart. The Shetland pony was named Nosy, a shapely and proud little gray with heroic mane and tail. She could be mean and ornery, baring her teeth and tossing her head in defiance. She came with a bright-red bridle and a black saddle, a perfect match to the contrasting qualities of charm and offensiveness in her character. Nosy led the way to a quarter-horse-Morgan crossbred horse named Traveler, a sturdy chestnut mare, that carried my daughter well into her adolescence. She used to ride the horse a few miles down the forested dirt road from our farmhouse to the IGA in Bakersfield, where she'd buy penny candy. She felt so cool, she now tells me, taking that long ride by herself, seeing the thick woods differently each time, alert to the strange feeling of trees all around her. Her memory of the land, she says, is largely on horseback.

"There's a preparedness," she says. "You have to give yourself over to the horse, believe the horse cares about you and doesn't want to hurt you." She describes how she experienced the world through the senses of the horse, the animal's attentiveness and readiness for flight, energy flickering through the flanks like a squall, eyes and ears taut.

"I went over her head a handful of times," she reports placidly. "We'd be galloping along. She'd stop."

One of the worst maternal terrors came on the day we brought Traveler home. The horse was nervous, pacing and skittish. So were we. We gentled the horse in the corral until she seemed at ease. My daughter climbed up on her back and the horse instantly bolted, yes, bolted. The word suits the electric charge with which the equine flew across the hayfield and veered off down the forest lane just short of the chokecherry hedgerow, a nine-year-old girl clinging with thighs and hands, leaning as low as a jockey and disappearing, a fearsome stillness closing in her wake.

But the girl, my ever-competent daughter, had her animal wisdom. As I ran after them, then gave up, then wept in maternal desperation, horse and girl slowly reappeared, walking calmly back toward the barn. They'd written their contract and they kept it, though it took argument and impatience and learning on both sides of the alliance. They entered an ongoing process of adapting to one another. My daughter always longed for a horse, as she would describe, "capable of hearing me." Traveler's quirks and insurrection were as deeply ingrained as the striations on her hooves and not to be corrected. My daughter longed for a perfect I-and-thou relationship with a horse. They learned to read each other well enough and together took on the task of reading the unknown that bordered their excursions.

When they returned from a ride, the ritual of brushing down the horse ensued in the hay-sweet barn. A horse's smell, rising with each brushstroke, is a comfort to horse lovers, something elemental that calls them into the animal's aura. The rider carries that scent into the house, molecules of natural oils that minutes ago were keeping the horse's coat healthy now clinging to her jeans and hands. It is a kind of sacrament to the horse lover, this sweetness of the other that lingers with her body. Decades after her horse period, my daughter now says she would pay someone just to go and smell their horses. Passing through the maple and pine forest together, she and the horse asked questions about the world and their part in it, teaching one another to feel safe in what was and always will be a dangerous and uncertain place.

D IS FOR THE DANCE OF THE HOURS: A PORTRAIT OF PREBANKRUPTCY DETROIT

Aisha Sabatini Sloan

M y father performed in his first and only opera while he was a college student working at the Detroit Public Library. He had no aspirations toward performance, just a crush on Leontyne Price. With politicians in the audience, he was warned not to disrupt the dignity of the opera as he played the role of pharaoh's guard in *Aïda*. But he found it difficult to keep a straight face while the men who played the high priest and the pharaoh gossiped about a sexual exploit with a female member of the cast, crass as they breathed between songs. My father was paid a dollar, and missed out on dinner with the company afterward because that dollar was all he had and he needed it to get home.

Both my parents are from Detroit. I grew up in California hearing stories about a city laced with more wonder than desolation.

We know it as the birthplace of gallerists and world famous choreographers, of raucous family dinners. Though they spent most of their lives in L.A., my parents began to spend more and more time in Detroit over the last few years, preferring to be closer to family. They moved there permanently this year.

Once my father and I drove across country from Tucson to Detroit. He put on "The Flower Duet" from *Lakmé*. Two sopranos sang bel canto as the night swelled black outside. Ground beneath us tilting downward, we fell through all that nothing toward a factory's blinking lights, car cascading into sound.

On a prolonged summer visit to Detroit three years ago, I played classical music in the car while running errands. Each time I turned on the stereo, the world seemed to click—to become suddenly whole. Colors pair best with their opposites: turquoise and vermilion, blood red and new-growth green. In this way, the east side of Detroit is complemented by music that comes from worlds away: burned wood and the entrance of the conductor. Overgrown grass and the sweep of a violin bow. A baby carriage tipped over in an abandoned lot and the hush that comes between a song's end and the applause.

In his essay "Detroitism," John Patrick Leary explains that most writing about Detroit tends to fall into one of three subgenres: a metonym for the auto industry, a lament, or an optimistic delusion. Given that the running metaphor of this essay is opera, I'll self-select: this is a lament.

MY COUSIN IS A POLICE OFFICER who often visits while she's on duty, scaring the neighbors. One day in the summer of 2012, I went with her to work. When I first stepped into the Detroit Police Department's ninth precinct, portraits of fallen officers greeted me. Elmer Cox died on May 5, 1925. His face is doll-like, or deerlike, his eyes sheened and shadowed. Alonzo Marshall Jr. died on September 1, 1971. In his portrait, he seems confused. I wrote down their names: Sypitkowski, Bandy, Steward. Somebody died on the year of my birth. I recognized the name of a man, Huff, who died after my cousin became this precinct's lieutenant.

My cousin tells us stories about her job, like anyone else would. But a normal day for her involves a woman who lived with her dead husband for two years. He sat in their living room as the woman went about her business, silent on an armchair in front of the TV. By the time they found him, he was mummified.

At one house, presumably one of Detroit's many mansions, my cousin says there was a branch the size of a large tree in the middle of the ballroom, home to a giant boa constrictor. Cops routinely answer calls about tigers and monkeys, pigs and birds. When I asked what the snake was for, she said, "That's where they bring people who fuck up." Certain animals are a form of exotic torture favored by drug dealers when people don't pay their debts.

"On the west side, they'll rob you and kill you," she says. "On the east side, they'll rob you, kill you, and rape your corpse." She'd been inviting me for years before I finally decided to ride with her for a day while she was on duty.

Although I began to write this essay then, I have hesitated to share it because there is an implicit understanding among people who love Detroit that you shouldn't talk shit. And I love Detroit more than most places in the world. A sense of possibility and kindness emanates from all that chaos in a way that is hard to explain. But censoring trouble doesn't make it go away. James Baldwin, not to mention the Buddhist scholars I've studied of late, have long argued that healing results only from staring struggle straight in the face. The late philosopher and activist, Grace Lee Boggs, spoke of Detroit as a kind of ground zero where we might visualize a new world order. So: here goes.

BEFORE SHE DIED, my paternal grandmother spent most of her life in my cousin's precinct. One of the last times I saw her alive, she told me a story she'd seen on the news. An elderly woman was found strung up and bled, like a side of beef, after two men who worked for her had stolen money from her purse. Perhaps because of stories like this, my father was always a little wary of the cast of neighborhood characters who passed through the house she shared with her younger sister, Cora May. So he kept close tabs on each of them. Pudgy visited out of grief. He couldn't make it to his own mother's funeral while he was in prison, so upon his release he devoted himself to my grandmother in penance. Gracie was attentive, but her eyes were glazed, and my great-aunt never failed to point out that she always arrived at mealtimes. Fred was known as an old-school hustler, but he kept my grandmother and great-aunt company for a morning cup of coffee, so long as they provided it.

After my grandmother died, Fred continued to visit with Cora May, and my father periodically called to speak with him. Because my dad and I have almost identical phone numbers, I often get calls for him. One day, I received a message that began, "Lester—ah, this is Fred," voice gruff like a heavy man's gait. I didn't think much of it then. That was the only time I heard Fred speak.

A few days later, Fred's body was found in the tall grasses across the street from my grandmother's house. He was bent and tipped over to the side, so it looked as though he'd died and entered rigor mortis while seated—dumped into the empty lot hours later. At the crime scene, my dad watched as Fred's daughter relayed what the police had told her to the gathering crowd of neighbors, wailing out the details of his situation like a distraught paperboy or a backup singer. "It was really quite moving," he repeated throughout the day.

We eventually found out that Fred had been drinking heavily and had a heart attack. Suddenly faced with a body, his friends panicked and dumped him in the lot across from my grandmother's house. But because he died under mysterious circumstances the day before I rode with my cousin, some part of me felt like I was embarking on a quest to solve his murder. Since I hardly knew him, his unexplained death felt like a symbol for the rupture of my grandmother's neighborhood. That day, I set out to collect clues that might reveal the phenomenology of the city's collapse. A kind of autopsy.

In a book on my father's shelves, the 1972 edition of *The Concise Oxford Dictionary of Opera*, *A* is for Azucena, a gypsy in Verdi's *Il Trovatore* who watches her mother get burned alive. *A* is for Giuseppe Anselmi, the Italian tenor who left his heart to the theatrical museum in Madrid, where it is being preserved.

ON THE DAY OF THE RIDEALONG, I am instructed to wear business casual, which is a variety of clothing I've always struggled with. So I borrow my father's bright white button-down shirt and my mother's trousers. My father had been unaware of my outing until this morning, and his concern hangs between us like an air-raid siren.

As I walk into the back door of the precinct with my cousin, an officer coming off duty points at his cheek for her to kiss. She gives a sideways smooch, then grabs at his wrinkled shirt and asks, "Was this in your car?" There is an eagerness for affection in his response, a childlike kind of purr. In a country full of awkward hugs and handshakes, my cousin greets people like a European.

I follow her into a large, white room. The floor is worn linoleum and a long, slanting pole connects the floor to the ceiling, which makes the room feel askew, as if just hit by an earthquake or flood. There are scattered desks at which nobody is sitting. File boxes are stacked precariously along the sides of the room. A fish tank sits next to a coffee pot, fake lilies, a box of green tea. It's like an empty, disheveled stage set. When I gape at the bright-red concentric vents on the ceiling, I am told, in a tone of disbelief meant to emphasize the extent of the disorder here, about the mice that sometimes fall out of them. A quaint photograph of a barn decorates the wall, as if it's a comment on the room.

On the water fountain in the hall, someone has taped a piece of computer paper with a large, typed warning: DON'T DRINK THE WATER. I sit down in a chair that will collapse if I lean too far to the right. At the public entrance, there is a sign that says, WELCOME TO THE EASTERN DISTRICT. TO BETTER SERVE YOU, THE DISTRICT WILL BE IN VIRTUAL MODE FROM 4 P.M. TO 8 A.M.

"The craziest thing to come in that door?" My cousin says, "A man bouncing a basketball, shooting."

A YEAR AFTER MY RIDEALONG, the city declares bankruptcy, and my cousin shows up in a brand new squad car. She shows us pictures of the department's renovated kitchen. By this time the city has hired two hundred new police officers and one hundred new firefighters. Crime rates, which are still horrible, have gone down about 20 percent. Police and EMS response rates have improved dramatically. Fingers are crossed.

But that day in 2012, the department was in a state of chaos. Seventy-five million dollars had been cut from the police department's budget. Officers were being warned to be on their best behavior because something in the realm of one hundred layoffs was rumored to hit soon. Precincts had been merged together. By the time officers made it across town for distant calls, the crimes they'd come for had become old news. The mayor announced that 164 firefighters would be laid off, despite the fact that arsonists kept the city lit like a bank of devotional candles. Fire stations received news of fire via fax machine and used a system of coins and soda cans to sound alarm.

Shadow figures from Kwame Kilpatrick's days as gangster-mayor still haunted the halls of government. Corruption was eating away at the infrastructure of the city like a termite infestation. Months after the ridealong, a friend sent me the link to an announcement made by the Detroit Police Union warning potential visitors to the city to enter at their own risk.

BEETHOVEN'S ONLY OPERA was *Fidelio*, which *The Concise Oxford Dictionary of Opera* calls "an uneven but magnificent expression of faith in liberty and loathing of tyranny." In it, a woman infiltrates a prison in the attempt to free her husband. Upon her urging, a group of men comprising the Prisoner's Chorus are led out into the sunshine for fresh air. They sing what has been described as "some of Beethoven's most radiant music."

The opera is often performed at houses that are being reopened "after destruction or enforced closure due to war." This association with war began upon *Fidelio*'s very first performance, during which French troops were marching on Vienna.

The war that is Detroit is not yet over, nor has it been officially declared. But *Fidelio* was performed at the Detroit Opera House in April two years ago.

IN THE BATHROOM, a woman helps me put on a bulletproof vest and says, of her lieutenant, "Listen to what she says. She's always into stuff." She pulls at the Velcro so that the vest fits tight against my body, emphasizing the words that I should keep an ear out for. *Duck. Cover. Run.*

The stories that my cousin told me before the ridealong could have come straight out of an opera:

Castrato. A woman protecting herself against the swinging arms of her brother picks up a knife and raises it toward him blindly. He falls dead and blood blooms underneath him, from what wound they cannot tell. When the heavy body is lifted for removal, the man's scrotum remains beneath, sliced clean off his body.

Chorus. A stolen car slams into and is wrapped around a pole. The driver's head is found in the street. After hours of searching with a helicopter and a fire truck, the body is found on the roof of a store. Someone sends a text message with a picture of the disembodied head to the victim's father, as though it were some kind of joke.

Crescendo. A naked man sets out in the direction of the ninth precinct office, holding an infant. He kills the baby and drops it along the way as he is walking. Biblical proverbs are found written in blood on the walls of the home he has left behind. So is the body of his wife.

As I reach for the soap in the bathroom, the vest snug around me, I try to imagine how I would react to each scenario. The dispenser is empty.

At the department's morning meeting, my cousin stands at a podium with her glasses down on the tip of her nose. "Name of the game is we back each other up, back each other up, back each other up." Each officer stands facing her in two rows. "Anything from the line for the good of the all?" she asks, and pauses. No one responds. She requests that an officer, a friend from her childhood, lead the troop in a prayer.

"Dear Lord," he says, "Let us come back in one piece. Amen."

She lists off the crimes that have taken place the day and night before. Shootings. Arson. Cocktails—I'm assuming Molotov. "Sweetie responsible for that," she says, lowering her glasses and looking at the officers for emphasis, referring to a recurring somebody that everybody already knows.

"Possible homicide. Man named Fred Young," she says. Upon pronouncing the name of my grandmother's friend, she looks at me and nods. When we walk outside, the garbage truck rumbles past us. The parking lot smells of rot. Apparently, when the incinerator across the street is burning, it rains trash.

ACCORDING TO *The Concise Oxford Dictionary of Opera*, opera has been performed in Detroit since the mid-nineteenth century, "when seasons were given by the Pyne-Harrison and De Vries Companies, and by an Italian ensemble under Arditi."

One winter, some year I can't quite remember, my family and I went to Greektown for dinner. Our waitress, most likely in her sixties, was short and round. She wore a tight bun and sat in the back of the restaurant, smoking a cigarette while we looked over our menus. Handing us our food, she had the grace and voice of a person who'd lived a big life, a quality my father can detect like a drug dog. I'm sure he asked her a question, but I remember their interaction as more accidental than that, as though without any kind of prompting the two of them began chuckling quietly about the temperament of a black soprano whose voice they both admired. She herself had spent much of her life as an opera singer. The night echoed a little deeper after she left us to our avgolemono soup. When we went back to find the restaurant the following year, it was gone. The casinos that light up the street offer free food, and many of the historic Greek eateries have been forced out of business.

Not far from Greektown, where Woodward meets Jefferson at the river, stands the statue of a seated man with his arms extended: *The Spirit of Detroit.* The man is muscular and cross-legged, made of bronze. In his left hand he holds a golden orb with rays shooting out of it, and in his right he holds a golden family with their arms upraised. The plaque states, "The artist expresses the concept that God, through the spirit of man, is manifested in the family." But you would be forgiven for thinking that he is holding the orb of light up and away from them, just beyond their grasp.

D is for Dresden, where Wagner served as the music director of the Royal Opera House one hundred and two years before the city was bombed. *D* is for "The Dance of the Hours," a short ballet in *La Gioconda* (and, later, *Fantasia*) "in which the eternal struggle between darkness and light is symbolized."

OUR SQUAD CAR makes a faint whining sound when my cousin starts it, so we switch to another. This one has no cage to separate the back seat from the front, but it's the better of the two. A cherry-scented air freshener, a Cheetos wrapper, and a blue bomb popsicle wrapper are stuffed into various pockets and creases of the car. I am struck by the way the belts and the glint of light off cuffs make male officers walking across the parking lot look so feminine, accentuating the natural twisting of their hips. "That's the morality unit," my cousin tells me, which means "vice," which means prostitutes. When she pulls on the panel with the lock and window buttons on the door of the five-year-old patrol car, the entire panel comes off in her hand.

"The car radios don't work, so if something happens to me, pull up this radio and start talking." She grabs at the radio attached to her uniform. As if she can sense that this information has freaked me out a little, she adds, "I'll try not to misbehave today." Given all the stories I've heard and all her bravado, I am surprised to learn that in over thirty years, she has only ever fired her gun at a firing range. She avoids using her baton too. As I yank at and click in my seatbelt, I glance over at her and notice that she's not wearing one. Feeling my gaze, she announces, "They're not gonna find my body shot up trying to unbuckle."

Our first task of the day is to back up two officers responding to a call about a twenty-seven-year-old with an AK-47. My cousin tells me that because of laws intended for rural Michigan hunters, it is perfectly legal for an eight-year-old child to carry a gun in the street, so long as he or she is accompanied by an adult. We scan the streets for a man who is five-foot-six, wearing a gray shirt and jeans. As we pass by the location he was seen departing from, the girl who made the call is standing in the doorway of a nondescript apartment building, wearing pajamas and glasses. "She's mad at him because he took her keys." There is something nerdy about the girl. The idea that she was just in close vicinity to an AK-47 puts the whole concept of an AK-47 in a new light for me. I try to imagine the way this kind of weapon will look, angular in what I imagine to be a flimsy drawstring backpack. We search for a figure darting through alleys, or walking in broad daylight, or hiding next to a dumpster, but find no one. Small blue flowers proliferate on the lawns we drive past, and I remark upon the color. "That's probably the state flower in some other country, but here it's a weed." One family has assembled out front of their house to pull the weed up. Their efforts are surprisingly arduous considering the delicate shade of their pale blue enemy. At another house, a woman with a yellow shirt and pigtails is combing her hair out on the porch.

"We all get up in the morning, come outside and comb our hair," my cousin narrates, mockingly. At the sight of a woman walking down the street, she says, "Out here, thirty looks sixty."

She doesn't expect much action this morning, not until around one o'clock, when more people have gotten out of bed. Still, the failed search has raised my adrenaline significantly. I am no longer curious to see anything extraordinary happen. I just want to get home alive. A man in an open blue dress shirt bikes through the blue weeds, scowling at the cop car.

In the years since, as I've wept at the sight of Michael Brown's body and Freddie Gray's body and Eric Garner's body on the news, I've wondered about the story behind that glare, and all the other stories I am not told that day. I think often how my white cousin negotiates the question of race when violence plays out in front of her, or on the news, since she herself has a half-black son.

I AM TOLD TO KEEP TRACK of street names. Lansdowne and Morang. Kelly and Moross.

Two attractive, clean-cut young men, one white, one black, stand in the street, in the middle of a transaction that they make no attempt to hide. They watch us pass with smirks on their faces. "Dope," my cousin tells me. She does not slow down. "There are some things you don't do alone."

We pass a Valero station where my cousin once arrived to

discover a man who had been shot just inside the entrance of the store. As he lay dying, his head was struck by the door each time a customer stepped over him to enter and exit, carrying on with business as usual. "Shut off the pumps," my cousin announced, infuriated, to the clerk when she walked in. Pacino-ish in the retelling.

We are on what my cousin calls Chedda Avenue, which means money. "Whatever the fuck you want you can buy on Chedda Avenue," she tells me. She pauses in front of a house decked out with balloons, T-shirts, candles, and liquor bottles, which serves as a memorial for a group of people who were recently killed. "That's a rip kit," she says. "R.I.P. Rip. One officer joked that he wanted to sell them at shootings." She pauses, chuckling to herself. "I know. That's sick."

Someone has called to report that a vandal is in the process of stealing aluminum siding from an abandoned house.

Chalmers and Elmdale. Chalmers and Maiden. Chalmers and Hayes.

"Nobody pays rent there, I'll guarantee it," she says as we drive past a series of apartment buildings. "Those assholes were shooting at us the other day."

On a well-maintained residential street, we pass a minivan that has been completely stripped. It looks like a war victim, no wheels, no nose, caved in and lopsided. A pit bull meanders down the block, wagging its tail.

IN THE DOCUMENTARY *Searching for Sugar Man*, folk musician Sixto Rodriguez walks down a street in Detroit, sun setting tangerine behind his slouching body. One of the most beautiful songs in his repertoire features his aching voice, singing of the drug dealer who sells him "silver magic ships" and adds color to his dreams. Jumpers, coke, and mary jane act as the cure for his lost heart, his false friends, and his lonely, dusty road. "Sugar Man," Rodriguez sings, "you're the answer"—his voice lilting—"that makes my questions disappear."

More than a few operas center on the theme of elusive pleasure.

Faust sells his soul to the Devil in exchange for a little youth.

Hansel and Gretel are sent to the woods to gather strawberries as punishment for playing, and instead of bringing the fruit back home, they eat to the point of exhaustion.

In *Irmelin*, a prince named Nils follows a silver stream, convinced that it will lead him toward true love.

At dinner one night, we go around the table making toasts. When it's her turn, my cousin says that if she could stop one thing in the world, it would be addiction. It is impossible to talk about Detroit without talking about intoxication.

In the squad car, my cousin surprises me when she says, "You wanna buy any kind of dope? Go to that gas station." I turn around, squinting back at the station in question, working hard to dismiss thoughts about a very stupid adventure involving a dime bag of weed. As if she can smell the curiosity on me, she adds, "Wanna get robbed or shot? It's gonna happen there too."

MY COUSIN'S FIRST DEATH on the job was at a hospice, due to cancer. The second was a man on a couch, whose body she saw out from the corner of her eye, perhaps because she was unwilling to face him. The third was a stabbing, at which point she took out her flashlight to better see the wound. "I got braver," she explains. The first shooting she witnessed "blew her fucking mind." The most recent death was self-inflicted. "My horrible," she explains, "is the nephew and the brother looking at the body."

When she started on the force, her brother told her, "Don't let them make you something you're not." And she took his advice to heart. Instead of going out to drink after a shooting, as is the tradition for many of her colleagues, she goes home instead. She has gone maybe once during her entire career. If only every officer had a brother like Ralph.

At the house we have come to investigate, there isn't a trace of a thief. We walk through to the backyard, examining the place where the siding has been taken. Stealing off of abandoned lots is a kind of home-and-garden pastime for Detroiters of all backgrounds. You can have some marble from the Packard plant for your end table, replant some long-gone woman's rose bush in the front of your house. Everybody does it. When he was young, my father helped my grandfather collect scrap metal to sell. But this was done with the owner's consent.

A cat meows as it enters the house next door, where trees are growing out of the windows and the entire front has melted. Across the street, a man trims his hedges. He has no idea who might have called the cops. This does not mean he wasn't the one who called, though. The graffiti and billboards in this city shout back and forth like a family argument, declaring the pros and cons of snitching.

We meet up with two other officers, both women. The conversation is idle, quiet, meandering. I feel like I am back in first grade, on the playground, playing make-believe with a couple of friends. We stand facing the charred and melted house and discuss the vegetation issue in this city. "See that?" my cousin asks me. "That's not a tree. That's a weed." She is pointing to the tallest plant near the house, a skinny, wild thing, but wide and high enough to be mistaken for a legitimate tree.

The degree to which the abandoned house has been overtaken by greenery verges on magical. It reminds me of movies about children growing up in the South, spending days investigating floor after floor of old barns and farmhouses. Except, in these films, there aren't two men breathing heavily behind the side door, hands calloused from ripping at the aluminum siding, waiting for the cops to leave.

One of the policewomen who has come for this call kicks at a tree stump. She has puffy neon stickers on the butt of her gun. We pile into our respective squad cars and go.

ONE NIGHT, on the front steps of our house, my cousin told my mother and me some of the most incredible stories we'd heard yet. In one, a man picked up and flung an eighty-year-old man onto the sidewalk before stealing his gold. The gold was the necklace of the old man's recently deceased wife, a loss that hit him much harder than the beating. A woman who watched this scene play out chased after the assailant, but he disappeared into a field of tall grass. "People are tired of this shit," my cousin said, laughing at the tenacity of the bystander who seemed so bent on bringing the fugitive to justice.

Sometimes we worry about her. That all this extremity and violence has hurt her more deeply than she's willing to admit. The stories she jokes about are sometimes so terrible, it seems impossible to summon a polite smile in response. My uncle, a retired psychologist, explains the necessity of laughter when it comes to stories like Detroit. Without the chance to find humor or beauty in these moments, such jobs would be completely unsustainable. But jokes can only heal so much. One day, after a home visit that rocked him badly, he drove to Lansing so that he could get out of his car and scream.

In *Jenufa*, an opera in three acts, the body of a child is found underneath the ice.

When this plot played out on my cousin's watch, counselors were called to speak with the officers involved. My cousin was the only one to speak at the baby's funeral.

SOMEBODY HAS BROKEN the window of a parked car. A husband is trying to explain what happened through the thick haze of alcohol—which he denies having consumed—emanating off of his body. The choreography of bodies is careful. My cousin, like a director maneuvering an actor's position on stage, tells the man to call for his wife and to come out of the house, but when she appears and he moves toward her, my cousin warns him not to go near his wife, using his first and middle name as though he were a child. A name that rhymes with Bobby Dee. His wife has the face of an exotic animal tattooed onto her arm, its head bent back in some kind of scream. Husband and wife both make attempts at constructing a narrative. Liquor makes his version a lot harder to follow.

"Whatever you had to drink, make sure it don't take you to jail," my cousin tells the husband.

The husband's drinking buddy is still sitting on the porch of the house. Without opening her mouth, my cousin looks at him and points, and he doesn't miss a beat, hustling down the steps. A toddler has wandered over to us from the porch full of watching next-door neighbors, and my cousin picks him up and delivers him back to them, scoldingly. Eventually, she gets the wife to go back inside so they can speak in private.

"C'mon, little Jess," one of the officers says as she passes, ushering me toward the house. Inside, the same animal that was tattooed on the wife's arm is everywhere. My cousin is waiting as the woman cries. I lower my eyes as she releases her story to a room full of listening women.

"That is mostly what your job is, huh?" I ask later. The capacity to listen and observe more than to bully and corral. "Yup," she says. Her branch of the family is known for being perceptive. Verging on telepathic.

"Don't disrespect your wife in public," my cousin tells the husband as we get ready to go. "Then you won't have to kick their ass if they disrespect her."

"I like you, you a good person," he says, still merry with drink. The other officer recommends that he take up fishing, and he laughs. His drinking buddy, hovering harmlessly near the scene, turns to me and begins to ask me if I'm in training. I nod my head, tight lipped, and move past him toward the car.

"That marriage is over," my cousin pronounces as we drive off.

My cousin explains to me in the squad car what had been whispered to her in the house. The wife in question was threatened at gunpoint at a fast food restaurant around the corner some time ago. Ever since, she's been on heavy medication, which keeps her sex drive low. This pisses off her husband, who has started to drink, and to flaunt his sexual exploits in front of her. "I won't give him any P-U-S-S-Y," she kept whispering. My cousin is positive that this is not the last we'll hear from this address today.

AS WE DRIVE PAST a crisis center with a crowd of people in front, a man flags down the car. We back up to see what he wants. He has zebra-shaved eyebrows. He asks her for a light. "Are you fucking kidding me?" my cousin asks him. We speed off. We are heading toward the foot of Alter, to the river.

"That was a bad mamajama," she says as we pass former mayor Coleman Young's old party house. For many Detroiters, this is a kind of epicenter for Detroit's downfall.

The neighborhood we move through has a Southern feel about it. "Like you fell off into Arkansas," my cousin says.

The lighthouse near Alter Road is a favorite spot for suicides. A five-hundred-pound woman jumped one winter, and officers waded into the subzero water to get her out. The fishermen tense up a bit as my cousin slams the door to the squad car and approaches. Awhile back, when she got wind that one of the cops in the squad was on their way to ticket the fishermen for fishing without a license, she would beat him to the waterfront and warn them.

I catch a glimpse of myself in the reflection on the car window. I look boxy. My hair is in a tight bun. I feel as though I'm in costume, and walk for some reason as though I am a robot. I am terrified that someone will require me to speak, and gaze off into the distance so as to look preoccupied. We approach one couple, and my cousin asks them about their luck that day. No crime has been reported here; the river is just a place where my cousin likes to be. But nobody knows that except for me.

As she talks about her fishing exploits, her philosophies on the psychological benefits of the pursuit, a man listens politely, holding his fishing pole, perhaps waiting to find out what it is that he's done wrong. Other folks farther down the way crane their necks to see what's going on.

The fisherman is accompanied by his vaguely high wife. She tries, like a double-dutch player, to jump into the conversation every chance she can get. But my cousin is waxing poetic: The ugliest fish she ever caught. The fact that she catches them and then gives them away. How sometimes she just throws them back in. I stand in silence, watching the man, wishing he were as at ease as he meant to be when he woke up and thought to head for the river.

ON A TRIP TO BAVARIA ONCE, I went on a tour of one of King Ludwig's castles. There was a cave, with a small pond at its center, which held a boat. He was a lover of opera, a fervent patron to Wagner, and it was from this boat that he would act as the sole audience for elaborate musical performances. Lit with red and green lights, the cave seemed an eccentric kind of loneliness. At the time, I scoffed at the extravagance of it. Now I wonder about the feeling of an orchestra quivering to life inside all that scooped-out stone and sorrow.

My father told me recently that the first novel he ever read was *Of Human Bondage*. Around that same time in his life, he had a paper route that took him past Goethe Street, which everybody pronounced "Go-thee." The word has come to symbolize the smallness of the universe he grew up in, something he was aware of from a very young age. Years later, he studied German authors, walked the streets of Frankfurt and Berlin, and learned how to pronounce Goethe correctly. Some days my vision of him flickers and he is still that child, murmuring his way through the unfamiliar expanse of a novel about feeling trapped. He's always said there should be an opera written for Detroit.

At the Heidelberg Project, Tyree Guyton's outdoor installation of found materials—boots, religious iconography, whole houses, shopping carts—my father is taking pictures of a pile of doors. I turn on the classical station and play it loudly for him out the open window of the car as he engages with the art and the wreck.

When I reach the words *magic flute* in *The Concise Oxford Dictionary of Opera*, part of me feels a flutter. As if the story of this city could be armed with some aura of the fantastic like these operas. Will Detroit ever be granted some secret power? Even I am lured into the possibility. That an instrument in the tall grass will lead this story toward its resolution. Set the dead man back to standing.

SOUTHAMPTON AND ASHLEY. Gratiot and Seymour.

A fifteen-year-old boy has been hit upside the head with a baseball bat. En route, we pass a public school, and my cousin tells me that even though the student body is getting smaller, the Detroit Public Schools' police force is getting bigger. When we arrive at the scene, EMS is there. It is apparent that this boy is older than fifteen. The man in uniform outside the ambulance is pacing. As we walk past, he is saying into his cellular phone, "She seems mad I haven't picked up the mail."

My cousin asks questions rapidly, as if simultaneously gathering information and keeping the young injured man conscious. He is hulking, crouched in the vehicle with the other EMT tending to his head. His elbow is bleeding. As the story goes, a man with dreadlocks hit him on the head with a bat while he walked across a gas station parking lot, and someone started kicking him in the head and face. An anonymous black Cadillac pulled up beside him and drove him to this address.

"You can't imagine why someone woulda done this to you?" she asks. *No.* "If we locked him up, would you tell a judge and jury, 'This is what he did to me?'" *No.* I wonder from the boy's manner of speaking whether he might be gay. He coughs. "You smoke?" My cousin asks. *No.* "Do you have asthma?" He shakes his head incessantly.

WHEN I AM VISITING with my father, I often find him watching a YouTube video in which an audience is told that Pavarotti will not be performing that night. A good friend of his will be on stage instead. With the crackling warmth and smokiness of a fire, Aretha Franklin sings "Nessun Dorma." My father begins to laugh and shake his head.

His best friend, Rodney, is an avid fan of old movies. He is often quoting films from the forties and fifties. He was the kid who wore the five-hundred-dollar suit he bought cheap from a thrift store to play in a pick-up basketball game.

The difference between their generation and the one coming of age in Detroit today, at least on the streets where they grew up, seems to have to do with a lost capacity for dream; for anticipating the unimaginable. There is no longer the same swagger that made Motown. No more energy for revolt.

And yet. One afternoon, when a friend and I drove down Jefferson, a man with long dreadlocks was skating with all the grace of a ballerina, headlong into traffic, swerving assuredly between oncoming cars.

The *O* section of *The Concise Oxford Dictionary of Opera* begins with a long list of laments. *O Carlo, ascolta. O cieli azzurri. O Isis und Osiris. O luce di quest'anima. O terra, addio.* Some are appeals. Some are love duets. Others are about a star, a death, a god or a place.

O patria mia, Aïda sings. O country of mine.

"I NEED TO PUT THEM on an island," a hostage negotiator for the police force told me. If he's not the only one communicating with a person on the verge, his work is compromised. Once, a man at Chene Park with a gun to his head spent five hours not killing himself or anybody else. But his phone kept ringing. Finally, he picked it up. He told the person on the other line, "I love you," and shot himself. The negotiator was standing ten feet away.

"There's an art to figuring out what's going to happen," a recently retired officer explains. "We didn't have a winter this year. Just spring, summer, and fall. And I hate to say it like they're animals, but they never rested."

The current economy paired with a poorly educated population "makes it easier for loosely knit people to commit crimes," he explains. And then there are the people who wear the badge. "You get a broke cop, in over his head, bad mortgage...soon they'll be able to get food stamps. You can go to McDonald's and get better benefits." The more they take away from an officer's pay, the more likely he'll be to dip into crime himself.

My cousin takes me to lunch at a restaurant with big black-and-white photographs of a long-gone Detroit framed and centered on the wall beside each booth. Two officers join us. Over French fries, coffee, and Greek salad, they lament the various aspects of a failing department. How a robot answers the phone when you call 911 after dark. How somebody's idea of a solution is that for your first year as a police officer, you work for free. How badly they feel for the firemen. How they suspect that, with the city getting a percentage of the profits made by the Tigers, the Lions, and three casinos, Detroit might not actually be broke. How camaraderie among officers is gone. And trust. How they used to love their jobs, and now they don't.

This is something that hasn't improved much since the bankruptcy. Officers starting on the force in Detroit make almost half of what you can make at the same job in Los Angeles—less than fifteen dollars an hour, after taxes. After it was announced that, as part of the post-bankruptcy plan, the force would endure a 10 percent pay cut, the *Daily Mail* published an article about a police officer named Baron Coleman who was consoled by the man he was arresting for robbery, who said, "I can't believe your city would do you like this."

SOME PEOPLE LIKE TO SAY that Detroit is going to seed. Reindeer have started to follow the train tracks into the city. Peacocks from the Detroit zoo can be found parading down the streets of the nearby suburbs. Whole families of quail and pheasants huddle and march through the empty lots that human families have evacuated.

A few days after my grandmother's funeral, we made an impromptu family trip to the Packard Plant, the same way we would go to a gallery or museum. Wandering through the halls of what had once been a major source of strength to Detroit, I took pictures of my father as he raised his camera to the decay. We stepped carefully up the once-marble staircases, read spray-painted messages and stencils as we would the labels beside paintings. We looked out over the expanse of that historic crumbling through huge holes that seemed to have been blasted into the wall.

Entire rooms glowed pink and green and yellow and blue as the sun seeped through fluorescent graffiti painted on the glass-brick walls. Archways led into rooms where rebar hung down from the ceiling, like an upside-down field of falling knives. In one room, I took video of the sound of dripping, of the birds that huddled and swooped through the pale, gaping expanse. We peered down empty elevator shafts as if into some underground world.

Goethe wrote a version of *Proserpine* as a tribute for his sister. Stravinsky made the music. Martha Graham set the myth into dance, as did Pina Bausch. In Bausch's famous version of "Sacre du Printemps," another story about a young girl who is sacrificed in the name of spring, the stage floor is covered in dirt. A red dress serves as the only vibrant color, carrying the eye as it is passed around from body to body, then tossed onto the ground.

On the last day I spent with my grandmother, I happened to look across the street, and caught a glimpse of something in the grass. It was an adult pheasant, feeding as his head feathers glinted red in the late afternoon sun.

WE GET A CALL about a stabbing. The call has come from the

same address as the domestic dispute we visited earlier in the day. "We're gonna see who got cut," my cousin says as we swerve onto the freeway on-ramp. When we pull up, the wife is standing on the curb with white cream on her face. "Noxzema face," my cousin mutters affectionately before opening the door. "What's on your face?" she says to her as we get out of the car.

A group of neighbors speak with an attractive female officer whom my cousin calls Malibu Barbie. One man explains that he observed the struggle, and screamed for the husband and wife to stop, but didn't want to come close because he could see that somebody had a knife. He wasn't sure who hurt whom. As Malibu Barbie walks away, he looks appreciatively at her behind and the group of people standing with him begins to laugh. Her beauty is about on par with Beyoncé's, and the incongruity of this given the grim scene makes me cough up a weak chuckle too.

"I told you I wasn't coming back here," my cousin tells the husband, who clings to his arm. He is no longer a fan of hers. "You wrong," he growls. "I ain't got to talk to you," he shouts. "That's another charge," my cousin says.

Inside the house for the second time, I notice that everything is green. A large photograph of a young man who shares his father's name is sitting on a mantel. I try to make small talk to get the woman to explain the animal whose effigy—knit, carved, and stamped; figurines, paintings, toys—appears in every available space in their house. But, understandably, she is unable to concentrate on my question. "I don't want to go to jail," she tells me, "but I'm afraid I'm going to kill him."

When it's time to tell her side of the story to my cousin, she shouts it. We find out that she was trying to take a bath when her husband tried to have sex with her. She resisted him and he locked her out of the house. He had already taken the battery out of the car, but now he hid the keys and her phone, so she had to go to a neighbor's house to call the police.

"That's another charge," my cousin says.

I wonder what would have happened here if the officers weren't all women. The wife swears that her husband cut himself. Whatever it is, it's only a scratch.

The whole scene has an unwittingly comic air to it because, as though in costume, the anguished protagonist is still wearing the Noxzema on her face. But nobody here thinks any of this is a joke. The policewomen assembled seem to have taken a special interest in protecting the woman who lives here. They articulate her options clearly and repeat them. Her husband, whose drunkenness has indeed worked against him, is going to spend the night at the station jail. Hopefully, my cousin says, they'll get a restraint against him.

"Mississippi and Alabama don't mix," she says as we drive off. She points out her window, where a house is facing backward, toward the alley.

BACK AT THE POLICE DEPARTMENT, my cousin's phone rings. The song "Boombastic" by Shaggy is her ringtone, and she begins to dance. Earlier in the day, in this same spot, a male officer was taking notes as a fourteen-year-old girl explained how she'd been forced into an abandoned house and raped.

In *Die Zauberflöte*, Mozart's Magic Flute, a man who seeks enlightenment discovers an instrument that can turn sorrow into joy.

When I think of the woman who could have killed her husband, I think of the wild animal tattooed on her arm, the way her house was filled with those tiny figurines. I wonder about that moment, long ago, before everything fell to shit, when she realized that this animal gave her some sense of strength, and that, one day, she'd need to be reminded.

ENTRY COVE

Lia Purpura

I say *entry cove* in ignorance, to name the world as I can, make-shift, by a phrase that lights on the skin—*entry cove*, a space made in tall grass and darted through, sound enough to constitute a hideaway in a meadow. A cove is generous in definition: a sheltering bay, a cave, gap, or hollow. As I near, an animal slower and heavier than a cat slips in. *Cove*, because I want to follow, everything outside too loud and wrong.

Here at the edge of this meadow, late summer, the goldenrod high, the sun warm and air soft, there's a motor, compressor, something violently chewing the quiet, shredding the peace. Hard to locate its origin. Overhead, a plane tears a path into blue sky. Then comes a far train whistle I make romantic to alter the imposition—until it turns back to the truck horn it is and I'm re-composed, on the outskirts again, making do.

You asked for my impression, you who once lived in this ruined town for years. After just a few days, I'm so hungry I'll take any-thing green. I sift for green moments, accept reduced portions, this circumscribed walk. Some stretches are fine: rows of stables have been made into offices and the worn-smooth silvery boards are intact. Near a once-barn, there's a real footbridge arcing over a trickle of creek. And this meadow-reprieve, preserve, conscious allotment of wild—it helps.

It was a woodchuck, I can see now. She's out and settled on the shorn path, fully adapted to the machinery noise, no wincing or twitching, just nibbling grass. As I move closer, she slips back into the green tangle. Then we do it again: I circle the meadow, and coming around, she's out on the path. I close in, she retreats—only partly though, now that she knows it's me. And just as she's wagered, I do move along. There's a name for me and the distance I keep. That I can't know it doesn't mean that I'm not, at this moment, being addressed.

THOUGH I GREW UP across the street from a parking lot, it did at least lead to a small county park and a lake—my fancy, my scrap, really, only a pond. Half the pond was belted by a path paved for walking and half was left wooded. Whole stretches had their microclimates, each distinct and brief as a shiver, or a stripe of afternoon sun in the eyes. At the path's beginning was a rocky area where fat white Long Island ducks gathered for handouts. Then a sadder stretch, treeless and too-bright, with splintery pilings where old men sat and fished in the murk. Then a relief-stretch where the pilings stopped and scrubby grass ran down to the water, willows shaded the banks, and the year-round geese slept. On the far side of the pond before the woods started was a rise, an open, mowed area I tried to believe in for years, thought could be used, it should have been used, made productive, *trod, tilled,* or *encamped*—but such language wasn't available to me, *plots* went undrawn, we weren't a *village*, there wasn't a *harvest*, we had dirt and not *soil*, and no one had *earth*. The space felt shunned—not left-to-reverence, not sacred-kept—and I couldn't get it to breathe or work or activate. Walking up there was an obligation, an attempt to restore I couldn't say what. Most days I'd focus past it, move quickly and try not to feel its need. The path ended in a turnaround, and beyond that loop, with its garbage cans, snarls of fishing line, rusty hooks, was the fence to the woods, called "the pit" by the neighborhood kids. But it wasn't a pit. It was never a quarry. It had no maw. There was no town legend telling its origin. By "pit" they meant only the interval—filler, like TV snow at the end of the dial—before entertainment resolved again.

If I felt like testing my footing, I'd climb out and swing around the fence, which leaned far into the water; usually, I'd just go over, get in fast and head to the steep, embrambled part, vast-feeling and farthest from home. So few were the raw places I could get to, spots no words touched, where language unhinged. And here, though the land had no name or story, I could read in the rock-cluster broods how light grew long and patted them, or touched the tallest trees' crowns so briefly. Ground gave. Wind found the undersides of leaves. Each spot was full of explanations—not answers exactly, I came with no questions—but still, ferns sprang into feather, the spines of fish and big-eyed skulls of birds bent me to them. The midway-through part was bright and exposed, so I moved fast there, past the rusty NO TRESPASSING signs, eye tuned for turtles and snakes—the neat holes of almost-never-seen snakes—so I could confirm my own ways of hiding. Then, coming fully around, there was the neighborhood side again, marked by another fence where I sat and waited for fish to surface, or a turtle to clarify on a log. Usually, after a rest, I turned and went back in for another dose. Though I knew nothing but the most basic tree names and a couple of grasses, that soft greens went by *moss* and floating greens *algae*, I applied these to the damage "the pit" had done. I went alone. I didn't want to play at hiding or being chased, or pass through quickly en route to some other activity. I wanted no chat to scuff the sounds of other lives. It wasn't a forest, it wasn't a marsh. I didn't measure or think in acres. It was the one place I had where land went rightful. Where I could finally stop converting.

*

WITH CERTAIN HABITS of mind engaged, ruin can be altered or even dissembled. Say I lived in upstate New York, say Niagara— the chronic, anxious hum of traffic might be recast, *that's just the falls.* Industrial grinding: *just the falls.* Flightpath: *falls.* Offloading: *falls.* I've long been in the business of converting, though not all cases are difficult ones. Some are sidelong or slant; sometimes the shift is agile-feeling, and not employed to salve or deflect. So a dark bank of late afternoon clouds might become mountains-at-sunset, plunging us into valley life: Baltimore at the foot of a range, the Cascades (in my car driving west into the city, I speak it, *Cascades*, that open, then tumbling, icy *a*, delicious double-click *c* outcropping) and the air goes hazy with snow-mist, the word *foothills* makes all worn things feel glacier-rubbed. How good to be, at the end of the day, overseen by something majestic. Or, in a childhood act of conversion, I could turn dim-winter-solitude to street-gaslit-by-Leerie, Leerie in his big brown coat who walked his patch of London at dusk with ladder and torch and waved to children having their tea, for whom I waited page after page, my own torch lighting my book in bed.

For a long while I called the churn of waves back home *old lace* and the rich biotic foam *bright spun* along the Long Island shore, until that wouldn't work anymore, and leaks or spills, which sound benign, household even, meant it was time to recast the froth— make it no longer of light and air, and not dissolvable, but dire. In this way a childhood ends, that is, some tactics no longer work.

SOME THINGS ARE IMPOSSIBLE to convert: what are trees with all their limbs cut? Mute stubs or thumbs. A field of pins. A hill of blunts. A very complete desolation. No right mind would draw a forest where a bird couldn't land, make the space leafless so the wind couldn't speak. *After a fire* is the best I can do—but a good burn doesn't work that way, and I can't slide a clearcut along the converter the way I used to, ruin carried along the moving belt of my hope. My urban versions are just as helpless: that heap of clothing, lamps, mattresses, TVs at the curb? Not the chaos of moving, but *eviction.* Those alley puddles? Not gathered from rain, with pins of ice forming, but used needles among the broken glass piles.

Real change, not conversion, abounds. It does. Here's a branch-ful of yellow on an otherwise still-green oak at the edge of the meadow, late summer, an actual herald, a season called in, not something to be reconfigured, in need of being eased or staunched. And the luminous parchment shells of cicadas, husks of sycamore bark, and black locust pods I step on for the satisfying crunch—all forms en route to their proper end. No need to see with a strategy, with habits employed to keep back the grief which, anyway, over-runs the banks I make.

YOU TOLD ME IT WOULD BE desolate here; I suspect it's gotten worse since you left—the downtown's nearly abandoned now, its main streets stretched wide by emptiness, no one out for a little air, no one meeting up for lunch. The tattoo parlors, cheap beer-&-pizza dives are brief stops along the interstate. Such loss makes anyone just-passing-through move along faster. Dusk here might be con-vertible if—no, let me stop. Dusk might be unto itself, if the light's allowed to catch a breath, if the rough of it's held against the body of a warehouse, loading dock, trailer, if the scene it colors has no name but I let the light work and the scene stays uncaptioned, purples and softens, iron peels like bark, like skin, every underside reddens and the oily puddles iridesce and I'm in, nowhere else, and it's awful, it isn't, and I don't want to stay, and I stay with it.

MONSOON AND PEACOCK

Aimee Nezhukumatathil

What monsoon can do is give you sweetness in spite of the heavy wet. Even when it rains in Kerala, India, people still ride their colorful scooters, and some even carry a friend or a love along with them. If it is a woman behind the driver, she will sit sidesaddle, wrapped in her sari or churidar. One hand grips only the padded rim of the seat for support, the other holds a black umbrella covering herself and the driver. The *thwap-thwap-thwap* of raindrops the size of quarters and the scooter's engine—the only sounds worth noticing on their damp course through the village streets.

This rain is never scary, though, even during monsoon. You can tell monsoon is near when you hear a sound like someone shaking a packet of seeds in the distance. A pause—and then the roar. You know it's coming when the butterflies—fire skippers and bluebottles—fly in abundance over my grandmother's cinnamon plants and suddenly vanish. A whole family of peacocks will gather up in a banyan tree, so still, as if posing for a seasonal portrait. Then the shaking sound begins.

If you could smell the wind from an ecstatic, teeny bat—if you could smell banana leaves drooping low and modest into the ruddy soil, if you could inhale clouds whirring so fast across the sky—*that* is what monsoon rain smells like.

Of the two monsoons that drench India each year, the Southwest monsoon, between May and August, is the heavier rain, while the Northeast monsoon in October is much more misty and light, feathering over people's faces from sunrise to dusk—like the mist machines in the produce section of my neighborhood grocery back in New York, which inevitably turn on just when I happen to be examining asparagus shoots or selecting a container of raspberries.

Monsoons transform the countryside of the southwest coast of India into a blaze of fierce-green verdure twice a year. The heavier rains etch metallic rivers such as the Periyar and the Bharathappuzha even deeper and wider, flowing westward from the rugged Western Ghats, until they lose themselves in milky conversation with each other in the deep backwaters, then, finally, into the Arabian Sea. Coconut trees swoop and tangle low at water's edge. From a distant bridge, the horizon is nothing but green stars.

Kill a black cobra and hang it in a tree so it will rain.
Rings around the moon mean rain.
Rain crow can tell of coming rain.
Cows lying down is a sign of rain.
If two doves sit in a frangipani tree, facing the same
* direction, it will rain.*
Swallow four seeds of a violet guava for rain.
Step on an ant and it rains.
Orange moon equals rain.
A dog eats grass? Means rain.

The rain is a constant companion during my stay with my

grandmother in Kerala, this land of coconuts. Kerala, land of rain. I am in my first year of grad school, and although I've visited India before—I was eight years old the first time—this trip is my first abroad without my parents to navigate me through extreme weather conditions I simply hadn't encountered in the States. Rain murmurs in my ears as I maneuver my way around the paths of the markets in Kottayam, the town where she lives. It trickles down my neck, repelling into beads on my waxy skin, freshly rubbed with mosquito repellent. In the space between my eyebrows, I am smudged with black: my painstakingly applied liquid bindi pools down the bridge of my nose and collects under my right eye.

Hot, fat raindrops drench my face even as I stand on our covered back porch. I spy three old women in saris stealing coconuts from my grandmother's grove just outside the village—the men who work my grandmother's land shoo them, but they just laugh, leaping gracefully like colorful birds scattering at the sight of a mongoose, up and over the cement wall edged with shards of bright and broken glass chips, without a single cut on their legs.

My eleven-year-old cousin Anjana and I sometimes watch MTV India on our grandmother's brown velvet couch. The television sizzles off—one of the many random power outages in the village. "No Current!" Grandma calls them. As in, "We must wash the clothes in the morning before No Current." "You finish the ice cream, or it will waste with No Current." "There are too many babies in this town because of No Current." We sit staring at the screen, the two of us—cousins who have only seen each other in pictures until just the week before. Anjana breaks the silence first.

"Sometimes, old ladies tie a frog to a fan. A small frog, yah? And then, they sing out loud that the frog is thirsty and needs water. All the family watches, even the maid. The frog is spinning, spinning from the ceiling, yah? Yuck, yah? Then, then—the next day there is rain!"

"What happens to the frog?" I ask.

"Nothing. I think the maid takes it down."

Any squeamishness or misgivings I had about bugs vanished within seventy-two hours of stepping foot in Kerala. I've learned the small skitter of insects knocking against the mosquito netting over my bed is loudest when the lights are on, so I make it a point to write aerogrammes to my friends back home only in daylight, to spare the insistent tapping against the gauzy cloth. Each night, I tuck and retuck the edges of the netting into a tight fit around my cool mattress. I brush my teeth with my right hand. My left hand grabs at the air around me, trying to spare my skin before bed from the black mosquitoes already heavy and obvious with someone else's blood. When I open my left hand, black asterisks cover my palm.

The next morning, my sister JoAnn and I beg our grandmother to let her driver take us to Vembenad Beach—anywhere from the house, damp and silent from the day's power outage. On the half-hour drive there, we pass by pantsless toddlers cupping dragonflies in their hands, faces exquisite with joy from watching the flutter of blue wings against the gray sky of monsoon. The roofs of their families' huts are made of empty rice sacks tied together. In the early mornings and afternoons, when the rains fall heavy and sure with the scent of bats' wings, I wonder how they keep dry.

WHEN THE RAIN STOPS, terrific smells—the kind that would make people at a food festival steam and sweat with envy—issue forth: curried eggs, thick steaks of broiled fish in coconut milk, chili chicken, payasam noodle puddings, and sweet honey bricks of halvas cooling on wooden tables. Although some of the residences are humble, people cook outdoors and neighbors find ways to share bounty with others less fortunate down the street. The kids playing outside here always look full, and everyone sleeps after the heavy noon meal. Whole households—distant aunts and uncles, maids, drivers, dogs, peacocks, and the family cow—lie down for a sweet afternoon nap and wait for the rain to subside so the evening meal can be prepared. Even if the family still feels a bit damp, they are sated and pleased, their round brown bellies full.

How the peacock grew his family: when a naughty boy mistook some oil for a rain puddle, his footprints became greasy little moons. And when those moons clustered and spun into an orbit of stars, like spilled sugar, they fanned out into a blue breast, and the breast begat milk, and the milk begat a cry—the bird's famous shriek like someone gargling hot cream and cinnamon.

WE ARRIVE AT THE LOCAL RESORT where people can rent house-boats for the day or week. It's the closest place in town that serves ice cream, and it is fortified by generators. A pair of male peacocks strolls near our car and pauses in front of us, a little too close. I'm used to birds scattering here at the first appearance of rain or people, but these birds stare straight at us and don't move until my grandmother fans her handbag at them. Kerala's famous coir houseboats line up along the edge of the resort, waiting for the next group of tourists to board before the rains start up again. I run out from our group, away from the restaurant. I stand on the silty beach, here at the southern tip of India, where the Indian Ocean begins a gentle whisk into the Arabian sea, while my four-foot-six-inch-tall grandmother shuffles the sand, trying to catch up with me. *Aimee, Aimee, you stay here and—ayoo! More bites on your face. What shall I tell your father when I send you home like this? Let's go inside and have your ice cream!*

Cornetto Ice Cream Parlour Menu

Vemby Special Sundaes—49R

The Boat—three scoop ice cream, strawberry crush,
banana pieces, fruits

Ice Cream Sandwich—three slices ice cream, marble cake,
caramel nuts, sauce, and jelly

The Apricot—vanilla, Spanish delight ice cream,
apricot sauce, apricot fruits, almond

The Pastry—vanilla and chocolate ice cream, pastry,
sauce, carmelised nuts, grated dairy milk chocolate

Vemby Cocktails—39R

Vembenand Beauty—three flavour ice cream, lychee
fruits, marble cake and black current sauce

Miss Ghulbi—gulabjamoon, vanilla ice creams, carmelised nuts and sauce

Cream Channel—mix of butterscotch and vanilla ice creams, jelly, crispy nuts, topped butterscotch sauce and dry fruits

Funcream—vanilla ice cream, jelly, fresh fruits, vermicelli, chickoo, and nuts

Pistafalooda—pist syrup, fresh fruits, noodles, jelly, almond nuts, and vanilla scoop

Joker 2000—it is a funny man for kids with ear, nose and cap

I choose the Joker because I hardly feel like smiling, with dozens of mosquito bites dotting my face, arms, and legs. Last count with a Q-tip and calamine lotion: seventy-five teeny warm lumps. Grandma gives me a quizzical look, like she suddenly smells spoiled milk, when I give the waiter my order, but I look away onto the shoreline of swooping coconut trees, trying to be dignified, grown-up, in choosing my dessert. Here the coconut tree trunks curve and swerve in a wild cursive, palms all full and bursting like green hands spread wide open.

GRANDMA IS RIGHT: the waiter returns with bowls of Miss Ghulbi and Pino Fantasy concoctions. He leaves and sprints back to our table with my Joker 2000 on a tiny blue saucer so small it could almost be a coaster. JoAnn looks at me half sympathetic and half embarrassed: this is what I summoned the family driver for? It is, of all the things on the sticky laminated menu, the only dish that comes premade from some factory in Madras. True to its description, it is a super-sweet concoction of pressed, solidified yogurtlike frozen cream, but pathetically shaped into the head of a man with glasses and baseball cap. Like Mr. Potato Head.

In this village where cold drinks are a novelty (refrigerators are used mainly for meats, and unreliable even then because of the frequent blackouts during monsoon), ice cream is nothing short of luxury. I savor every last cold bite, but I'm finished before JoAnn has had two bites of her Miss Ghulbi.

I try not to covet her tantalizing bowl of ice cream, the sugared nuts steaming in this humidity. In my disappointment, at least I forget all the mosquito bites swelling on my body, focusing instead on the screeching of peacocks in the distance and my grandmother clinking her spoon on her ceramic bowl, scraping the last remnants of pineapple.

Thankfully, Grandma offers to buy me something else, and suddenly I am eight years old again—quiet and smiling, all traces of my impatience with the heat, the mosquitoes, or the stares of villagers vanished. I am so grateful. I let her choose and order for me in Malayalam—the language of my father only when he is angry with me—and I don't even frown when she shares a joke with the waiter where I am so obviously the punch line. JoAnn thinks I'm eating a Vembenand Beauty, as there are moist vanilla and chocolate cake slices layered into the ice cream, but then there are no lychee pieces, and instead, a kind of dark, fruity syrup, like a thinned jam, that blends so sweetly with the pure vanilla ice cream on my tongue.

The peacocks continue to trill-call in the distance. Rain begins to fall again. Lean, tanned boatmen use bamboo poles to steer large two-story houseboats along the backwaters of Vembanad Beach. A small splash of pole—and then quiet. The splash—and then quiet. Splash—and quiet. As a houseboat solemnly glides past our table, past our slice of beachfront ice-cream parlour, I think I catch the white flash of teeth from the brightest of smiles. I find myself smiling back at him, and my grandmother watches the whole scene as she scoops the last of her ice cream from the bright aluminum bowl.

✳

I'M EIGHT AND I'VE JUST RETURNED from my first trip to southern India to visit my grandparents. During that time, I've fallen completely in love with peacocks—*Pavo cristatus*, India's national bird—in spite of hearing stray ones in my grandparents' courtyard shriek like a cat being dragged over thumbtacks every morning. The bright and bold turquoise and jade feathers, and the memory of the peacock's bright blue neck, curls over my shoulder as I listen to my new third-grade teacher in suburban Phoenix announce an animal drawing contest. We've just moved here from a small town in Iowa, where I was the only brown girl in class. And although my classmates stared hard at me when I first was introduced to everyone, even now I remember how happy I was to see kids of all shades in the room. My knees bounce at my desk when I hear the announcement of the schoolwide drawing contest. Of *course* I know what animal I'm going to draw.

She sends us off to the library to search for an animal, and I ask if I can just stay and get started on my drawing. She fumbles in her purse, and I see a pack of cigarettes. *No, you may not. We all need to be on the same page*, she says.

I scan the library shelves. There are no books on peacocks. My friends choose various dog breeds, small reptiles, lots of kittens. In my notebook, I write in careful cursive, PEACOCKS ARE THE NATIONAL BIRD OF INDIA. Then the bell rings and summons us back to class.

My teacher walks up and down the aisles, checking our notebooks. When she stops at my desk, I hear a smoky sigh, and her long maroon nail taps on my notebook: two short taps. I have no idea what this means.

When we draw our animals on thick sheets of white construction paper, I fill the page with a sea of bright teal green and purple. I outline the dramatic eye of the peacock in black, like he's wearing eyeliner. The rest of the page blooms with peacock feathers, dozens of violet eyes. I can see the drawing the kid next to me is working on—a mostly blank page with a single squiggle-line on it: a snake.

My teacher continues to stalk around the rows of our desks. *Some of us misunderstood the assignment*, she says. She reaches the front of the room, and clears her throat. *Some of us will have to start over and draw American animals. We live in Ah-mer-i-kah!* Now she looks right at me. My neck flushes. *Anyone who is finished can bring your drawing up to my desk and start your math worksheets. Aimee—* The class turns to look at me. *Looks like you need a do-over!*

I turn my drawing over and blink hard, trying not to let tears fall onto the white page. To this day I have no idea what she was talking about. "American animals" was not even part of the original assignment. Did she think peacocks couldn't live in this country? I had seen them at the San Diego Zoo the summer before, and my father had told me they even block roads in Miami, where they can be seen strolling across lawns in the suburbs.

I pick up a new sheet of paper and slink back to my desk. I draw the most American thing I can think of: a bald eagle perched on a branch at the edge of a cliff, two eggs peeking up from the nest delicately balanced on the branch. I know the nest looks like a basket of Easter eggs, but I don't care anymore. I just want to be done with the drawing so my classmates will stop staring. I color in the wings with the saddest sepia in my crayon box. Before I turn it in, I add an American flag—as big as the one hung outside the school—its pole poked into the tree's branches. Nothing about it looks natural, especially since the flag itself is so much larger than the eagle.

WHEN I GOT HOME THAT DAY, I parked myself on the couch and stared at the television. When my dad called me to dinner, I told him I wasn't hungry. When he walked into the living room to ask me to come to the dinner table anyway, I said, *Why do we need to have all these peacocks all over the house? Wooden peacocks, brass peacocks, a peacock calendar, a peacock painting—it's so embarrassing!* My dad said nothing, just walked out of the room, then called back, *Your dinner will be cold.*

The next day, all the peacocks in the house were gone. *All* the peacocks, except for our family calendar: twelve months of peacocks, in front of a waterfall, a museum, a wall of bougainvillea. The calendar remained, marking our time with its little squares, a new set of dramatic eyes looking back at me each month.

Weeks later, after announcements and the Pledge of Allegiance, my teacher announced the results of the drawing contest: my eagle drawing had won first place. It was displayed in the giant glass trophy case, right outside the principal's office. I always hurried past it on my way to class.

I WAS A GIRL WHO LOVED TO DRAW. I was a girl who loved color, who loved a fresh box of crayons, who always envied the girls who had the box of sixty-four colors, but made do with my off-brand box of twenty-four. I was a girl who loved to draw—and yet I don't think I ever drew a bird again, not even a doodle while I was on the phone, until well into adulthood.

This is how I learned to ignore anything from India. The peacock feathers my grandfather had carefully collected for me on my last day in India grew dusty in the back of my closet, instead of sitting in a vase on my white dresser. This is how for years I pretended I hated the color blue.

But what the peacock can do is remind you of a home you will run away from and run to all your life. My favorite color is peacock blue. My favorite color is peacock blue. My favorite color is peacock blue.

GOING DOWNHILL FROM HERE

Laurie Clements Lambeth

NUDE DESCENDING A STAIRCASE

The nude in Marcel Duchamp's famed 1912 painting *Nude Descending a Staircase, No. 2* does not appear to need a railing. She seems quite capable of walking down stairs, multiplied as she is into several incarnations, a body for each stair. Division of labor, rendering the task of each step far less daunting. As Duchamp parcels out her golden motion, the nude is anything but graceful, her body—or bodies—serviceable, put together more efficiently than we are, with the bulk of her in the calves, the feet: sturdy, working legs. Her head, translucent waves of motion, all flurry at higher elevations, weighs little on her arm-pumping shoulders. She doesn't even need to think until she reaches the lowest step, where her head appears as she carefully looks down, leans back, holding all those previous stages of her movement steady, saying—if she had a mouth—"Don't worry about this, ladies. I've got it all under control. I'll stop your fall."

This is how I see the painting today, when the scars in my brain and spine delay and suspend each downward step, confounding the entire process. I'm trying to work out how she does it. How she descends, machinelike, functional, on such a rickety staircase, without holding on to anything. I want to dissect it, which is a bit of what Duchamp was after—conveying motion in a static, painted image during cinema's infancy—except I'm searching for instruction in weight distribution and balance. In where one arm goes when the opposite leg moves. In how to do it without bracing, without thought, without fear.

But then I get confused in the blur of her. At some point her upper torso becomes a golden, shining, eyeless horse head, leaning over the lowest figure's shoulder, and I can't unsee it. She is human and animal at once. And all of a sudden, the entire scenario is knocked off balance, too much horsey weight pressed upon her shoulder—the way I've known foals to do, not knowing their own strength. (How many horses' jaws have pressed down upon my own shoulders, claiming, pushing?) The horse-head part of her could knock them all down.

When I revisited the painting on the Internet, my search also produced various homages to Duchamp—C-3PO from *Star Wars*, Bender from *Futurama*, and Superman, all descending in the same manner as the original—as well as a photograph of a silver-haired, smiling woman on a staircase. The woman looks down the stairs as her shadow rises behind her, stark against the wall. The shot reminded me of cinemascope films from the 1950s—Hitchcock came to mind, as did staircase sequences in two Nicholas Ray films, *Rebel Without a Cause* and *Bigger Than Life*.

The woman is, as it turns out, seated. She is modeling the Picasso stair lift, manufactured by HandiCare Stairlifts in the United Kingdom. As she descends, I imagine her gliding, the machinery conveying her safely from floor to floor. Shadows of the banister rails rise like prison bars across her lower body. The metaphor's no doubt unintentional. The woman, like Duchamp's figure, defies it; she needs no banister at all. Her body changes shape, molds into the chair on a track. I find myself between these two bodies—chairless, trackless, but unsturdily small-footed and weak-limbed. Not cut out for this sort of thing unless I change shape, redistribute myself into parts.

DECLINE

"We really don't want to be on a downward path, do we," my husband, Ian, said after I asked if I should call the neurologist about my latest multiple sclerosis relapse. I'd already dusted off my canes, ready for that third leg—wooden, Lucite, or carbon fiber—to extend from my right hand and unstagger me. "Calling the neurologist" is our shorthand for getting put on IV steroids to nip the flare-up in the bud, before more damage occurs in the brain, spine. Too often, I'd delay that call to the doctor, thinking the episode would resolve itself on its own. By the time I called, the steroids would be of little use, the damage already done. And damage has been occurring more often than before, so flare-ups have felt less like a rarity, more like the norm, the distinction between them more osmotic than fixed.

I suspect we've been on a downward path for quite some time, like those roads that seem level until fatigue sets in and you realize it's been an uphill climb all along. But how do you know, traversing a slight downward slope, that you're slowly sinking? When you look up, or look behind you to see each horizon, hold your hand level before your eyes? But what if that's tilted too?

Apparently, 90 percent of people living with relapsing-remitting multiple sclerosis experience progression within the first twenty-five years. And I'm past that. What I can't quite work out is whether there is an automatic shift in category, maybe a new sash presented to signify your place as "secondary progressive." Those who can, take a bow. Those who are unsure, remain seated. I raise my hand, ask if I am now progressing.

"Depends on how you define progression," says the neurologist. How you define decline?

✳

If I have just crested a hill like the one I took so often back home in California, heart pounding, lungs swooshing so fast the air cuts in my throat, and if I have done so in long strides (a condition often unavailable to my body now, but once my pace of choice), lowering my eyes down the hill's opposite side will come as relief: it's all downhill from here. If I am on my way home, dog panting beside me as I walk, the comfort of descent is all the greater: we are nearly there.

If, however, I begin my excursion at the top of a hill and head down a long, possibly uneven surface, "all downhill from here" means something else entirely: there is a lack of control, an uncertainty, like entering the dark wood in a fairy story. The fully functioning body leans differently, as if repelled from gravity's pull. Still, the foot may occasionally pause—itself uncertain of the ground—before the heel plants and the toes automatically follow.

There are no hills where I live in Texas. The hills I know reside in the memory of my cells, passed down from one cell to another, like stories. Some found their way into my legs, from horseflesh and hoof, long ago. Horsehair lining my calves offered proof.

If I say things are going downhill, it's clear that the grade of my descent, metaphorical or actual, is fraught, steep, confusing. I may place each foot lower and lower in succession, but the feet might not plant themselves where my mind plans. They might, for instance, hover and step wide, too close or too far, or I might feel as though the ground is nearer than it actually is. I might stumble, each foot separately questioning the ground in a different language, not hearing the other foot drop. The toe might drop first, forgetting that's the heel's job. Going downhill is an unstable act of speculation.

I can find hills in this city if I try. The floor in this house where I write—its terrain of uneven floorboards and swaying carpet—is the most complex topography for miles. My body knows it by heart and yields here, braces there, although someday it may forget entirely, or the floor may bottom out. The bathtub, with its deep valley, slippery, flooded floor, and rims sometimes missed by the foot so I'm pawing at air, is another matter.

Mine are educated feet; mine are Ivy League legs—over and over they learn (or, more accurately, my central nervous system learns) what walking is like, how it works. They graduate from physical therapy only to forget everything they've learned a few months later. "How did that story go?" my neurons ask the muscles. "What about that part when you go—what is it called? Downhill? Decent? Descent?"

"I think I missed that part," each muscle cell responds.

"Ask the eyes," one of them says.

The eyes keep their secrets.

WANDERING

The final days of Edgar Degas are often characterized with the words "blind," "nearly blind," or "wandering the streets of Paris." Some argue about the distinctions between blindness and near blindness, and I wonder what they must think blindness is: when the lights go out, or in Degas's case (and, for a time, mine) when they are too bright to see, to open one's eye. His spectacles helped shield his right eye from painful glare, and by his forties he had lost the central part of his vision, so that the subject he was painting would need to be seen around, rather than directly. It would not seem incongruous for Degas to wander the streets of Paris in his later years; if the eye could be trusted only through wandering, so it must be for the feet as well.

I once took part in an imaging study trying to establish new ways to map the brain's cerebral cortex. That outer layer of brain tissue is unclear on MRI, the imaging technique that scans the brain in monochrome, breaking it down into a series of thinly sliced wholes, pushing layer by layer from the top down, back to front, and in profile, ear to ear. The MRI prefers the direct approach, looking into the center of things, smearing the nuances of the periphery. Contrast between lesions in the cortex's gray matter, the home of certain cognitive processes, and those in the brain's inner white matter, the home of everything else, is low, the study indicated, on MRI. To map the scarred brain's topography, wandering is required.

Researchers laid me down on a table and moved my hair out of the way. One looked at a screen while the other scribbled—yes, scribbled—all over my head with an instrument that felt like a pen. Periodically, the researcher monitoring the screen's 3D image of my brain would tell the one scrawling over my cranium that he'd missed a spot, or that something needed to be filled in; there were holes. So he would literally retrace, returning to areas of my head that he'd visited before, filling in gaps with his roaming scribbles, the instrument's pattern inscrutable to me but capturing a sharper image of my gray matter—my conscious, working mind—than ever had been previously seen, than I will ever see. The contrast between the brain's thinking outline and its interior was something they kept for the study and never shared with me. They did not steal my thoughts, though. They paid me.

The most common misspelling of wonder is wander, and vice versa. It's been one of my pet peeves in student papers, but now I see it a little differently. When my pace is slowed and I drag my leg, I become far more absorbed in my surroundings, in the wonder of sap droplets on a tree, of ants moving through a fissure in the tree's bark. At such times I usually seek out the least difficult, most direct path—but my mind wanders, wonders. It has time to. I must believe there is some sense in the error, that through uncertain wandering there comes a kind of clarity.

VERTIGINOUS PATTERNS

The layout of an opulent art deco Chicago hotel, which housed a big writing conference I was attending, twisted into a maze of hallways and staircases, short and long, many of which had no elevator. A new flare-up hit the evening I arrived. I had been walking well for a while and had decided not to bring a cane, so for the next few days I staggered through peacock-themed, lushly patterned hallways, choosing whether to take the stairs or the open, temporary metal elevator by estimating the amount of steps and energy it would take to go one way or another. When I couldn't see the elevator I took the stairs, which was most of the time. People passed, not needing the stair rail, hurried marvels of balance and strength. The interior managed to confound my stride to the point that the vined and peacock-feathered pattern of the carpeted stairs twisted all the more. I couldn't tell where one stair ended and the other began, or how far down it was. My feet sometimes tipped in their boots—or hovered, waiting for the floor to rise. I braced myself on the brass railing, then slowly lowered my body until the stair's spongy surface welcomed (slightly) my foot. And the next, again and again.

On ramps, stairs, on an unfamiliar texture, such as the studded curb meant to inform blind people of the street's proximity, my feet are known to swim, even in their shoes, suddenly strangers. And it's not necessarily my feet's fault. They're not lazy, just forgetful, unable to communicate. In turn, my brain cannot discern the most polite way to tell the feet where they are and where to go. Or perhaps the brain has forgotten the password to unlock each foot's motion, which now I imagine as sparkling and jewel-encrusted, precious, inaccessible, nearly glowing from its own light source.

When I say the brain might have forgotten the password, what I mean is the neural pathways have been interrupted and traffic has slowed between brain and foot, or spine and foot. I do not mean that the conscious mind has forgotten how to move the foot, although the longer my motor function is impaired by MS, the more foreign the idea of an even stride. *How do they do that?* I ask myself, startled as a crowd of people pass me in a hall, all dart and hurtle and assured spur.

SCENE FROM THE STEEPLECHASE: THE FALLEN JOCKEY

He lies beneath the horse, the man in the pink silk shirt, his softly bearded face angelically rendered by the artist. The light on that face is warmed with a glow so otherworldly that he couldn't possibly be directly beneath his charging steed, where he would no doubt be engulfed in shadow. His helmet lies open beside his head, useless, white silk lining reflecting—what light? It seems as though he exists on a different plane than the rest of the painting. Perhaps he does, concussed, in danger, possibly dead or maybe just sleeping. They have cleared a hedge, the horse midair, in the process of landing. The rider has fallen, no struggle upon his placid, detailed face, no blood.

Two of the horses in this large and imposing painting by Edgar Degas have lost their riders. Or are the two horses actually the same horse in motion, the nude descending a staircase parceled out into two beasts? And that blur of tail above the higher horse's tail, yet a third—everything coming down, one horse in each stage of descent, or many. They continue to run. All motion, nearly animated by a series of loose, bold outlines and broad strokes, the horses are dashing out of the picture, while this man, said to be Degas's younger brother Achille, will remain, a finely wrought inert figure amid the landscape's wash of green.

"He looks like he's *dreaming* the horses," Ian whispers, so patient in the museum as I am again called back to the painting and stand before it for what must be the third time. I dream horses often, the ones I know have died or have been sold, horses that for years I fed, trained, rode, and nursed through their injuries—favorites. They return to me in sleep, where I no longer ride but walk as an equal beside them, lean against a shoulder, blow greetings into their nostrils. I can imagine them running through the dark above my bed, the gray one luminous, the two sorrels flashing copper.

Horses are said to avoid trampling their riders at all costs, yet in the painting it appears that the angelic head of Achille Degas will soon be knocked by a rear hoof. The animal engine rushes forward, past this still moment.

I have been stepped on only twice by horses: once, leading a troubled horse across a muddy natural spring on a trail ride with my mother, whose level-headed horse did not balk an ounce when we passed over it on our way out. My mare, next in line, was frightened. I got off, but she refused to be led through, so I climbed the side of a hill to lead her around the mud, and she rushed past me to catch up to her stablemate. I maintained my hold but was nearly slammed into the hillside. On the way back, I led her to the spot first so she wouldn't feel the urge to catch up and might walk calmly through the mud. My mother waited behind. I stepped in. The mud pulled my leg down deep. Rein in hand, I called the mare, still hoping she'd walk through. From behind me, she made a huge standing leap over the spring, passing me, and pulled me out, launching me onto the dry trail, where I lay belly-up like the jockey in the painting, watching while the mare danced and fretted, as skittish horses do, around my body, hooves everywhere. She gingerly stepped once on my stomach, ripping my shirt. Then she galloped up the trail a few paces, grazed and waited.

The second time I was trampled was after a jump, as Degas depicts, although more artificial and confined. The horse I was riding heaved her abdomen sideways into the jump's right vertical post. My stirrup knocked it, and the whole jump tumbled after us. I fell with it, A hoof grazed my ankle—no huge injury, just bewilderment. I imagine the horse was tottering, needed a step to regain balance, and I was in the way. I know now the necessity of that extra, stabilizing step. She may have otherwise fallen, too, on me.

Horseless now, I often tilt sideways without planning. Sometimes it's the only way to stay upright.

For both horse and rider, a fall simultaneously disorients and liberates. Among equestrians, falls signal experience, grit, hard work, and commitment—bragging rights—not only because they reflect more demanding and rigorous training, teaching a rider how to react and improve, but also because after every one, the rider must dust herself off and get back on the horse. Unless, as is probably the case with our fallen jockey in the painting, the rider is too injured or concussed to remount the horse just yet.

Falls happen quickly, but certain images or sensations in their whirl are indelibly etched in memory, stopping time. In what other context are we hurtled unknowingly into the air, turning? From beneath the horse's stomach, the rider might catch glimpses of angles never before seen: the ovoid shape of the horse's abdomen, the dark wrinkle of sheath or teats, the legs and hooves a maze of odd angles, and then gone to sky. In Degas's painting Achille's legs are still in the position of riding, knees out, heels spurring only a blade of grass.

Now, though, my attention drifts to the horse. It is easy to recognize the freedom the animal feels without a rider's weight, but harder to know how directionless the horse might feel without it. Degas returned to this painting at least three times over a span of nearly forty years, making changes here and there, getting the anatomy just right. You can see his meticulous attention: between the front legs of Achille's horse hangs a shadow of the foremost leg, the artist's way of correcting a less dynamic, heavier stride in the original painting.

The shadow leg—that's my leg. That's my movement: blurred, dark mistake. A correction made to look intentional.

Surprising I find it here in painted shade. In animated mistake and the vigor of correction. But didn't my stride glow with its own light, my foot's wavering motion? Maybe it fits in the jockey's brightly lined helmet. Or better, my movement is the bewildering pace of four legs—five, including the shadow leg—floating and rushing over a motionless, supine human form.

As confusing as movement can sometimes be for me, or rather for my legs and feet, or rather for my brain and spine's scarred axons, what I find so compelling in the painting is that even in a state of physical certainty—the athletic jockey, the galloping horse—the world can turn upside down, and the body is suddenly unfamiliar. In that way I don't need to enter the painting. It is already in me.

BIRTH

When a horse is born—and I have been lucky to be present at several foalings, have felt one wet, black foal slip into my lap, have lifted the placenta from the colt's frantic, gasping nostrils—its hooves are not yet hardened, having spared the mother the pain and rupture of that kind of merciless kicking in utero. The hooves at first resemble fingers or tentacles that glisten at the end of each leg. I remember each one moving aimlessly in the air, feeling the dry air change them before they turned to stone. Remarkable that within two hours the foal will rise and stand, wobbly and new. The next day it will spring from one end of the paddock to the other.

Like those newborn tentacles that harden to hooves, my feet sometimes search in air for their shape. Like the foal but much older, I am repeatedly born anew, find my feet and learn again to walk, but it takes far longer, and my feet feel the beckon of an old tentacle from time to time.

TODDLER

"And so walking begins as delayed falling," writes Rebecca Solnit, observing the first steps of toddlers. Forward motion, propulsion, is all that stabilizes us when first we try to walk, hurling our little bodies from one point to the next. Remarkable to think of our first bipedal accomplishments as delay, but it's true: we delay the inevitable through constant motion. Arms outstretched, bowlegged babies, we stagger against topple, against stillness. And so it has seemed, each time I've learned to walk again. Once the wires between brain and leg fray, the rest of the body attempts to make up for it: the abdominals pull the knee as though connected through a taut pulley system. The arms stretch, the stance widens. Compensations are made without conscious control. I toddle. I sway. I reach for walls, for edges. My arms keep me vertical.

"Laurie, why do you have your arms up by your shoulders like that? And your legs are so wide apart. I mean, it's like you're a toddler learning to walk for the first time," said one physical therapist, suppressing her laughter. "I mean, that's really how toddlers walk!"

I can't remember whether she imitated my gait or not. Her level of surprise indicated that she had only just arrived at the idea that young adults may occasionally drift into zones of necessity when their bodies stop moving as designed, widening their stances to survive, hands up for balance—because the world at times is a wavering tightrope. Though her words stung, I thought about the months leading up to this moment—my prolonged acceptance of my slowed stride as a sign of disease progression, against the glimmer of a chance that I could indeed learn again to walk here, at this world-renowned center. So I acted as though I was in on the joke.

"Exactly," I said. Because learning to walk was precisely why I was there. Didn't she know that?

I was walking for her without my cane, equal parts sideways and forward motion, inching my way along the hallway that surrounded the main therapy room. She left for a moment and returned with two long wooden dowels—the size of thick broom handles—which she inserted into my hands. We then began slowly, methodically walking, the physical therapist behind me, holding the dowels' ends, pushing them forward and back as she swung her arms, which in turn swung my arms, like an old-fashioned toy train with its long bars alongside the wheels, keeping everything moving forward together. It felt so unnatural. Over time, it began to feel more natural, but the timing between arms and legs can astonish and perplex me to this day.

I was reluctant to come to my next visit, but thankfully, I was passed to another physical therapist, Meg, who stuck with me until I graduated. In place of wooden dowels, she handed me weighted balls to swing with my stride, and she walked beside me, coaching and praising. Mostly, we focused on strengthening my core—abdominals, hips, and buttocks—to help me remain upright without tipping. Each step powers you forward, but it also opens a hovering moment when you are standing on one leg without anything to hold onto, ready to tip, unless your hip can hold you, or your side can still your sway.

One session, I spotted a short wooden stairway nearby that we'd never used. Even though my house has about four steps between the porch and the ground, stairs were something I wasn't "ready for" yet. Pointing to the staircase prop, I said, "So strange—going downstairs has become harder for me than going up."

"That's because it *is* harder," she said. "Going downhill or down stairs is a form of controlled falling."

The idea seemed so counterintuitive; for most of my life with MS, I'd look up a flight of stairs with dread, gauging whether each climb was worth the energy. I yanked myself up staircases, assimilating the railing as part of the machinery of my body, buildings and their towers quite literally incorporated into my propulsion, their very inaccessibility transforming them from their original concrete, wood, plaster, or brick into fleshy components of my ratcheting motion, my hand gripping higher up the rail every few steps, the banister blooming an extension of my arm, all climbing, all huff and puff. Going back down was usually the reward. How had it become so disorienting? Downstairs, downhill, down, down, down, now an entirely different story. Controlled falling, without much control.

"For you," Meg added, "the falling is all around you." Which is actually how it felt. Anything carried the potential to set me off balance, tip me. Over time, the idea took on new meaning. As my ability to walk without assistance strengthened, that falling all around me became more and more pronounced. Impaired proprioception—I'd experienced it before, but never in such immediate flurry. My perception of my entire body's position within the blur and hum surrounding me, where the "me" began and the cushion of space around me ended, disintegrated. People and objects—walls, even—would all of a sudden enter my frame of vision, my space, uncomfortably close. In a grocery store I would—and sometimes still do—cling to a rack of shelves, my husband running interference, blocking any stimulus hurtling toward me.

As my motion gained speed, so did the world. To address this, Meg found a small, slightly shriveled yellow balloon, and from a couple paces behind me she threw it into my space as we moved down the hall. Once it passed my ear I threw it back, all the while keeping my eyes ahead. How can I convey the sense of this most difficult game of catch, except to say that the falling was all around? Around each corner, therapists rushing, patients trying a new prosthetic or brace, and this sudden yellow, which grew less sudden over time.

The falling is still everywhere and a constant possibility. In a crowd. In an unfamiliar room. In a hall. In shoes. On a grassy surface. A ramp. Stairs, of course. Thresholds. In a grocery store aisle. Before paying attention to anything else when I traverse a space, I try to scope out what I can hold on to, what I can grip or lean against should I lose balance. Always a step ahead when I'm actually many steps behind, looking for corners and railings. Wallflower.

With my feet wide apart and my hands in the air clutching at an invisible safety net, balancing the way toddlers do, I'm bound to catch up eventually, I tell myself. Until I learn otherwise. Again.

All is downhill from here. I try to control the falling.

If the falling is indeed all around me, and if going downhill or down stairs is a form of controlled falling, could every surface be essentially a hill flattened, no distinction between crest and valley? Falling, their constant potential? The ease or instability of decline, the exhausting, steep climb upward, the steps across a room, or the controlled fall into the unknown, all one?

SURFACES

When I was a Girl Scout, my troop camped once at Newport Dunes, a sandy campground surrounding a small, tideless Pacific lagoon. I loved water, and although we lived steps away from that same ocean, I yearned for a certain stillness in water, just wading out into it and beginning to swim, rather than diving beneath wave after wave before reaching calmer seas. So the first thing I did after setting up my tent was to step into the lagoon, each step a little deeper but not deep enough to swim yet. Then the wet ground suddenly moved beneath me. Stunned, I flinched my knee up. I took another step. The seabed shifted. It oozed and slid, too slippery, no grain to it, slimy mounds everywhere. This tranquil lagoon was actually teeming with motion underfoot. I ran out of that water as quick as I could.

But not before catching a glimpse clear through to the seabed: giant, disk-shaped, speckled sea slugs populated the lagoon floor, and I was walking on their backs. No wonder they were moving. I had invaded their territory, unwittingly stepping on their bodies because there was nothing else to stand on. How was I to know then that the ground beneath me could change so quickly, or that years later it would do so over and over on dry land, to such a degree that although I could not see any difference in a floor's surface, could not run away from it or point to it, the substance of ground beneath me could be altered by my own body's faulty wiring and shifting sense of touch and stability, the perceived changing surface underfoot dependent more upon time's returning relapses than on the physical substance I stand on?

DECLENSION

Time declines all, they say. Progression inevitable, they say. Hills that rise slant down. You have the floor, they say. How far down, I say. They say how low can you go. How steep a slope, I say. Slight drop, they say. Plateau. Slump, not flatline, they say. *You understand, these were words before: up, down,* I say, words I do not own but feel I should. Downward, they say, is normal, but plateau is where we'll put you. Stay flexible. Incline toward this wind. Go ahead and Zanaflex, they say. Progress, the way of the future, they say. We are inclined to say it's relatively stable. Mesa, not mountain, they say. *The fall-off hills rise in masses, flat on top. White clouds bite down on them like teeth,* I recall, chomping. What's the grade of incline, I say. They say mild decline. They say they feel inclined to know. Come down here, I say. Take a tumble. Slide. Incline your ear. They decline my invitation. Making progress, they say. An upgrade. Very busy. *Your health has reached its quota and is no longer available,* they say. Have I been downgraded, essentially going downhill, I say. A positive result yields a negative outcome, they say. They decline to know for sure. Testing negative, they say, has a positive outcome. A decline in contrast sensitivity, I say. They say slow descent, the good kind. A little tip. Lucky dip. I assent and say all's downhill from here. I say downhill into the flood. Dive, I say, not cannonball. Controlled fall. I am inclined to take a dip, I say, from time to time, but always rise to the surface. Dip down, they say. Tip forward. Don't let us (drop now) push you, they say, a nudge. I say it is our policy to decline tips, a pleasure to—Arching off the incline, I incline to a different wind.

*

FIRST LESSONS: LEANING

When you ride a horse up a hill, you lean into the hill. The steeper the hill, the steeper your lean, your hands giving the rein to the horse, your shoulders hovering above the neck, until you are rising fully out of the saddle and into air, the animal beneath you all sweat and snort and heave; by rising, you lighten its load.

When you ride down a hill, however, you lean against the incline. You contradict it. The steeper your descent, the steeper your lean back, as though you've lost part of yourself behind you. You sit deep and become heavy. Rather than driving the horse into the dirt, your lean lifts pressure from its front legs and distributes the effort back to its powerful haunches. The horse's motion becomes more controlled.

To lean into a hill, you relinquish control to the air and the hooves conveying you. To lean against the hill, you gather all the control you can muster and do the impossible: lift the front end of a horse.

If I've learned anything from these elementary lessons so deeply ingrained in my body's memory, I hope it is this: when anything starts going downhill, lean against it, counter its weight, look up, and raise the world sinking before you.

Or at the very least this: whether walking downstairs or down a hill, lean back against it to keep yourself from falling. Your action must counter the slope, if at all possible.

FALLING ACTION

The slope changes without notice. My father-in-law, who'd always outpaced me (even when he started using a cane) during our visits on England's Isle of Sheppey, began falling in his mid-seventies, a dozen years after I met him. He was bewildered more than anyone, could never explain how it happened. He fell about once a month at first. Then once a week, multiple times in a day, until mentions of the falls grew more incidental because of their frequency. His doctors called it "normal aging" when tests results were inconclusive. It must be normal, this steep decline, this falling into age, going downhill.

The family bought him a rollator, an advanced form of what Americans call a walker and British people call a Zimmer frame. We all thought it would offer him stability. Eager to give it a spin, he stepped out alone with it one day, turning down the main road's sidewalk. The road seems flat there but it has a slight downhill grade, the kind you barely notice, the kind that makes you feel stronger because the distance traveled requires so little effort.

He leaned into the hill's downward lightness, gaining speed, perched like a jockey on the rollator's handles, feeling once again the wind generated by his own motion blowing cool against his face. Liberated, he released all of his weight to the miraculous aluminum tubes and wheels supporting him, this new, lean, wheeled extension of his body.

He lost control. The rollator flew out from his hands. He tipped. A passerby found my father-in-law crumpled in the gutter. The road is narrow there, so this person certainly saved his life. Sometimes I imagine the stranger as a truck driver who stops his rig, leaves the door open, its chime merging with the calls of wood doves and blackbirds as he blocks traffic; sometimes it's a blonde with curious children in her car; sometimes an old woman sitting at the bus stop, kerchief over her curlers. Someone called the paramedics who lifted him into the ambulance and drove him home, where his wife was ironing, unaware that anything had happened until the colored lights flashed against her house.

Hearing about the fall from a continent and ocean away, my shoulders shifted back instinctively, as though I was riding a horse downhill, trying to lift its front end from gravity's pull, trying to lift a man from a downward path, his shoulder bending to the wind. It turned out that his body was becoming more forgetful than mine.

Months later, I sat with him one afternoon at their dining table. We talked about what it's like to lose power, to release the body's past strengths and mourn their absence. I was glad he brought it up, because he didn't talk much about such matters with the rest of the family, and it felt awkward to push for more. He had fallen many more times by then. His geography, his radius for living, had narrowed: this recliner, these rooms, that room with assistance only, the garden if supervised, never alone on the stairs. Who could catch him if he fell?

In a year my father-in-law would rise from this table where we'd talked together, fall and hit his head on the radiator, be placed in hospital for weeks, get shifted from one hospital to another, and lose the ability to stand altogether, never to return home again. Nowadays, when I sit at that table, the radiator's warmth rising up my back, I imagine what that fall was like, and I remember the time we sat alone there together as I listened to his vulnerable observations of his new, mysterious physical limitations. He felt responsible for and ashamed of his inactivity, as though exercise could have maintained his strength.

Our conversation trailed to silence. He watched his wife outside the window, her lithe, energetic body stretching up and up, hanging laundry on the clothesline with colorful pegs. "That is one amazing woman," he said, as though her devotion and energy had just struck him, as though the very notion of easy movement was already becoming a source of wonder. Down she bent to her basket, up she reached again.

DISTRACTION

One horse I trained and loved, the sorrel who was later sent to slaughter without my knowledge, feared the shadowy, murky base of certain hills. Instead of moving forward, he would often reverse at high speed, legs all a tangle. This once resulted in the two of us backing into the street at rush hour—me raising my hand apologetically, hoping we wouldn't get hit, his irregular hoof beats striking the pavement, both hearts racing—simply because the horse would not descend the trail's slope. If there was mud, all the worse. His refusal to walk down a particular hill sent the two of us through a neighbor's fence once. His fear of that hill knocked me unconscious.

The base of a hill is dark and mysterious to horses, quite possibly a jagged chunk removed from the earth, a hole a horse could tumble right through, its descent a fearsome flight. Or maybe, after a rain, the puddles at the bottom of a hill become shimmering broken windows to drop into, the many hoof prints sloshed through the mud evidence of other horses' falls, their hooves swallowed up in unstable ground. Or maybe we fade to nothingness at the end of the slope. The longer I worked with this horse the more accepting—but still wary—of going downhill he grew, perhaps trusting me a little more, and the better prepared I became as we approached.

I understand his fear now, facing decline. I must be prepared, gather up my reins.

Depending upon the circumstance and slope, I chose one or more of the following strategies to move this horse downhill:

1. Stop and watch, gently coaxing with my spur, giving him the rein;

2. Sing to him, "Both Sides Now" a particular favorite that set his ears twitching;

3. Turn the horse around to reverse down the hill, a frightening experience but one that distracts the horse from his source of fear until we've passed it;

4. Slow his stride and turn his head—again, distraction;

5. If all else fails, dismount and lead him down through it.

Beginning our descent down a long, steep, usually contentious, shady path, I noticed a family of skunks waddling down a few paces in front of us. I chose option four. He remained calm, didn't see the skunks. No black and white tail raised in alarm.

Once, riding him home from a show, descending a hill that usually coiled this horse's stride and raised his fears, I noticed a foal running in a paddock next to the path. I sat back, all of my weight leaning against the hill, preparing for the worst. The foal was young, probably a week old or less, frantic. I turned my horse's head away from the spectacle. Somehow I remember the foal wailing, but if it did, my horse would have surely balked. Or maybe not. He sometimes surprised me with his calm when the stakes were high. Although my left rein insured that he couldn't see the foal, I had to look, quick, sidelong glances: the foal's mother lay on her side, legs outstretched, stiff, and raised above the ground a couple inches. She was entirely motionless, most likely dead. Unaware of the hill's real drama, my horse calmly carried my backward-leaning body down the narrow path.

Which would you choose when facing a downward slope: to turn away or to face what lies ahead? To be surprised or to be prepared? Could one ever be fully prepared? Can the grade of descent be measured? What if it's terraced? What if you can't tell the difference? When I was small I loved ladders, climbing the vertical one that led to my brother's attic room when he wasn't home, my hands each grasping the smooth, polished wooden rungs all the way to the top and back down, like crawling, only up, higher than anyone in the house. The ladder to my attic today folds out at an angle, with rails on either side closer to the top. I've stopped going up there, not because of the climb up, but because of the climb down, not knowing where my feet will land when the eyes can't see what's below. Each foot unwittingly dangles, trembling, waiting—hoping—to hit a rung. Unsure, unaware, I'm all the more frightened of the drop.

I'm tempted to say this: the difference between "going downhill" and "all downhill from here" does not lie in one's perspective on decline, awareness fueling fear versus distraction breeding ignorance breeding its own fear. "All downhill from here" nestles in the curled embrace of "going downhill." Both lead to the same destination. What the ground there feels like, or how long it will take to get there, is another matter.

TIME

When I began writing this essay, an MS relapse had weakened the arm and leg on my left side. I hadn't been able to type for months; the left hand could barely press the keys. Not being able to walk evenly was something I could handle. Not being able to write was another matter. When I finally sought physical therapy, I was more motivated to get back to writing than to walk.

At some point I realized that I could write by hand, because, hello, I'm right handed. I could at least write a rough draft. Ultimately, this essay began in red ink scrawled across smooth, wide pages in my notebook, arrows emerging from one page to another, words and sentences crossed out, sentences trailing off to nowhere. Coming back to it was like entering a maze.

In between the red-inked beginnings and now, my steps have slowed at least twice a year for no less than one month each time. I wrote some of this when the prospect of going shopping in a single grocery store was daunting. I wrote some of it while I was capable of walking two miles. Like an actor, I had to get back into the character that was me, as though my body was an old costume—method acting through memory, only it's not an act. Today my body hobbles once again and has done so for over a week. Tomorrow it may change again.

When I began writing this, my father-in-law had fallen about a dozen times. He could still stand up. The cause for his falls had been neither diagnosed nor treated. As I write now, he has been gone from this world for four months and twelve days. This occurred after a couple of years when he was unable to walk at all, one year unable to sign his name, and months attempting to speak and hopefully be understood. Progressive supranuclear palsy (PSP), a rare, progressive neurological condition, was diagnosed a little over a year before it took him. The passage of time burns deep, especially when I—from my seemingly eternal returns of movement and loss, those slowly deepening hills and valleys—stop and behold the entire disease process, of a degenerative neurological illness so similar and yet so different from my own, go from its late diagnosis to death in less than two years.

I'm still on the same chapter.

MEET ME TONIGHT IN ATLANTIC CITY

Jane Wong

L et's begin here: on the sand. Or, rather, on the slabs of wood above the sand. On June 26, 1870, the Atlantic City boardwalk opened to the public. Sixteen years earlier, the first tourist train had arrived on the newly minted Camden and Atlantic Railroad. Tourists came to stick their toes in the Atlantic—steel blue, the color of whales they'd never see. They came to lean against each other in the high dunes and make promises they couldn't keep. They let the wind lift those promises up, to be caught in the chandeliers of expensive hotels or the beaks of passing seagulls. The women who came held frilled umbrellas—jellyfish along the shore. And when they returned to their jobs and errands and thumb-sucking babies, they carried sand with them, making the train car a beach in and of itself. Glitter of the sea. This is how the boardwalk came to be:

a fed-up railroad conductor and simply too much sand for his own sweeping sanity.

Just to be clear: this is not our story. Not yet. Our story moves across that steel blue world, from another continent, from a place where there is no such thing as "vacation." My ancestors would repeat that word, 假期, as if it were a cloud and could disappear at any point. On this continent, there are herds of oxen and lily pads the size of unkeepable promises. As a small child in central New Jersey, I dreamt of this story. Of oxen, my mother riding the back of one, the hair on its hide so coarse, it makes your throat hurt. Our story, our history, holds a different version of Atlantic City.

In 1988, my mother was still dreaming in Cantonese—not a single word of English wormed its way through her open-mouthed sleep. My brother Steven had just been born, howling like a wolf who knew he was a boy. Four years earlier, when the nurses placed me in my mother's arms, my mother says I stared at her silently. She held me up to the fluorescent light and declared: "I'm afraid. She knows too much." By 1988, my father had been holding mahjong gambling circles for five years, in the basement of my grandparents' apartment in Matawan and then in our house in Tinton Falls, where my parents had settled that year. Cigarette smoke escaped like doves from underneath the floorboards. And the shuffling. The shuffling sound of mahjong tiles, a porcelain earthquake. I learned later that these tiles used to be made out of bone, backed by bamboo. Now: Bakelite, plastic. My father always invited the same people to play: Uncle Jimmy, the Chicken Bone Man, and Balding Uncle.

Just to be clear again: our story is not about small enterprises. Our story goes beyond the little batons of twenty-dollar bills, passed around the mahjong table. Beyond the table's green felt, stained with cheap Tsingtao and sky-high piles of gnawed bones from the Chicken Bone Man's eponymous pastime.

Our story is Atlantic City. We are talking Taj Mahal, Caesar's Palace, Bally. Casinos depicting worlds my father couldn't fathom, but kept returning to, like a moth drawn to a blinding bulb. At Caesar's Palace, there were towering white columns so extravagant, they held up nothing at all. There were white statues of horses braying, a ceiling painted like the sky with white clouds, the busts of white people we assumed were famous but were really just white. My parents didn't even know where Rome was on a map, or that Rome existed. But Caesar's Palace was irresistible in its whiteness. Who could say no to the patina of wealth? This is how we arrived: on that Chinese tourist bus where you have to fan yourself with your ten-dollar gambling voucher and put your cigarette out in a Dixie cup. Or, if you hit it big like we once did, you can arrive in the dolphin-colored leather of your BMW, before you inevitably crash it into the Parkway median. No air conditioning and the windows down, to save on gas mileage, of course. We arrived over a century after those first tourists, to a boardwalk full of nonwhite faces. Shoulder pads, pinstriped suits, and an amalgamation of languages punctuating the salty air. The poor, the working class, the hopeful, in red-tag sequin dresses from Marshalls. Here we are! Yes, here, with self-serve wine and crab legs at the Palace Buffet—all of which we marveled at, but never touched.

THE BOARDWALK WAS STRICTLY a summer affair. In the 1870s, it was broken down for safekeeping during the winter. The boards stored like quilts packed in a trunk, like pickled radishes, like a family who won't look each other in the eye.

For repeat patrons—the ones who threw enough money away—casinos offered free hotel stays for the whole family. Each Christmas, Thanksgiving, Valentine's Day, Memorial Day, July 4, my father disappeared into the red velvet of spinning roulette tables. We made other plans. Steven and I tested the structural soundness of hotel beds by jumping on them. Once, a cockroach flew out of the mattress, disturbed in its sleep. "How is this fancy?" my mother moaned. She was used to crushing cockroaches, and punched its antennae lights out. K.O. Game over.

Steven and I traded the remote back and forth like a secret, marveling over the gluttony of cable television. We spent hours watching channels we didn't have: Nickelodeon, MTV, Disney. We made up a dirge for basic television and sang it over and over: *Rest in peace, you piece of shit.* Rest in peace, you piece of shit. In the afternoon, we walked the boardwalk back and forth with the other

Chinese American kids who were never allowed to play that wa-ter-gun race game, even though we knew there had to be a winner. No stuffed dinosaurs for us, no Dippin' Dots. The game operators, home from college and tipsy on Pabst, were always shouting at my mother, words she didn't understand. "Hey gorgeous, lemme get your number while the brats play!" and "I'd let you play for free any day, baby!" and "Hey pretty lady, you speakee any Englishee?" At twenty-six, my mother was all pink lipstick and confused by the attention, but knew to accept gifts from white people: an ice-cold Coke pressed against her cheek, a stuffed orca whale for Steven.

Here is one scene, on a shore of many: on the way back to Cae-sar's, my mother sits on a boardwalk bench, the dune grass behind her like the back of a throne. From her purse: bread rolls stolen from the Palace Buffet. She chews out all her anger on those rolls, on the gnarls in the crust. Soft middles demolished by her patent leather heels as they dig into boardwalk cracks. Seagulls swarm near her in full praise. Glitter of the boardwalk.

"I'm tired, Mommy," I whine, pulling on her earrings with my sandy hands. Next year, both her earlobes will split open from too-heavy earrings. The infections will heal and yield scars I will grow jealous of.

"Tell that to your father."

The sky is lavender and dragon fruit. Everywhere around us, people marvel at the swirling sunset and take pictures. Later, when I ask my mother for baby pictures of me, she'll tell me we were too poor to have a camera. She'll simply repeat: "I held you up. You didn't blink and you had the biggest eyes I've ever seen." *I'm afraid. She knows too much.*

I lean my head against her sharp shoulders, which will always vacillate between sharpening and softening. Steven joins the seagulls and starts eating breadcrumbs off the ground.

"What's it like in there? Where daddy goes?" I ask her.

My mother stares at my brother. He has my father's eyes—big and shining like a dying flashlight. He will grow to be as tall as my father: six feet, to be exact. He will be a handsome man and he won't know it. A man who has to shave every day. But at this moment, his tongue is speckled with sand and gluten. "Stop that right now," my mother screams at him. "Stop that, stop that!" Soon, Steven is wailing, and that unrelenting sound stops all my questions. Meanwhile, an off-duty clown strolls down the board-walk with his date for the night. She is holding one of his oversized juggling pins and laughing like something is stuck in her belly. The boardwalk shifts underneath our feet. Is winter coming? Yes, but not now: the woman's hair is coiled cotton candy. "Show me that new trick," she sings in the dwindling light.

I did not know, at that time, what my mother thought of At-lantic City. What she thought of that fake blue sky at Caesar's, of transparent lettuce with Russian dressing, of my father—a man she barely knew—throwing money on a table to prove his worth, to show he could do whatever he wanted. Not long ago, she'd been a farm girl, sucking on sugar cane after hiking up the mountains to gather wood for the stove. This was before she was arranged to marry my father at nineteen. My father: a tall stranger who moved to a country where a piece of plastic could buy a car. My mother would follow him soon after. Their names, because they are real: Jin Ai and Hung Foo.

Another scene, this one for Jin Ai but not for us: at 6 a.m., my mother wakes up in our comped room from a dream in a lan-guage she doesn't understand yet. *Hey gorgeous, hey pretty lady, my baby.* She walks past our sleeping forms—consumed in white down feathers—and puts on her heels. With purpose, she takes the elevator down to the first floor. She walks into that red velvet world and follows what her heart does not desire. My father is whiskey-eyed and half-asleep—hunched over the blackjack table like a drowsy raccoon. His shirt is unbuttoned one too many and his wallet is an open window. My mother clenches her fists and imagines raising them to the false sky above. Her eyes swirl like a crystal ball. No one will ever know if she's crying.

My father doesn't say her name or look up. "One more game."

Dozens of floors above, we are still dreaming. *K.O. K.O. K.O.*

REMEMBER: THIS STORY is not about small enterprises. This story expands like an oil spill; it touches the fins of every faraway shore. This is a story poor immigrants share, like those packed bunk beds shared with false uncles and aunts. We are targeted. This is no mistake. This can't be boiled down to "cultural proclivity for luck." Casino buses roll into Chinatowns across the country like ice-cream trucks for a reason.

Cache Creek Casino in Brooks, California, as John M. Glionna reports in a 2006 article for the *Los Angeles Times*, has a tank that holds a two-foot-long dragon fish named Mr. Lucky. Dragon fish have round scales like coins, and are purported to be worth upward of $300,000. The owners' apparent vision: Chinese gamblers rubbing the cool, blue tank with dollar signs in their eyes. Glionna quotes Wendy Waldorf, a spokesperson for the casino: "Asians are a huge market. We cater to them." According to NBC News, approximately thirty thousand Chinese gamblers take cheap buses from New York City's Chinatown to casinos in the surrounding tristate area, including Atlantic City. In 2011, a bus on a return trip from the Mohegan Sun in Connecticut crashed and killed fifteen passengers. After the accident, the *New York Times* reported, police officers who spoke Chinese visited the survivors to speak with them about the disaster. With mangled limbs and empty pockets, whose grandmother was lost, whose father?

In "How I Got That Name," poet Marilyn Chin writes of her own father's gambling addiction:

> While my father dithers,
> a tomcat in Hong Kong trash—
> a gambler, a petty thug,
> who bought a chain of chopsuey joints
> in Piss River, Oregon...

In a 2012 *MELUS* interview with Ken Weisner, Chin speaks about her "gambler bigamist father," about her siblings and the necessity of humor in her childhood home: "We had to laugh deep from our guts to keep from crying."

Across the country, mirroring Chin's Piss River, Portland, my father played all night in Atlantic City. He did not stop to eat or go to the bathroom or ask where his family was. My father owned a Chinese American take-out restaurant on the Jersey shore, and he'd disappear from work for days, sometimes a week. My mother ran the restaurant without him, her arms scraping the fryer, grime peeling like bark. Her anger: strips of wonton wrappers seething in the hot oil, slow and dangerous. She was a motionless alligator ready to strike. We avoided her gaze during those days. Years later, in 1997, the restaurant finally closed its doors. Eventually it would become Panda House, a new Chinese restaurant run by a new family that looked remarkably like mine.

As we drove home from Atlantic City together, my father would glow over his winnings. He'd flail an arm back in that poorly won BMW and toss a couple of twenty-dollar bills at us. "Liar," my mother would say, staring out the window. "You lost. You always lose." The new leather burned our thighs as we watched the Parkway smokestacks grow bigger and closer.

My father always lost in the end. We all lose in the end. The next year was when he rammed the BMW into a median on his midnight way to Atlantic City. What he would lose beyond money—his job, family, sobriety—would not be clear to him until much later. Perhaps it's still not clear to him; I wouldn't know. Underneath the boardwalk, there is so much rotting trash.

In his article "The Vulnerable Faces of Pathological Gambling," published in *Psychiatry* in 2005, psychiatrist Tim Fong takes a close look at gambling and its impact on communities of color. "Specific reasons for why certain minority groups are more vulnerable," he writes, "may be related to higher group gambling participation rates, location of gambling establishments (they tend to be in urban settings), and relationships to lower socioeconomic status." Fong homes in on immigration and gambling in particular. Requiring no English skills and offering the possibility of quick money, gambling has a problematic allure in new immigrant communities. It could seem like a source of confidence, of hope. Did my father hope for all of us, or just for himself? One truth: the sky was always blue at Caesar's. A director at the NICOS Chinese Health Coalition, Michael Liao explores the relationship between immigration, gambling, and social status. From his article "Asian Americans and Problem Gambling": "Studies have often pointed to decision-making opportunities as motivation for gambling—particularly among marginalized populations who feel a lack of control over their daily lives." My father could ask a blackjack dealer to hit him with another card. But he couldn't ask for a cup of hot water instead of ice water because he didn't have the language for it.

After we lost the restaurant, my father was unable to hold a steady job. He would spend a few days working for someone else as a cook, only to storm out shouting and throwing spatulas. His apron tossed in the trash, ties dangling in the wind like snakes. It was the same story at that factory job, that A&P job, that dim sum waiter job. "I'm the boss," my father would snarl beneath a plume of cigarette smoke. His brown leather jacket slumped around his shoulders as if he was unable to shed his own hide. I always found it funny that, below the brand name, his jacket's interior label read: I DON'T WANT TO GO TO WORK. And so he didn't. My father rarely spoke to us, even more rarely in English, and this is what we remember him saying the most. I'M THE BOSS. Translation: What can I hold on to?

Our shared story moves away from the past and closer to the present. In 2016, the Lucky Dragon Casino opened in Las Vegas, an "Asian themed" paradise of gambling. A 1.2 ton gilded dragon hangs from the ceiling, its scales glimmering. David Jacoby, the casino's chief operating officer, was clear when speaking to the *Los Angeles Times* about its target market: the larger Asian diaspora, particularly the Chinese. Modeled after street markets in China and Taiwan, the food court, Dragon's Alley, features a brick wall taken from an alleyway in Beijing. If you touch the wall, you could practically go home. "This place is heavily feng shui'ed," Jacoby told the *Times*. I haven't visited the Lucky Dragon or any of these new casinos—now that I can choose not to, I will never find myself in one again. Newspaper reports are as close as I need to get. But I know Jacoby is right: the kitchen is blessed in the sheen of the American dream. Cleansed in luck, in that steel blue water we all traversed.

MY MOTHER TRIED TO LEAVE many times. She woke up in the middle of the night and packed a suitcase, folding each dress like a present for no one in particular. Each time, she failed to get out the door. My brother wouldn't leave his dinosaur blanket behind and refused to pack it. I begged for us to go, to walk out into the blinding snow. I dreamt of the icicles stinging my cheeks: relief. By the door, my grandmother crumpled like a poorly made bed. If she had to endure her arranged marriage, why couldn't my mother?

It was my father who ended up leaving. That day was like any other ordinary day. I went to school, my mother slept since she worked night shift for the postal service, and there were lunches and leaves falling from trees and ants crawling through a maze in my brother's classroom. We got home and he was gone. Just like that. Breaking down the boardwalk for the season. Except this was a perpetual winter, and we were thankful for it. That week, my mother opened the windows of our house, to let the cigarette smoke out. To air out each promise, each day my father had disappeared in Atlantic City. She changed the locks. She surveyed the brilliant brass doorknobs in her hands and maybe she thought: *These would make beautiful earrings.* All three of us carried the dirty floral armchair replete with cigarette burns down to the basement, and shoved it into a corner we could all forget. Disappearance is a strange choice; I would grow to learn this as an adult, when a parade of men would suddenly leave me and each, then, try to reconnect. My father made one attempt, in the months that followed. He broke into the house through the basement window and left half a rotisserie chicken, a red packet with five dollars in it, and a note: HAPPY BIRTHDAY, JANE. My birthday had been months ago. I thought of the Chicken Bone Man as I tore the glistening skin from the leg; yes, I ate it. I was grateful, even for this. I wondered how my father, at six feet tall, had climbed into that tiny basement window. He must have finally transformed into a raccoon.

One summer when my father had taken us to Atlantic City, my mother bought us hermit crabs on the boardwalk. After trip after trip of no ice cream and no boardwalk games, which truly were a scam, this was a sign of utter generosity. We loved the crabs dearly. We kissed their shells and let them strut along the hotel room floor. In the morning, my father was passed out in bed, still in his cheap button-down shirt and too-big slacks. He had been gambling again all night. My brother and I watched, our hands over each other's mouths, as one of the hermit crabs crawled all over his back. Manifest destiny.

Decades later, when I asked my mother why she bought us those hermit crabs, she talked about waiting. "I remember standing outside of the gambling floor, watching you both run around. And I remember looking around me—at the other wives and husbands waiting with children. How I looked just like them. Tired. And thinking: Why? Why am I standing here?" She paused, removing the daggers from her eyes, thrown in the direction of my father. "I felt bad for you both. I bought you hermit crabs."

IN SEATTLE, WHERE I CURRENTLY LIVE, it's the Snoqualmie Casino. The casino buses are luxury coach, with toilets and air conditioning. They pick up patrons in the International District, right behind Uwajimaya. When I'm grocery shopping for anything that reminds me of home—persimmons, sour dried plums, Chinese pickled vegetables—I swear I see my father boarding that bus, loafers polished in kitchen grease. I take one step closer to see better, hugging my groceries to my chest. But then: another. He looks like my father too, leather jacket and all. In this misty city, it's hard to tell. They're all my father. Do I care if they are? Regardless, I wish they'd look at me. This is what I think, as these aging Asian gamblers take the vouchers from the casino bus driver and hold them tightly in their hands. *Do you see me?*

This is a story of lost enterprises. I was thirty-one when my grandmother passed away. She had dementia for years and only remembered two people toward the end of her life: my father and me. She'd repeat the same story about taking me to the swing set at a park. "Jane wouldn't get off the swings, not even when the sun went down." I imagine that when my father listened to that story, it was as if he were on that swing set, playing with his mother as a child. Underneath this story is my father's story: his love for his mother, the only person he never left. Layered on one another like mud, these stories of care and comfort overlap. When my father abandoned our family, he moved in with my grandmother and stayed with her for as long as he could. He peeled her grapes; he brushed her hair; he cupped her feet in his hands and clipped her toenails. When he was a child, my grandfather and my uncles left home and moved to Hong Kong; my grandmother raised Hung Foo back in the village, the baby of the family. When my grandmother died, I was visiting Shanghai to read from my first book of poems. As she was lowered into the dirt, 7,403 miles away in New Jersey, I was restless from jet lag and staying in a hotel that smelled like recycled air.

A couple of months later, when I returned to Jersey for the holidays, my father called my mother out of nowhere and asked if I was coming home. "I can't remember the last time he called. Something's not right," she said, half laughing, half suspicious. "He said he wanted to see you. I told him it was up to you."

How the scene goes, after all is lost: my father arrives through the garage door as if he's lived here all along. It's been many, many years since I've seen him. My father has grown old. He's not how I remembered him as a small child or teenager. All his rotten teeth have fallen out. One golden crown hangs in his mouth like a crescent moon. He is in sweatpants and holding a gift of four giant oranges—the size of small planets. We sit awkwardly at the kitchen table. My brother weaves his hands together as if they were glued. My mother peels her own orange—an orange she bought—and nurses a slowly brewing growl. My father, all laughter, tells us how he makes his own wine. That it tastes terrible, like dirty feet. He announces in mixed Cantonese and English: "I can do whatever I want now." None of us say it out loud, but we all wonder if he's drunk. My mother feels like she needs to use a knife and begins beheading apples. It's time for my father to go.

Steven, now twenty-eight and fully bearded, bought a bottle of merlot when he heard that our father was coming. As our father puts on his shoes—stained white sneakers covered in grass cuttings—I watch as Steven offers him this gift. Steven laughs, deep from the gut, to stop himself from crying. He is sweating and I hope that the bottle slips right out of his hands and breaks open in the hallway, sputtering everywhere like pomegranate seeds. At least, then, our father won't take it. When I ask my brother why he gave him the bottle, he says in the gentlest voice: "To pass the time."

As I watch the NBA playoffs, I think of my father drinking too much and watching them too. Of drinking himself to sleep and dreaming about his mother, her purple jade bracelet shining deep within the earth. Of how he needs to see his daughter, right this instant. He'll remind himself not to talk about how much money he won or how she hasn't grown or any memories really. *Maybe*, he'll think, *I'm better now*. And the giant oranges. *Don't forget the oranges*.

THIS IS A STORY OF LOST ENTERPRISES. Of boarded-up pizza joints, lonely stuffed animals sans tipsy game operators, echoing parking lots with floating trash, and neon lights toppled over like sand castles. A ghost city. In 2012, the Revel, a $2.4 billion casino, opened. This was a most anticipated undertaking in Atlantic City; the Revel's entire exterior was built with glass so that it would discreetly disappear at night. A casino that disappears into thin air—which it did, just two years later.

It's fair to say that the Revel did not have luck on its side. During construction, lightning struck a worker's bucket and killed him. Six construction executives died in a freak plane crash. Another world my father could have dreamed in, abandoned in rotting, unlucky luxury. Hotel rooms with punched-out windows. Echoing concert halls with families of soprano rats. Seagulls building velvet nests, declaring their own American dream in feathery glory. "I always say Atlantic City is like Dracula," Jim Whelan, former mayor of Atlantic City, told NorthJersey.com. "You can't kill it, no matter how hard we try." These days, if I close my eyes, I can hear Bruce Springsteen playing in Tony's Baltimore Grill, a surviving Atlantic City pizzeria, or maybe in our old Chinese American take-out amid the hiss of the wok firing: *Everything dies, baby, that's a fact. Maybe everything that dies someday comes back*. The hope for resurrection, for return. Sometimes I imagine my father in the future: in his nineties, strolling along an empty boardwalk with me. We walk, and he points out how the waves sound just like they do in the South China Sea. What kind of luck do I need for this to come true?

Why do I need these landscapes? The image of the sea draws me out of myself, forces all my attention to the surface so that I can cast my thought into the depths once again... The roots of my astonishment at the world cling tight to my inner life, in a tangle of memories, experiences, atavisms from both my own childhood and that of our species.
—ANNA KAMIENSKA, "In That Great River: A Notebook," tr. Clare Cavanagh

BECOMING EARTH

Eva Saulitis

I t's April again, and I'm still here, and I still have cancer, and "the roots of my astonishment at the world" sink deeper than ever past last fall's leaf litter into the muck of breakup and resurrection. This year, spring is early in south coastal Alaska. Every morning, I step outside, and the woods around my house are already awake, speaking through the throat clearings of varied thrushes, earliest of songbirds to arrive. On Facebook, people are reporting things like *One greater yellowlegs in Beluga Slough*. And *Today I saw my first sandhill crane*. Just one crane is big news, gets a hundred likes.

LAST NIGHT, my husband Craig and I hiked around the nature trail near our home for the first time since fall, and a north wind blew across the Beluga wetlands, pressed down on the dead wheat-colored grasses, wrinkled the standing water. We were bundled up in scarves and hats. On the viewing platform, we could see ducks on Beluga Lake through binocs. We heard Canada geese fly over. In spring, during migration, over a hundred species of birds visit this place. Trumpeter swans and red-necked grebes nest along the lake. In winter, you can see a hawk owl, or even a gray. Though I know these basic things, I'm not a serious birder. More than anything these days, it's the sounds I'm after, the voices; it's mere presence or absence that matters.

THIS TOWN IS FILLED with serious birders, people who can identify the peeps, the migrating shorebirds of various species that for most of us are indistinguishable little mottled scurriers lifting from the mudflats into sheets-drying-in-wind flights. People from all over flock to town for an annual shorebird festival, some hoping to spot rarities like bar-tailed godwits, red knots, red phalaropes. For me it's not about IDs, but the way the landscape, speaking in the winter tongue of branches creaking and resident birds—chirring natters of redpolls and pinched-lipped insistences of chickadees—gives way to these transient presences, these temporary inhabitants.

WHEN I WAS YOUNGER, I kept a life list of birds. In college, I worked as a naturalist, and it was my job to name things, to know all the species of a place—the plants, the trees, the insects. In college, I studied botany, mammalogy, ornithology, ichthyology, dendrology, taxonomy; I learned to identify, classify. I learned stories, where the veery builds its nest, how the grape fern replicates its kind.

I WAS A TWENTY-YEAR-OLD NATURALIST undergraduate student the spring I got pregnant—I can't even say by accident. I was an educated dumb-fuck those days, lost my senses in an alcohol haze by night, regained my senses in classrooms, labs, and woods and fields by day.

THE OTHER DAY, I started to burn old letters. A whole boxful. And certain journals, the ones from those college years. I sat in front of the woodstove and tore out journal pages and talked reassuringly to my younger self and said good-bye and stuffed the pages into the flames. I made a lot of ash this way. I was not without second thoughts, and made a small pile of them to stash for later. The pages on which I'd written out my drinking and drugging stories, my love-lust stories, were interspersed with pages of field notes, sketches of great blue herons, poems to lakes, data gathered at beaver ponds for a project I worked on one summer. Something in me was trying to build a soul, and something in me was dismantling it, desperate for a boyfriend to keep me safe, for a high to make me feel alive, not shy, not bookish. I'd like to claim the budding naturalist as my true self. I'd like to claim the woods as my true home, my actual safe place. I could tear out just the embarrassing pages and leave the nature bits, but who would I be fooling?

WHEN YOU HAVE METASTATIC CANCER, the incurable kind, you stop fooling yourself so much. You start to think about letting things go, including the old shames. You think about unfinished business and how to finish it. And if you can't finish it with people for whatever reason, you invent ways to finish it inside yourself. At the same time, you have present-tense business with the world, and it's the world outside me that pulls hardest. In my limited time on earth, I have trails to walk and birds to hear and words to put to paper. The past, I realize, is imbedded within me. The letters—the paper and ink—don't matter. The people who wrote them are inside—my past with them goes with me everywhere I go, along with the past selves I carry, the nature-girl and the druggie and the musician. I feel more and more like a tree. The way growth rings not only enumerate, but depict, in a very crude form, the lay of the land, the good and bad, the years with and without sun or water, the years of stress and disease. The details, the stories of those years, are not discernible. They are secrets of the tree. It's what we call dignity.

THE OTHER DAY, on another trail near my house, a friend and I saw a black winged shape about six feet up a cottonwood tree. From a distance, it looked like an angel. Up close, it turned into someone's glove. In another part of that cottonwood stand, we found a tree with a wound, low-down near the ground. A slab of bark was missing, revealing a near-white, pale scar, feathered with brown, shaped crudely like a pair of flared wings. Later, my friend sent me William Arrowsmith's translation of "Black Angel," by the Italian poet Eugenio Montale, a section of which ends this way:

> great ebony angel
> angel dusky
> or white
> if, weary of my wandering,
> I clutched your wing and felt it
> crunch
> I could not know you as now I do,
> in sleep, on waking, in the morning
> since between true and false no needle
> can stop biped or camel,
> and the charred residue, the grime
> left on the fingertips
> is less than the dust
> of your last feather, great angel
> of ash and smoke, mini-angel
> chimney sweep.

I CLUTCH LIFE, feel it crunch. After burning letters, my fingers smell of ash and smoke. I realize, in truth, that an accurate journal of today would be similar to the burned journals of thirty years ago—nature as a steadying force in the path of a stumbling soul. You think you're constructing your soul, when it's not that simple. It's being made, and you're only partly the maker. As a child I was taught the soul was given by God, unmarred. Each blot must be accounted for, confessed and forgiven, the soul made clean again. As the soul, so the body, gifted, under my care. This is still my way. Only sometimes now the soul feels outside me, something I am trying to embody, or become: this now blank-white sky of thickened cloud growing grayer as the wind shifts to the east. If I stare at it long enough, it blots out my thoughts of past or future. Anna Kamienska, the Polish writer, put it another way: "The soul has two distinct layers. One is the 'I'—capricious, fickle, uncertain, it hops from joy to despair. The other, the 'soul,' is steady, sure, unwavering, watchful, ready, aware." Her definition of *soul* fits the sensation that comes over me when I'm alone in the woods. I become aware of a presence that is "steady, sure, unwavering, ready, aware"—pure life force. Into that window, which I want to make a mirror, I stare and stare.

IT'S A PARADOX, two paths I walk. If to let go is to become one with earth, then the burning, the giving away, the throwing out. If to let go is to become one with earth, then the want, the walking, the seeds I plant and the plans I make, knowing they can be forsaken.

THE YEAR I TURNED TWENTY, in my college naturalist job, with an older student, I walked the trails of a place called the Herbert C. Mackie Camp, in western New York State. The two of us sketched ferns, identified trees and plants, marked sites for interpretive signs, took notes for the field guides we would write, for nature hikes we would lead. The older student dressed the naturalist part, and she knew a lot more than I about many things. While I was a slump-shouldered hippie, she was upright. She wore cargo pants and work boots and a fly-fishing vest to hold her expensive binoculars and Rite-in-the-Rain field notebook. A hand lens to examine fern spores dangled over her breasts. Her long blonde hair hung in a thick braid to her butt, and she lived with the guy who worked as a maintenance man at the camp. She was an adult, though only a few years older than I was. I was not an adult; I was unformed, more a chrysalis. Besides my sister and my boyfriend and the swamp, she became the only one to know of my pregnancy. She'd told me about her abortion. In the way of growing and dying things, she mentored me.

THE NAMES AND FACTS I memorized on the nature trails that year didn't help me the day I peed on a stick, and with my sister, read the news it delivered. What helped me was the pull of place. After the shock, after the phone call to the older student, who gave me the number of the clinic I should call, I drove out to the nature center and I headed down the trail a couple miles through the woods, half-running for the swamp, and I sat on the ground at its edge and cried and listened to the swamp-sounds that preceded and would continue on after me and wished myself into the heart of that inaccessible place, where creatures knew their purpose and carried it out unwatched. They did not question. They did not fail at their lives. I wasn't there at the swamp to make a choice; I knew I'd end the pregnancy. I wouldn't have been able to name my reason until much later. I went there to grieve, partly yes. All my life I've grieved that child, though not the circumstance she would have entered. (*She*, then as now, is how I think of that life.) But perhaps I was doing something else there, compelled to that swamp, heart-pulled to a knowing I couldn't verbalize. I went there to gather my resolve. I went there to be witnessed and forgiven. The fact is, I acted out of a sense of survival, like any animal. Swamp child, I call her. I left the possibility of her in that place; buried her under moss, as I would one day, two and a half decades later, imaginatively bury my lost breast in a cove in Prince William Sound. What I didn't realize was that to let her go made her completely mine, internalized and eternalized, an inaccessible wetland I carried forward into the rest of my life. My black angel. An ache reawakened even now by frog-croak, swan-bleat, crane-rattle. My body never carried any child but her.

THE SPRING MY CANCER came back, two years ago, I walked almost daily the rickety boardwalks of the Beluga Wetland nature trail to the viewing platform. Once, I heard the muted trumpet jazz riffs of swans ghosting through the spruce lowlands. I didn't know what was happening to my body at first. Over time, it had become harder and harder to breathe. I didn't know the lining of my right lung was gradually filling up with fluid from the cancer lesions growing and weeping there. I just knew I could no longer run or walk uphill; even the gentle incline of my driveway left me winded. Then as before, I went instinctively to standing water, to the flat, muddy reek of a trail winding through wetland, where almost no one else ever walked. The land trust that managed the trail had put up benches hewn from beetle-killed logs here and there, and

I'd pause and sit to catch my breath. The day I learned my malaise was metastatic cancer, I walked the trail with my husband and a friend. It was June by then, and the swamp was flushed green. A doctor had drawn three liters of fluid from my lung lining in the emergency room, uncollapsed my lung, and I could breathe again.

I CAN'T WALK THE TRAIL without remembering. I barely glance at the interpretive signs placed at points of interest by the land trust, signs to explain the facts of this meadow, that stream. Memory of two springs since cancer's recurrence has constructed its own signs in me, and those I read. One tells me to slow down at a particular bend of the boardwalk. I want to hear again the calls of swans I can't see. I want to see swans at the back of the lake where yesterday we saw only mallards. My call not so different than the swans': *I want, I want.*

I'VE BECOME LESS ATTACHED to names and facts, more attached to reasonless reasons, to the tug inside me telling me which way to go. Underneath my various identities, that tug has remained a constant all these years. The other day, driving to town, the wanting toward Prince William Sound, archipelago where I've gone to study orcas every summer since 1987, was so strong in me, I almost wept with its force.

In many respects, it's hard to know what to do with your life when you have a terminal illness with unknown terminus. You are no longer to be relied upon, as the disease trajectory is cagey. You cancel out of things. You say yes with caveats. The median survival for metastatic breast cancer is two to three years. It's been over two years now since my metastatic diagnosis, five since doctors found cancer in my right breast. Each spring since then imprints a unique set of tracks on my map of where I've been, and who I am keeps revising. So I keep burning journal pages, and letters written by people who are now strangers, to a stranger who was myself at twenty. This spring, I am burning and walking and planting seeds in plastic six-packs for another garden Craig and I will be planting. I'm spritzing the soil with water. This morning, the first green shoots broke the surface. I'm purging things out of my house, clothes mostly. I'm sewing old fabric into long strings of prayer flags and giving them away. I've consolidated my letters down to one box, from three. As time passes, I'm wiling to give up a little more, and at the same time, I'm more wedded to things outside my body, outside my house, things from which my body—and perhaps my soul—is made—muck, swamp water, wind, bird call. I used to try harder to explain these things to other people, but they are becoming less explicable. I'm hanging on, but not like I did to those men of my twenties, my holding tight with desperation, nascent and human.

THERE'S DESPERATION, but it's the desperation of cranes rising ahead of the first big fall storm to migrate. It's the pull, the want built into our bodies and the bodies of other animals. It's the desperation of spring, of nesting, of territory defense, of yearling moose driven away by their pregnant-again mothers. It's the want of one clueless, newly kicked-out-of-the-nest juvenile moose so desperately baffled, he reached his snout toward me, standing on my deck, then snorted and charged, kicking, around the yard. It's his want toward who-knows-what. It's the want of diving creatures for air. Only my memory of the swamp—with its heron rookery tree, and the heron I watched that long-ago day stalking frogs, and its pileated woodpecker hammering through the quiet, and the day's heat rising in waves from the surface of stagnant water—that feels still, held in suspension, its desperation so quiet, so hidden and inner, it isn't sensed by the likes of me. It's the desperate resolve and the desperate grief I carried away.

TODAY THE BARE TREES ARE A MESS against the glaring backdrop of sun through thin high clouds, and the branches move in a cold north wind. They seem to scrape the sky and my face skin when I go outside to hang sheets to dry.

AS I WRITE, two swans fly past. Their long necks stretched out. I want, I want. I want to be the earth. They vanish into the broken light, urging me toward the place they are surely heading.

NOTES ON CONTRIBUTORS

BELLE BOGGS is the author of *The Art of Waiting: On Fertility, Medicine, and Motherhood*, a finalist for the PEN/Diamonstein-Spielvogel Award for the Art of the Essay, and *Mattaponi Queen*, which won the Bakeless Prize and the Library of Virginia Literary Award. She teaches in the MFA program at North Carolina State University.

MAY-LEE CHAI is the author of ten books of fiction, nonfiction, and translation, including the memoir *Hapa Girl* and the recent story collection *Useful Phrases for Immigrants*, which won the Bakwin Award for Writing by a Woman. Her writing has been awarded a National Endowment for the Arts fellowship, a Jack Dyer Fiction Prize, and the Asian/Pacific American Award for Literature; named a Kiriyama Prize Notable Book; and given honorable mention for the Gustavus Myers Center for the Study of Bigotry and Human Rights Book Award.

ALISON HAWTHORNE DEMING is the author most recently of *Stairway to Heaven*, from Penguin Poets in 2016, and *Zoologies: On Animals and the Human Spirit*, from Milkweed Editions in 2014, which includes the essay reprinted here. She is the Agnese Nelms Haury Chair in Environment and Social Justice and Regents' Professor at the University of Arizona.

CAMILLE T. DUNGY is the author of four collections of poetry, including, most recently, *Trophic Cascade*, winner of the Colorado Book Award, and the essay collection *Guidebook to Relative Strangers: Journeys into Race, Motherhood, and History*, a finalist for the National Book Critics Circle Award. She has edited anthologies including *Black Nature: Four Centuries of African American Nature Poetry*. A Colorado State University professor, her honors include an American Book Award, NEA fellowships, and NAACP Image Award nominations.

CAROLYN FERRELL is the author of the story collection *Don't Erase Me*, awarded the Art Seidenbaum Award of the Los Angeles Times Book Prize, the John C. Zachiris Award given by *Ploughshares*, and the Quality Paperback Book Prize for

First Fiction. Her stories are anthologized in *The Best American Short Stories of the Century* and *Children of the Night: The Best Short Stories by Black Writers, 1967 to the Present*. She is a recipient of a grant from the National Endowment for the Arts and teaches at Sarah Lawrence College. She lives in New York with her husband and children.

TONI JENSEN's first story collection is *From the Hilltop*. Her stories and essays appear in journals such as *Orion, Catapult,* and *Pleiades* and have been anthologized in *New Stories from the South, Best of the Southwest,* and *Best of the West: Stories from the Wide Side of the Missouri,* among others. She teaches in the programs in creative writing and translation at the University of Arkansas and in the low-residency MFA program at the Institute of American Indian Arts. She is Métis.

AMY LEACH is the author of *Things That Are*, published by Milkweed Editions. She holds an MFA in creative nonfiction from the University of Iowa, and her work appears in *The Best American Essays 2009, The Best American Science and Nature Writing 2016, A Public Space, Orion,* and *Tin House,* among other journals. She has been recognized with the Whiting Writers' Award and a Rona Jaffe Foundation Writers' Award. She lives in Bozeman, Montana.

CARRIE MESSENGER lives in West Virginia. Her work appears in literary magazines including *Fairy Tale Review*, the *Florida Review*, the *Literary Review, Pleiades,* and *Witness*. She has been a fellow at MacDowell and the Virginia Center for the Creative Arts. She is an associate fiction editor for *West Branch*.

Preoccupied with earth science since childhood, AIMEE NEZHUKUMATATHIL crafts her research-based poetry using curious phenomena of the natural world. Her award-winning books of poems include *Miracle Fruit, At the Drive-in Volcano,* and *Oceanic*. Other honors include fellowships from the MacDowell Colony and the National Endowment for the Arts. She serves as the poetry editor of *Orion* and teaches in the MFA program at the University of Mississippi in Oxford, where she lives with her husband and sons. Her essay in this anthology also appears in her collection *World of Wonder*, from Milkweed Editions.

LIA PURPURA is the author of eight collections of essays, poems, and translations, most recently a collection of poems, *It Shouldn't Have Been Beautiful*, from Penguin. *On Looking*, a collection of essays, was a finalist for the National Book Critics Circle Award. Her awards include Guggenheim, NEA, and Fulbright Fellowships, as well as four Pushcart Prizes. Her work appears in the *New Yorker*, the *New Republic, Orion,* the *Paris Review,* the *Georgia Review, Agni,* and elsewhere. She lives in Baltimore, Maryland, is writer-in-residence at the University of Maryland, Baltimore County, and teaches in the Rainier Writing Workshop's MFA program.

JILL SISSON QUINN is a nature writer and teacher living in central Wisconsin. Her essays appear in *Ecotone, OnEarth, Orion,* and many other magazines. Quinn's first book, *Deranged: Finding a Sense of Place in the Landscape and in the Lifespan*, was published by Apprentice House of Loyola University, Maryland. Her work has been reprinted in *The Best American Essays 2016*, and she is the recipient of a John Burroughs Essay Award and a Rona Jaffe Foundation Writers' Award.

SHUCHI SARASWAT's writing and photographs consider landscape, place, and the spaces we call home. She received the 2012 Gulliver Travel Research Grant, and has received scholarships to Djerassi Resident Artists Program, Ledig House, and Bread Loaf Writers' Conference, among others. Her work most recently appears in *Tin House* online.

Poet and essayist EVA SAULITIS worked for nearly thirty years as a marine biologist studying killer whales in Prince William Sound. The essay reprinted here comes from her book *Becoming Earth*, which was published after her death. Her first book of essays is *Leaving Resurrection*, and her memoir is *Into Great Silence*. Her books of poetry are *Many Ways to Say It* and *Prayer in Wind*. Saulitis lived in Homer, Alaska, and Kapaʻau, Hawaii.

Tracing memory threads LAURET EDITH SAVOY's life and work: unearthing what is buried, re-membering what is fragmented, shattered, eroded. A woman of African American, Euro-American, and Native American heritage, she writes about the stories we tell of the American land's origins and the stories we tell of ourselves in this land. Her books include *Trace: Memory, History, Race, and the American Landscape*; *The Colors of Nature: Culture, Identity and the Natural World*; *Bedrock: Writers on the Wonders of Geology*; and *Living with the Changing California Coast*. *Trace* won the 2016 American Book Award from the Before Columbus Foundation and the 2017 ASLE Creative Book Award, was a finalist for the 2016 PEN Open Book Award and the Phillis Wheatley Book Award, and was shortlisted for the William Saroyan International Prize for Writing and the Orion Book Award. Lauret is the David B. Truman Professor of Environmental Studies and Geology at Mount Holyoke College, a Fellow of the Geological Society of America, a photographer, and a pilot.

AISHA SABATINI SLOAN was born and raised in Los Angeles. Her first essay collection, *The Fluency of Light: Coming of Age in a Theater of Black and White*, was published by the University of Iowa Press in 2013. Her most recent essay collection, *Dreaming of Ramadi in Detroit*, was chosen by Maggie Nelson as the winner of the 1913 Open Prose Contest and published in 2017. A contributing editor for *Guernica: A Magazine of Art & Politics*, her writing can be found in the *Offing*, *Ecotone*, *Ninth Letter*, *Identity Theory*, *Michigan Quarterly Review*, *Terrain.org*, *Callaloo*, the *Southern Review*, *Sierra Nevada Review*, *Essay Daily*, *Tarpaulin Sky*, *Drunken Boat*, *Catapult*, *Sublevel*, *Autostraddle*, and *Guernica*.

JONI TEVIS is the author of two books of essays, most recently *The World Is On Fire: Scrap, Treasure, and Songs of Apocalypse*. Her work appears in *Orion*, the *Oxford*

American, Poets & Writers, The Pushcart Prize XXXIX: Best of the Small Presses 2015, and elsewhere. She serves as the Bennette E. Geer Associate Professor of English at Furman University in Greenville, South Carolina.

ARISA WHITE is the author of *Black Pearl, Post Pardon, Hurrah's Nest, A Penny Saved*, and the Lambda Literary Award–nominated *You're the Most Beautiful Thing That Happened*. Her chapbook *"Fishing Walking" & Other Bedtime Stories for My Wife* won the inaugural Per Diem Poetry Prize. As the creator of the Beautiful Things Project, she curates cultural events and artistic collaborations that center narratives of queer and trans people of color. A Cave Canem graduate fellow, she is an assistant professor at Colby College.

TERRY TEMPEST WILLIAMS is author of seventeen books, including the environmental literature classic *Refuge*, and most recently *The Hour of Land: A Personal Topography of America's National Parks*. She is currently writer-in-residence at the Harvard Divinity School.

JANE WONG's poems and essays can be found in *The Best American Poetry 2015, American Poetry Review, Third Coast, jubilat, Black Warrior Review, The Pushcart Prize XLII*, and others. A Kundiman fellow, she is the recipient of fellowships from the Fulbright Program, the Fine Arts Work Center, Hedgebrook, and Bread Loaf. She is the author of *Overpour*, published by Action Books in 2016, and is an assistant professor of creative writing at Western Washington University.

RAFIA ZAKARIA is the author of *The Upstairs Wife: An Intimate History of Pakistan* and *Veil*. She is a columnist for *Dawn* in Pakistan and writes the Alienated column for the *Baffler*.

We offer our thanks to *Ecotone* founding editor David Gessner, for his ongoing support and leadership; to former editors Beth Staples and Ben George, for their thoughtful stewardship of many of these essays; and to the following current and past MFA editors, whose work has helped make this book possible:

Kathryn M. Barber, Arianne Beros, Douglass Bourne, Jason Bradford, Nicola DeRobertis-Theye, Nina de Gramont, Eli Didier, Elle Drumheller, K.N. Flora, Meredith Fraser, Hunter Hobbs, Ashley Anne Howard, Kinzy Janssen, Sally J. Johnson, Ryan Kaune, Peter Kusnic, Kate McMullen, Catey Miller, Laurel Jones, Joanna Mulder, Katie O'Reilly, Nicholl Paratore, Miriam Parker, Adam Petry, Meg Reid, Aurora Lee Shimshak, Cathe Shubert, Elliot Emory Smith, Rachel Taube, Caitlin Rae Taylor, Stephanie C. Trott, and Carson Vaughan

Emily Louise Smith, Publisher   Anna Lena Phillips Bell, Editor

SPECIAL MENTIONS, NOTABLES, AND REPRINTS

"Imaginary Children" by Belle Boggs
Notable in *The Best American Essays 2015*

"The Pony, the Pig, and the Horse" by Alison Hawthorne Deming
Special Mention in *The Pushcart Prize XL:
Best of the Small Presses 2016*

"Differentiation" by Camille T. Dungy
Special Mention in *The Pushcart Prize XL:
Best of the Small Presses 2016*

"Going Downhill from Here" by Laurie Clements Lambeth
Notable in *The Best American Essays 2017*

"Sign Here If You Exist" by Jill Sisson Quinn
Reprinted in *The Best American Science and Nature Writing 2011*
Special Mention in *The Pushcart Prize XXXVI:
Best of the Small Presses 2012*
John Burroughs Nature Essay Award, 2011

"The Journey Home" by Shuchi Saraswat
Special Mention in *The Pushcart Prize XLII:
Best of the Small Presses 2018*

"*D* Is for the Dance of the Hours: A Portrait of Prebankruptcy
Detroit" by Aisha Sabatini Sloan
Special Mention in *The Pushcart Prize XLI:
Best of the Small Presses 2017*
Notable in *The Best American Essays 2016*

"What Looks Like Mad Disorder: The Sarah Winchester House"
by Joni Tevis
Special Mention in *The Pushcart Prize XLI:
Best of the Small Presses 2017*
Notable in *The Best American Essays 2015*

ACKNOWLEDGMENTS

"Imaginary Children" from *The Art of Waiting* (Graywolf Press), copyright ©
2016 by Belle Boggs. Originally published in *Ecotone* in 2014, vol. 9, no. 2.

"The Pony, the Pig, and the Horse" from *Zoologies: On Animals and Human Spirit*,
copyright © 2015 by Alison Hawthorne Deming. Originally published in *Ecotone* in
2014, vol. 10, no. 1. Reprinted by permission of Milkweed Editions, milkweed.org.

"Differentiation" from *Guidebook to Relative Strangers: Journeys into Race,
Motherhood, and History* (W.W. Norton), copyright © 2017 by Camille Dungy.
Originally published in *Ecotone* in 2014, vol. 10, no. 1.

An earlier version of "Summer, 1959" appeared in *Choice: True Stories of Birth,
Contraception, Infertility, Adoption, Single Parenthood, & Abortion*, edited by Karen
E. Bender and Nina de Gramont (MacAdam/Cage), copyright © 2007 by Carolyn
Ferrell. The original essay from *Ecotone* vol. 3, no. 1. (2007) is published here.

"Carry," copyright © 2018 by Toni Jensen. Originally published in *Ecotone*
vol. 14, no. 1.

"Going Downhill from Here," copyright © 2016 by Laurie Clements Lambeth.
Originally published in *Ecotone* vol. 11, no. 2. The section "Declension" originally
appeared in *Poetry*, October 2016, as "Cusped Prognosis," and includes italicized
passages from Anne Carson's *Plainwater*. Reprinted by permission of the author.

"Memorandum to the Animals" from *Things That Are*, copyright © 2014 by
Amy Leach. Originally published in *Ecotone* in 2010, vol. 6, no. 1. Reprinted by
permission of Milkweed Editions, milkweed.org.

"Hypää Järveen!" copyright © 2011 by Carrie Messenger. Originally published in
Ecotone vol. 7, no. 1.

"Monsoon and Peacock" from *World of Wonder*, copyright © 2018 by Aimee
Nezhukumatathil. Originally published in *Ecotone* in 2017, vol. 13, no. 1.
Reprinted by permission of Milkweed Editions, milkweed.org.

TEXT JANSON TEXT LT PRO 10/13.2
DISPLAY HELVETICA NEUE 19